DIARIES AND JOURNALS OF LITERARY WOMEN FROM FANNY BURNEY TO VIRGINIA WOOLF

Diaries and Journals of Literary Women from Fanny Burney to Virginia Woolf

Judy Simons

University of Iowa Press, Iowa City

University of Iowa Press, Iowa City 52242
International Standard Book Number 0-87745-291-1
Library of Congress Catalog Card Number 89-52172
First edition, 1990

Printed in Great Britain

For my mother and father

Acknowledgements

I should not have been able to complete this book without the award of a Research Fellowship from the Leverhulme Trust and for this I am most grateful. In addition I should like to thank my academic colleagues who have supported and encouraged the project, in particular Ian Baker for his patience in reading the manuscript and Shirley Foster for her continued enthusiasm and helpful advice. I should also like to thank the women members of Network and of the Research Group in Women's Studies 1600–1830 for allowing me a stimulating forum for discussion of work in progress.

The extracts from the unpublished diaries of Louisa May Alcott and Abigail Alcott are quoted by permission of the Houghton Library, Harvard University. Extracts from the unpublished diaries of Edith Wharton 1905–1926 are reproduced by permission of Watkins/Loomis Agency Inc. In addition I am obliged to the Curator of the Collection of American Literature, Beinecke Rare Book and Manuscript Library, Yale University, for permission to quote from the Edith Wharton manuscript material in their possession. I should like to thank the staffs of both these libraries for their help in locating material. I am grateful to the Executors of the Virginia Woolf Estate and the Hogarth Press for permission to quote from the five volumes of *The Diary of Virginia Woolf 1915–1941*, ed. Anne Olivier Bell; to Oxford University Press for permission to quote from *Fanny Burney, Selected Letters and Journals*, ed. Joyce Hemlow (1986) and from *The Journals of Dorothy Wordsworth*, ed. Mary Moorman (1971); to Clarendon Press for permission to quote from *The Journals of Mary Shelley 1814–44*, ed. Paula R. Feldman and Diana Scott-Kilvert (1987), and from *The Journals and Letters of Fanny Burney (Madame D'Arblay) 1791–1840*, vol. IV (1973).

Contents

I never travel without my diary. One should always have something sensational to read in the train.

— Oscar Wilde, *The Importance of Being Earnest*, Act III.

1

Secret Exhibitionists:
Women and their Diaries

Diarists, that shrewdly innocent breed, those secret exhibitionists and incomparable purveyors of sequential, self-conscious life

— Gail Godwin

I

'Do you really keep a diary?' Algernon asks Cecily in Oscar Wilde's *The Importance of Being Earnest*. 'I'd give anything to look at it: May I?' 'Oh, no,' she answers, covering it instinctively with her hand. 'You see, it is simply a very young girl's record of her own thoughts and impressions, and consequently meant for publication. When it appears in volume form I hope you will order a copy.'[1] Wilde's play was written during 1894, five years after the publication in English of the *Journal* of Marie Bashkirtseff, the Russian artist who had died of tuberculosis at the romantically young age of twenty-four. On its appearance, Bashkirtseff's diary, with its startling, candid tone and its unabashed personal confidences, had caused a literary sensation, and had started something of a vogue for intimate confessional reminiscences among well-bred young women with imaginative aspirations. *The Importance of Being Earnest* contains several references both to diary-writing and to other literature written by women – Miss Prism, the governess, has in her past produced 'a three volume novel of more than usually revolting sentimentality' and Wilde makes suggestive connections between these forms of women's private and public writing. As Marie Bashkirtseff had herself written most provocatively shortly before her death, 'The record of a woman's life, written down day by day, without any attempt at concealment, as if no one in the world were ever to read it, yet with the purpose of being read, is always interesting: for I am certain that I shall be found sympathetic, and I write down everything, everything, everything. Otherwise why should I write?'[2]

1

Both Bashkirtseff and Wilde's Cecily addresses significant critical issues relating to diary-writing, firstly in their association of a
particular use of the diary form with women, and secondly in their
implications regarding audience. Cecily's apparently spontaneous
gesture of shielding her diary with her hand from prying eyes is at
odds with the idea of authorship itself, a contradiction which
Wilde is keen to point up. Similarly the paradox enshrined in
Bashkirtseff's entry, that she is writing 'as if no one in the world
were ever to read it, yet with the purpose of being read' is a crucial
signpost for twentieth-century critics interested in the strategies of
textual interpretation. As Margo Culley has observed, 'The importance of the audience, real or implied, conscious or unconscious, of
what is usually thought of as a private genre cannot be
overstated.'[3] As Culley indicates, the awareness of who might read
the personal journal determines both its subject matter and its
approach and consequently calls into question the whole status of
the diary as a private literary construct. Bashkirtseff's own emphasis on self-promotion through her journal discloses in addition
her real need for a public reaction to the persona she presents to
the world. As the American novelist Gail Godwin has pointed out,
confessing somewhat guiltily to her own obsession for diarising,
diarists, 'that shrewdly innocent breed, those secret exhibitionists'[4]
are paradoxes in themselves.

Indeed there does appear to be an almost indecent aspect to the
publication of a private diary. We read avidly, our interest verging
on the prurient, records of individual lives apparently written in
seclusion, hoping for glimpses of secrets never intended for our
perusal. 'I don't mean that any eye but mine should read this. This
is – *really private*',[5] wrote Katherine Mansfield in her 1921 journal,
now a world bestseller. And 'Only let it *Never* be printed! oh never,
never, never',[6] wrote Hester Thrale passionately a century earlier,
aware of the dangers that lay in wait for her diary after her death.
In 1767 the adolescent Fanny Burney addressed her first journal to
'Nobody', since only 'to Nobody can I be wholly unreserved – to
Nobody can I reveal every thought, every wish of my heart, with
the most unlimited confidence'.[7] In later life Burney went through
her own journals and edited them, an action which somewhat
counteracts her original claim for secrecy, but her early terror when
she mislaid a page of her manuscript is undeniable.

As ill fortune would have it, papa went into the room – took my poor Journal – read and pocketted it. Mama came up to me and told me of it. O Dear! I was in sad distress – I could not for the life of me ask for it. .... I was so frightened that I have not had the heart to write since, till now, I should not but that – in short, but that I cannot help it! As to the *paper*, I destroy'd it the moment I got it.[8]

For Fanny Burney, the thought of other eyes reading her un-guarded thoughts was an intrusion too dreadful to contemplate – she could not even bear to keep the page whose sanctity had been so violated. Yet the urge to write remained with her for reasons that she could not fully explain. She was not alone in this, for it was an urge that many women in the eighteenth and nineteenth centuries succumbed to. In an age when silence was generally considered to be a female virtue, and modesty a characteristic young girls were encouraged to develop, it was to their journals that women turned, when other channels of communication were closed to them. For some, even the act of writing a diary was considered to be subversive, with its emphasis on self-aggrandisement and its invitation to articulate clandestine thoughts. Burney, for instance, at the age of fifteen, was warned that 'journal keeping is the most dangerous employment young persons can have'.[9] Writing her memoirs in 1748, Laetitia Pilking-ton remembered how in her youth even reading was felt to be a potentially seditious employment for women, a pleasure which consequently she 'was obliged to enjoy by stealth with fear and trembling'. Having taught herself to read, so she claimed, she was then discovered by her father reading aloud to herself (from Dryden!) at the precocious age of five. Immediately 'I burst into tears begging pardon and promising never to do so again.'[10]
Given this context, it is not surprising that women's diaries of this period were often covert in their expression of a personal identity, nor that Laetitia Pilkington should compare the irresis-tible impulse to write, 'this scribbling itch', to 'an incurable disease'[11] which afflicted women who found themselves addicted to literary activity, despite its associations of guilt. Just as publicity was to be shunned, so privacy became a precondition of women's literary development. Accordingly, the private journal, which had gained credence as a genre because of its spiritual associations, became one of the few forms that women could adopt as less shameful than writing poetry or polemic, areas where they might

appear to be competing with men and thus disowning their sex. The influential twentieth-century diarist, Anais Nin, formulating her theories of female expressiveness, has described how 'it is feminine to be oblique'.[12] So, for many eighteenth- and nineteenth-century women, their personal journals became indirect means of resistance to codes of behaviour with which they were uncomfortable, allowing for a release of feelings and opinions which had no other vent. By modelling their diaries on the patterns of diary-writing already established by, for example, Quaker diaries or spiritual conversion narratives, early women diarists could appear to be following a well-worn path, validated by religious precedent. Yet within this format, used by men as well as women, they were also able to contrive opportunities for personal statements. Felicity Nussbaum has demonstrated convincingly how by the mid-eighteenth-century, women's reliance on formulaic utterances in the private journal allowed them both to comply with the accepted conventions of published diaries and to find ways of circumventing those conventions to suggest a personal authority. 'Was it not for her diary she would neither know what she did nor who she was nor what she had',[13] wrote one such woman tellingly in 1721, admitting to the fundamental importance of the diary in her own life as a means of self-definition. Ultimately, then, as Nussbaum has remarked, 'In writing to themselves, eighteenth-century women could create a private place in which to speak the unthought, unsaid and undervalued.'[14]

However, despite the associations of privacy, women diarists were not always as solitary in their writing as we might suppose. In the eighteenth and nineteenth centuries for instance, journals, while intended to be frank and accurate records of individual lives, were also often thought of as a collective activity, sometimes shared between members of a family, or shown to a close friend as a mark of special intimacy. 'My diary is not meant to be read by any person except myself', stated Elizabeth Barrett categorically, going on in the same sentence to make an exception of her sister for '*she* deserves to be let behind the scenes'[15] In a more demanding tenor, Louisa May Alcott's parents in 1842 expected to read their daughters' childhood journals and to be free to criticise them according to an ideal standard of Puritan daily self-examination, a scrutiny which permanently inhibited Alcott's capacity for unreserved self-expression. The youthful Mary Godwin, in the first raptures of romance, started a journal as a joint enterprise with her lover

Shelley, on the day that they eloped together. Begun as a tribute to their mutual passion, the journal's gradual change in character, as it fluctuates between reticence and effusion, reflects the changes in the relationship and in Mary's own available outlets of communication. George Eliot too wrote entries directly into George Henry Lewes's travel journals, reporting on sightseeing trips they had shared and scenic beauties they had enjoyed together. Dorothy Wordsworth's journal provides yet another example of this collaborative approach to journal writing. In part she took upon herself the responsibility of keeping a journal, as she accepted so many other household tasks, so that it could be used as source material for her brother's poetry. William was allowed free access to it, a personal reference library for him to rifle as he wished. That Dorothy's journal contains not just a catalogue of information, but an interpretative record of experience, together with a revealing psychological portrait of its author, testifies to the seductive power of diary writing itself.

Women frequently took upon themselves the role of family historian, their diaries providing a communal chronicle of domestic life. Although she had been keeping diaries since she was a young girl, Hester Thrale began a *Family Book* in 1766 specifically to document the growth and progress of her children. 'She can walk & run alone up & down all smooth Places tho' pretty steep', she reported proudly of her eldest daughter, Queeny, aged two. 'She is neither remarkably big nor tall, being just 34 inches high, but eminently pretty. She can speak most words & speak them plain enough too: but is no great talker.'[16] This sort of diary has to some extent been replaced in our own day by the family photograph album, and like those annals, Mrs Thrale's *Family Book* provides accounts of birthday parties, the children's height, their first dancing lessons, and their witty sayings. Her diary, however, also reveals the uncertainties of domestic life as it affected women in the late eighteenth century and the resilience with which they met crushing blows to their equilibrium. Mrs Thrale's *Family Book*, as well as listing her children's achievements – 'Sue . . . has worked a fine map sampler', she noted with a flourish in December 1777[17] – gives details of family illnesses, childish earaches and fevers, and conveys the terror with which she greeted signs of incipient disease. In a book which tells of a series of unwelcome pregnancies, difficult births and infant deaths, including her baby Ralph's drawn-out suffering and death from hydrocephalis, and the shock of her beloved son Henry's sudden death at the age of ten, we find ample evidence of the agitation and the traumas of maternal experience.

Although journals did not necessarily have the confessional status we now so frequently attach to them, this does not mean that they avoided personal confidences. The sort of intense subjective analysis that we tend to associate with records of an inner life did not come fully into fashion until the twentieth century, post Bashkirtseff and the psycho-analytical revolution. The general assumption that there was, as Nathaniel Hawthorne pompously asserted in 1830, 'a certain impropriety in the display of a woman's naked mind to the gaze of the world'[18] inevitably contributed to women's reluctance to express themselves too boldly in print. Nonetheless, women were still able to use their journals to unburden themselves of feelings and views they felt prevented from voicing in public. On a very practical level, Hester Thrale records, with the frankness of her age, the physiological discomforts which accompanied her day-long outing canvassing on her husband's behalf when he was standing as MP for Streatham.

> I worked at Solicitation for ten Hours successively, without refreshment, or what I wished much more for – *a place of retirement*. This neglect, wch. was unavoidable, surrounded as I was with *Men* all the Time, gave me an exquisite pain in my Side – wch tho' relieved at my return home of Course, has never quite left me since –[19]

But journals also offered much needed opportunities for psychological release. Abba May Alcott, Louisa's mother, a model of saintly womanhood in her obedience to family duty, found in her journal a welcome outlet for suppressed anger and frustration. 'I am almost suffocated in this atmosphere of restriction and form', she recorded bitterly in November 1842. During a winter of extreme depression in her life, her diary became the repository for her dissatisfaction when friends, husband and children all seemed 'most stupidly obtuse' in their failure to understand her misery, and when their demands on her time and her patience were deeply resented as an 'invasion of my rights as a woman and a mother.'[20] Abba's diary, in its engagement with a self that was kept hidden from public view, provides a fascinating complement to the representation of her as serene and self-controlled that we find in her daughter's fictions. It also reflects intriguingly on a dynamic matrilineal inheritance of duality, for Louisa, more restrained than her mother in her conversation with her journal, yet makes frequently reference to the 'double life' she leads and the tensions that existed between her private and her public experience.

Practised writers were understandably self-conscious about what they told their diaries, sensitive to the distinction between private and public modes of expression. 'He is tight & shiny as a wood louse', wrote Virginia Woolf of T. S. Eliot in her diary, adding carefully in parentheses, '(I am not writing for publication)'[21]. The dividing line between degrees of privacy is a delicate one, and the nature of the implied audience inevitably determines the tone and content of the text. In addressing their diaries to members of their family or to imagined correspondents, like Burney's trusted Miss Nobody, women created for themselves a literary format that helped to justify an otherwise unforgivable obsession with self. In a juvenile autobiographical fragment, Elizabeth Barrett makes clear that there were stringent moral overtones attached to this sort of self-indulgence which could not be easily excused. 'Perhaps these pages may never meet a human eye', she wrote at the age of fourteen, '– and therefore EXCESSIVE vanity can dictate them tho a feeling akin to it SELF-LOVE may have prompted my not unwilling pen.'[22] Like Fanny Burney, however, her pricking conscience was ultimately less powerful a force than the irresistible impetus to put pen to paper.

The picture is further complicated when we take into account the merging of the journal and the private letter such as we find in Fanny Burney's diaries. Burney, during times when she was separated from her family, kept meticulous notes on what she did each day, wrote them up in journal form and then sent packets of papers to her sister, so that she would be able to gain some insight into experience she could not share at first hand. Burney's journals consequently vary in tone according to her expected readership, and sections of her later diary, written with an eye to posterity, are much more formal than the familiar tone of the first volumes. In this study, the terms 'journal' and 'diary' themselves become interchangeable. Although strictly speaking 'diary' can be used as a generic term to cover both a daily record of engagements and more intimate writing, while 'journal' tends to refer more specifically to a personal chronicle, writers themselves do not always keep to such nice distinctions. Elizabeth Barrett's 'diary' is as full and indiscriminate an emotional record as it is possible to find while Mary Shelley's 'journal' seems too often irritatingly composed of laconic one-line entries and inscrutable coded references, perhaps indicating her nervousness in case it should fall into the wrong hands.

Yet whether or not writers had a specific audience in mind, the format of the diary, with its record of routine personal activity, naturally encourages introspection in its conscious recall of individuals' encounters with others or, more usually, with themselves. Repeatedly women's diaries document their loneliness, highlighting the lack of comfort and understanding available to them in their daily lives. The young Queen Victoria describes, with pathetic excess, in her diary of 1834, her parting from her half-sister, Princess Feodora of Leiningen.

> I clasped her in my arms, and kissed her and cried as if my heart would break, so did she dearest Sister. We then tore ourselves from each other in the deepest grief . . . When I came home I was in such a state of grief that I knew not what to do with myself. I sobbed and cried most violently the whole morning . . . My dearest best sister was friend, sister, companion all to me.[23]

In training for a life dominated by public protocol and adherence to form, Victoria learned early the lessons of solitude, and like other women of her time found relief in written expression. As Sophie Tolstoy, the wife of the Russian writer, explained, 'I am so often left alone with my thoughts that the desire to write my diary is quite natural. I sometimes feel depressed, but now it seems wonderful to be able to think everything over for myself without having to say anything about it to other people.'[24]

Partly because the scope of their lives was often restricted to the domestic environment and personal relationships, and partly because other outlets for written expression were for so long closed to them, women developed a tradition of diary writing that was informed by seclusion and their response to it. 'We live at home, quiet, confined, and our feelings prey upon us', says Anne Elliott to Captain Harville in Jane Austen's novel *Persuasion*, speaking of the distinction between men's and women's lives. 'You are forced on exertion. You have always a profession, pursuits, business of some sort or other, to take you back into the world.'[25] In the same chapter Austen goes on to make explicit links between women's cultural limitations and their exclusion from literary expression and to argue that the popular image of women's nature is nothing more than a male fiction constructed from a model which women themselves have not been allowed to contribute to. The veiled anger and sadness which permeate this novel in its deeply felt depiction of female neglect and a woman's inner life emerge more personally through the medium of diaries and journals, which reveal women's eagerness to provide authentic records of lives which were too often in danger of misinterpretation.

In her *Journal of a Solitude*, the twentieth-century poet May Sarton experiments with the journal as a form of writing that grows naturally from a self-imposed isolation. 'I have an idea that women are far more interested in self-actualization than men are. Women internalize their lives to a greater extent',[26] she concludes, having spent several months as a virtual recluse. It is this internalisation of experience (although Sarton does not attribute it as firmly as does Austen to cultural and historical conditioning), which has had such a powerfully determining effect on women's writing through two centuries. The diary form as bourgeois women have used it since the mid-eighteenth century grants us access to a world normally hidden from view, and to constructions of womanhood which often demonstrate a surprising estrangement from conventional female images endorsed by other literature of the period.

It is worth noting as well that this dynamic can work in reverse, as women compile their private writings according to a scheme imposed upon them. An entry in Jane Welsh Carlyle's diary for 21 October 1855 shows her making a deliberate effort to avoid introspection as an approach which might prove dangerous in its encouragement to emotional extravagance.

> Your journal all about feelings aggravates whatever is factitious and morbid in you; that I have made experience of. And now the only sort of journal I would keep should have to do with what Mr Carlyle calls 'the facts of things'. It is very bleak and barren, this facts of things, as I now see it – very; and what good is to result from writing of it in a paper book is more than I can tell.[27]

Interestingly, Jane Carlyle's attempt to adapt her own writing to a masculine formula as a means of controlling despair is treated sceptically even as she embarks on it. The wry manner in which she views the enterprise clearly reflects her own suspicion as to its effectiveness. In the very act of writing the journal then, women can show themselves fully aware of the problems they are engaging with, both in terms of the interrogation with self (and the related problems of evasion), and in terms of the choice of literary format they adopt.

For by their choice of mode as written documents all diaries imply readership, even if the reader and writer are one and the same. Many diarists, both male and female, in fact call deliberate attention to their anomalous position as authors, engaged in an activity that invites audience response, while concurrently endorsing the secretive nature of what they are about. As Virginia Woolf, one of the most prolific as well as one of the most self-aware of literary diarists, commented in her diary of November 1928, 'And this shall be written for my own pleasure. But that phrase inhibits me; for if one writes only for one's own pleasure, I don't know what it is that happens. I suppose the convention of writing is destroyed: therefore one does not write at all'.[28] Throughout her five published volumes of diaries Woolf continues to make reference to herself as the reader of her own text, imagining herself transformed by age, as a woman of fifty re-examining the work she has produced fifteen years before, the thought of this audience encouraging her to maintain her entries regularly. 'I fancy this old Virginia putting on her spectacles to read of March 1920 will decidedly wish me to continue. Greetings! my dear ghost; & take heed that I don't think 50 a very great age,'[29] she writes with mocking self-irony. For the act of reading the journal can be as significant as writing it: both activities validate personal experience, attach importance to the daily round of mundane events, and by so doing establish the diarist's own sense of worth. Many diarists consequently write knowingly to themselves, verifying the fact of their own identity in the habitual dialogue they conduct with themselves. Edith Wharton was only half joking when she wrote in her journal notebook of 1925, 'I love to be with my friends; with four or five of them I feel my wings, but, oh, when I'm alone how good the talk is!'[30]

In anticipation of an audience of one, diarists were naturally sensitive to the falsification of experience their diaries were subject to. 'It is unfortunate for truth's sake', wrote Virginia Woolf in her diary, 'that I never write here except when jangled with talk. I only record the dumps & the dismals, & then very barely.'[31] Mary Shelley, aware that her diary might well present a picture of her life that would only distress her unbearably on re-reading, consciously tried to redress the balance. 'As I have until now recurred to this book to discharge into it the overflowings of a mind too full of the bitterest waters of life', she wrote in March 1823, 'so will I tonight ... put down some of my milder reveries; that when I turn it over, I may not only find a record of the most painful thoughts.'[32] The novelist Barbara Pym, writing her diary, 'my clever book', as she termed it, in 1943, noted how 'I seem to write in it only when I am depressed, like praying only when one is really in despair'.[33] Realising the fallibility of their diaries as objective or accurate records of their lives did not prevent writers of both sexes from being drawn to the form, recognising its therapeutic and its metonymic value, its ability to recreate vast areas of experience through recall of particular detail, and its concomitant exposure of the fluid and protean nature of the self.

As critic Sidonie Smith has observed, 'The autobiographical text becomes a narrative artifice, privileging a presence or identity that does not exist outside language. Given the very nature of language, embedded in text lie alternative or deferred identities that constantly subvert any pretentions of truthfulness.'[34] For women writers, whose social utterances were often constrained by patriarchal impositions of female propriety, the medium came to have special value as a personal space in which to negotiate that delicate boundary between private opinion and its open articulation.

Virgina Woolf's remarks on her inveterate habit of re-reading her journal help to shed light for us on the entire practice of private writing and its problematic status. She wrote in April 1919;

> I got out this diary, & read as one always does read one's own writing, with a kind of guilty intensity. I confess the rough & random style of it, often so ungrammatical, & crying for a word altered, afflicted me somewhat. I am trying to tell whichever self it is that reads this hereafter that I can write very much better; & take no time over this; & forbid her to let the eye of man behold it.[35]

As well as the personal insights afforded by this comment – Woolf's rather awkward stance as both artist and critic, and the incipient feminism of the final phrase – the statement illuminates a fundamental difficulty besetting all diarists, as the production of their text forms for them an active demonstration of their split identity, whose unity the act of diarising might well be intent on affirming. 'It would be curious to discover who it is to whom one writes in a diary', speculated Beatrice Webb in her journal, addressing the problem head on. 'Possibly to some mysterious personification of one's own identity, to the unknown, which lies below the constant change of matter and ideas, constituting the individual at any given moment.'[36] The painter Ivy Jacquier's realisation that the reason she keeps a diary is that it helps her to understand 'the fluctuations of self. One never is, one has been or is becoming'[37] emphasises this ephemerality. For as in all autobiographical writing, the diary constructs a fictional persona, a version of the self that the diarist wishes to project, however unconsciously. So the critic James Olney, writing about formal autobiography, has commented, 'In the act of remembering the past in the present, the autobiographer imagines into existence another person, another world and surely it is *not* the same, in any real sense, as that past world that does not under any circumstances, nor however much we may wish it, now exist.'[38] The same can be said of diaries. Marie Bashkirtseff remarked with interest in 1880 how reading about the passions and sufferings of adolescence in her old diary left her now quite cold. Devastated by thwarted love, she had described in 1873 her feelings on hearing that the man she adored was to marry another. 'And I have to take a Latin lesson! Oh, torture!' she had scribbled furiously at the age of fourteen. 'Oh, I detest him! I want to see them together. They are at Baden-Baden that I loved so much! Those walks where I used to see him, those kiosks, those shops!'. Six years later, she wrote impassively in the margin, '(All this on account of a man whom I had seen a dozen times in the street, – whom I did not know, and who did not know that I was in existence . . . All this re-read in 1880 produces no effect on me whatever.)'[39]

Thus the sequential organisation of the diary, with its emphasis on the passage of time and the process of ageing confronts the writer with a simultaneous demonstration of her own continuity *and* her discontinuity. 'I have written, therefore I must have existed',[40] insists the novelist Joyce Carol Oates, her use of the past tense in itself testifying to the slippery nature of personality. The self who reads past entries, be they the entries of yesterday or of ten years ago, is significantly different from the self who initially wrote those entries. Yet they are the same, the process of growth indicating a development within the present identity which is conditioned and determined by the past. It is often asserted that all forms of autobiographical writing help to impose a sense of wholeness on the disparate and transient concept of selfhood. Indeed, as Margo Culley has noted, events in women's lives, such as marriage, travel or widowhood, are all occasions which confront women with the intermittent nature of self and 'keeping a life record can be an attempt to preserve continuity seemingly broken or lost.'[41] In reading the diaries of rural women in America, Elizabeth Hampstein has noted how some diaries depend upon pattern and repetition, using the basic technique of daily reportage as a strategy for controlling disturbances in individual lives. She quotes a delightful example from the diary of one woman, Grace de Con, married to a sick husband. T. H. Zintgraff, as an illustration of the way in which adherence to the diary formula can imbue even extraordinary events with a sense of normality.

> Sunday 2 May 1935. Quite nice. T.H. is no better, just as crazy as ever, broke a window pane with rocking chair. Mrs Fisher, Mrs Alexander called, Miss Stanzel came to see my new store. T.H. passed away this evening at 8pm.[42]

Yet one can just as easily argue that diary-writing, for women in particular, who take on so many roles in a multiform existence, emphasises the very fragmentation of self that they are trying to keep at bay. For the notion of self as it exists in twentieth-century literature is at best a cultural construct, an arbitrary fiction partially if not wholly determined by the language employed to define it. Continually, literary diarists, struggling to clarify their own relationship with language and what lies beyond it, show themselves sensitive to the potential breakdown of this fiction that the forms of personal writing invite. In her journal, Katherine Mansfield playfully visualised herself in

> a huge cavern where my selves (who were like ancient sea-weed gatherers) mumbled, indifferent and intimate ... and this other self apart in the carriage, grasping the cold knob of her umbrella, thinking of a strip of white paint and the wet, flapping oilskins of sailors.[43]

Notoriously unstable, but exceptionally lucid in her analysis of her own inconsistencies, Mansfield draws attention to the particular problem that besets the writer of a journal, the narrator of the self's story, whose detached, critical persona regards and records the more unthinking protagonists of everyday.

In examining the private diaries of women who were also engaged in more canonical forms of creative writing, this multiplicity and sense of personal division becomes a marked focus of study and stimulates a number of critical questions. What relationship, if any, can be traced between personal writings and texts for publication by the same author? What is the nature of the 'self' that diarists are engaged in constructing and how does this reflect contemporary images of womanhood? Do writers' diaries offer insights into methods of literary production, and those of women writers into the distinctive problems they, as women, might have encountered? What status did women grant their diaries and how does that affect their approach to the medium? These issues are all addressed in the succeeding chapters on individual diarists and their work. In the eighteenth and nineteenth centuries in particular, individual women's lives, perhaps more notably than men's, were subject to continual change, as differing ideologies of femininity were imposed upon them. The successive stages in their lives – as daughter, sweetheart, wife, mother, widow – were defined through the appropriation of certain codes of behaviour, each considered suitable for one of these roles. Eighteenth-century fictions are full of incidents which testify to the confusions of identity that women experienced during this period. Fanny Burney, whose journal so teasingly offers ambivalent images of its author, created heroines in her novels whose stories follow their search for a stable and socially acceptable identity. Her works all contain key moments of panic, when the heroine finds herself the victim of mistaken identity – Evelina assumed to be a prostitute; Cecilia and Camilla taken for madwomen; Juliet masked, disguised and ignored by her family – with disastrous consequences. These portraits accurately reflect the fragility of women's position in a world where gender was their main identifying characteristic, and their stories are repeated in Burney's narrative of her own life in her journal which mirrors the same fears and uncertainties in a different form. When Jane Austen's Elizabeth Bennett says at a crucial turning point in *Pride and Prejudice*, 'Till this moment I never knew myself', her statement embodies the fraught search for self-discovery that beset thinking women of the time and that was so eloquently conveyed through their most reliable resource, the personal journal.

If we accept that women have had a particular tentative hold on the prevailing idea of a unified self, then we can see that for those women who have also had professional careers, involving a series of images which veer away from the domestic roles which have traditionally defined women, the division between public and private aspects of self becomes intensified. It has become almost a truism to speak of the public and private worlds of the eighteenth and nineteenth centuries as reflecting in turn masculine and feminine spheres of activity. Certainly it is undeniable that women's writing has most often been associated with the private sphere, focusing on the home as subject, and utilising literary perspectives which have evolved from the literature of privacy: the letter, the journal, the nostalgic memoir. The diary itself has been designated a distinctively 'feminine activity ... a personal and personified creation, the opposite of masculine alchemy'.[44] To some extent this female talent for exploiting undervalued forms has inevitably perpetuated women's exclusion from the artistic canon, and sharpened the sense of otherness that certain twentieth-century feminist theorists have identified as determining women's capacity for articulacy. Women writers then have inevitably had a special relationship with that 'female' form, the diary, both drawing on it as substance for their own public writing and retaining it as a mechanism in their own lives in its traditional role as therapy, consolation and a means of expression of their own divided sensibility. Making a similar point, Suzanne Juhasz goes on to remark, 'Hence both the logic and the conflict that comes when women validate their lives as meaningful and the diary form as an appropriate model for the expansion of their lives; in the process bringing such lives and such genre out from the private into the public world.'[45]

Ironically, the act of writing the journal aggravates this sense of dichotomy, the concentration on one's personal life forcing an analysis and a detachment which inhibits the spontaneity normally associated with diarising. Although it is generally true that in contrast to the autobiographer looking back over a lengthy period of experience – 'the perspective of the diarist is immersion not distance'[46] – the retrospective view of experience is common to both forms, inevitably requiring selectivity and self consciousness, and creating problems for the author of the text who is also its subject. A dramatic instance of this subject/object division is provided by Samuel Richardson's novel *Pamela* (1740), much of which is presented in the form of a fictional journal. As Pamela is increasingly threatened by her seducer, Mr B., and her avenues for protest narrow, so she hides her journal entries about her body, sewing the papers into her clothes, an emblematic signification of her grasp on her individual identity and the psychological difficulties it encodes. That novel, a male creation, testifies to the growing interest in the existence and nature of a female voice in the eighteenth century, and the inevitable association of that voice with a personal literary medium. It is highly relevant that women's first major emergence into the public literary world in the eighteenth century was through fictions which reiterated the autobiographical and familiar forms of writing – the diary, the letter and the memoir – which had supplied them with an informal tradition of writing they could easily transpose.

The eight women writers who give their names to the succeeding chapters all help to illustrate the complex nature of these issues. Fanny Burney was one of the first women who operated with success in two separate literary spheres simultaneously, the public and the private. With an enormous critical reputation, she relied on her diary for a form of expression which was not satisfied by her imaginative creations. In addition we should note that her first published writing grew directly from the diary form she was familiar with. Burney can be credited with bringing respectability to women's fiction and for establishing a literary method for women which relied on subterfuge for its full effect, the mutinous subtext constantly threatening to erupt from beneath the conformist exterior. So the two halves of her writing experience, the personal journal and the imaginative fictions, form a single literary entity. The subjects who follow Burney in this book do so because they all illuminate some aspect of this literary relationship which has been fundamental in determining women's writing and the forms of resistance to patriarchy that writing has embodied. Dorothy Wordsworth's journal actively, albeit unconsciously, challenges the patriarchal literary tradition, in asserting an alternative literary mode to the Romantic poetry which it engendered. Dorothy's continual downgrading of her journal is ironically subverted in its own artistic power and, when set against Wordsworth's lyric poems, the same subjects can be seen transformed in alternative structures. Mary Shelley's journal, like Dorothy Wordsworth's, is an example of a document which has been considered of value in the past because of its insights into the work of a male poet. If, however, the journal is examined in the context of Mary's own role as author, it takes on a completely different aspect. At the time of what many have thought her most creative period, the writing of *Frankenstein*, Shelley's journal is surprisingly covert, but its laconic treatment of events and ideas that take on monstrous shape in her fiction, gives a new slant to the public/private dimension of writing.

The mid-nineteenth century diaries of Elizabeth Barrett and Louisa May Alcott tell us much about the forms of imaginative writing these women selected, Barrett-Browning as a poet, and Alcott as a children's writer, Elizabeth Barrett's diary was produced at a critical turning-point in her life, both as woman and as artist. It marks a point of maturation in the development of her poetic identity, and its place in her complete *oeuvre* as an important literary experiment cannot be overlooked. In its obsessive analysis of both emotional and literary crises, it reveals the ambivalent connections between romantic absorption and literary development, and in its ultimate breakthrough towards artistic independence it is one of the few diaries that comes to a triumphant conclusion. Alcott, writing in a different country and culture, yet exhibits some of the same signs of strain we find in the works of the English women writers in their journals. Her own hostility to the fictions for which she became famous sheds light on the constraints that operated on nineteenth-century women writers, writing for a market that demanded a product which forced them to compromise their own artistic integrity.

The three early twentieth-century diaries show women who had each broken to some extent with the conventions of Victorian womanhood, yet who were still moulded by those conventions. Edith Wharton's love diary, the record of her passion for Moreton Fullerton, contains a sexual directness which would have been quite unthinkable for public expression and which provides a heady counterpart to the controlled satires on contemporary society that formed the bulk of Wharton's published work. It shows the tensions that existed for her between the separate identities she created for herself, the authoritative doyenne of European society and the passionate solitary individual, aware of her own internal division. Katherine Mansfield, also an expatriate, exhibits the same interest in writing and in sexual identity as does Wharton. Both women kept journals only sporadically, and both left a mass of uncollated personal material behind them. Mansfield's published *Journal*, assembled by her husband, John Middleton Murry, shows how skilful editing of such material can produce required images which may falsify the self-portrait. The vulnerability of women's reputations, so marked a theme in Fanny Burney's journals, remains a real concern even in the twentieth-century, as the posthumous career of Mansfield's manuscripts frighteningly illustrates.

Virginia Woolf is perhaps the most famous of the women diarists studied here, and her diaries the most widely read. They also most consciously resist interpretation, as Woolf, with her delicately balanced psyche, determined not to use her journals to explore her mental or emotional condition. Instead, Woolf's diaries, when placed in the context of modernist experiment, offer a consummate demonstration of the diary as art. In showing the development of a writer over a lifetime, they also show Woolf, like her predecessors, juggling the personal and social dimensions of identity to accommodate her sense of herself as a woman with her position as a writer. It was an exercise that she found one of the most challenging of her entire literary career. In writing of Virginia Woolf's diary, Lyndall Gordon has commented that 'It was not a background to her work, it was a creative work itself'.[47] The same is true of all the diaries studied here, for, in the eyes of the women who kept them, private journals formed a necessary part of their literary existence, not just a corollary to their other work but often taking over from it as the most developed, continuous piece of writing they were to engage in. Diaries could not only absorb the attention but could also extend the boundaries of female creativity, giving their authors a licence for uncensored expression that was prohibited elsewhere. In her diary of 1855, Jane Carlyle remembered 'Charles Buller saying of the Duchess de Praslin's murder, "What could a poor fellow do with a wife who kept a journal but murder her?"'[48] Given the compelling power of the journal and the intimate nature of women's attraction to it, the violence of such a male reaction is not perhaps altogether surprising.

2

The Fear of Discovery: The Journals of Fanny Burney

The fear of discovery, or of suspicion in the house, made the copying extremely laborious to me: for in the day time, I could only take odd moments, so that I was obliged to sit up the greatest part of many nights, in order to get it ready.

— Fanny Burney. *Early Diary*, 1777

At the age of fifteen in 1768 Fanny Burney began writing her diary with a delight that came from a mixture of nervousness and exhilaration. Yet by the time she made her final entry in 1840 that same diary had become her major literary work. Between those two dates she had participated in, and recorded, some of the most dramatic events of her time. She was a best-selling novelist by the time she was thirty, fêted by the most celebrated intellectual and artistic figures of her day. Appointed later as lady-in-waiting to the court of Queen Charlotte, she became a privileged member of the inner royal circle at a time when the reverberations of the French Revolution seemed to threaten the entire institution of royalty. Following her marriage to a French refugee, she went to live in Paris after the Terror, but was prevented from returning home by the outbreak of war, and in 1815 she witnessed at first hand the terrible aftermath of the battle of Waterloo. Despite a reputation for frailty, she not only survived a horrific operation for breast cancer at the age of fifty-nine, but lived on to eighty-seven, having nursed her husband during his last agonising illness. All these events are described in her journal which forms a dynamic portrait of an age in turmoil as well as of the woman who lived through it.

Although Fanny Burney began her journal as a semi-satirical chronicle of her life, purely for her 'most genuine and private amusement', its purpose changed as she grew older. Separated from her family, when she was at Court and later in France, she used to send her journal entries to her sister Susan at regular intervals. When Susan died, she followed her husband's instigation and wrote much of her later journal deliberately for posterity, months or even years after the events it describes had occurred. We can therefore identify three stages in Burney's journal, each with its own distinctive character. The early diaries (1768–86) cover the time of Burney's literary apprenticeship and the subsequent publication of her first two novels, *Evelina* (1778) and *Cecilia* (1782). Their exuberance, reflecting her youthful, high-spirited approach to writing, and in particular to uncensored self-expression, is balanced by a more tentative tone, as if surprised at her own daring. The journals of the next stage (1786–91), however, were written during her years at Court, the most isolated period of Burney's life, when, depressed and exhausted, she turned to her journal as her only form of emotional release and her only means of contact with the outside world. The third and longest section of the diary was written after Burney's release from the confinement of the Court, and records her marriage to Alexandre D'Arblay and her adventures in post-Revolutionary Europe. Despite its multiformity the journal of these years (1792–1839) establishes its own unity, communicating both the rhythms of Burney's daily life and a sharp sense of historical perspective. Often less casual and more conscious in composition than the earlier entries, it shows Fanny Burney's literary powers at their height. At a time when her public writings were conventional and constrained, her private diaries form a distinct contrast in their powerful and dramatic renderings of deeply felt experience.

Fanny Burney's journal is thus remarkable for the variety of literary genres it incorporates: it is a personal memoir; it is a series of letters to an intimate friend; it is a political and social history; it is a working notebook; and it is also a fiction, creating a narrative of compelling intensity with a central character of heroic stature. As a record of a life it is unique, kept up with remarkable regularity over seven decades. In recreating the shape of that life it gives us both substance and pattern, with gradual changes in style and interests as its writer moved from adolescence to old age, from lively girlhood to the more sober and responsible roles of wife and motherhood. Above all, Fanny Burney's journal is an outstanding work of art, not just offering insights into the mechanisms of Burney's creativity, but forming a sustained and controlled series of discrete texts, connected by virtue of the central character who features in them, but demonstrating above all her range and flexibility as a writer in her sure handling of the forms of personal narrative.

In many respects the first entry in Fanny Burney's journal is one of the most revealing.

ADDRESSED TO A CERTAIN MISS NOBODY

Poland Street, London, March 27.

To have some account of my thoughts, manners, acquaintance and actions, when the hour arrives in which time is more nimble than memory, is the reason which induces me to keep a Journal. A Journal in which I must confess my *every* thought, must open my whole heart! But a thing of this kind ought to be addressed to somebody – I must imagion [*sic*] myself to be talking – talking to the most intimate of friends – to one in whom I should take delight in confiding, and remorse in concealment: – but who must this friend be? to make choice of one in whom I can but *half* rely, would be to frustrate entirely the intention of my plan. The only one I could wholly, totally confide in, lives in the same house with me, and not only never *has*, but never *will*, leave me one secret to tell her. To *whom* then, *must* I dedicate my wonderful, surprising and interesting Adventures? – to *whom* dare I reveal my private opinion of my nearest relations? my secret thoughts of my dearest friends? my own hopes, fears, reflections and dislikes? – Nobody!

To Nobody then will I write my Journal! since to Nobody can I be wholly unreserved – to Nobody can I reveal every thought, every wish of my heart, with the most unlimited confidence, the most unremitting sincerity to the end of my life! For what chance, what accident can end my connections with Nobody? No secret *can* I conceal from Nobody, and to Nobody can I be *ever* unreserved. Disagreement cannot stop our affection, Time itself has no power to end our friendship. The love, the esteem I entertain for Nobody, Nobody's self has not power to destroy. From Nobody I have nothing to fear, the secrets sacred to friendship Nobody will not reveal when the affair is doubtful, Nobody will not look towards the side least favourable.

I will suppose you, then, to be my best friend, (tho' God forbid you ever should!) my dearest companion – and a romantick girl, for mere oddity may perhaps be more sincere – more tender –

than if you were a friend in *propria persona* – in as much as imagionation often exceeds reality. In your breast my errors may create pity without exciting contempt; may raise your compassion without eradicating your love. From this moment, then, my dear girl – but why, permit me to ask, must a *female* be made Nobody? Ah, my dear, what were this world good for, *were* Nobody a female? And now I have done with perambulation.[1]

What an elegant beginning! Fanny Burney is almost precociously self-aware, carefully structuring her statements to fit their well-shaped framework while projecting an impression of easy naturalness. Her first sentence gives a simple enough justification for the journal – that it should act as a record when her memory should fail. But as she warms to her theme, it becomes clear that the journal must serve a more complex function. A confidante is needed, and the fact that Burney already has a human one in the shape of her sister, Susan, does not invalidate her need for self-expression in writing. Secrets are to form the acknowledged subject of the journal, personal thoughts and opinions which she felt were too seditious to be uttered aloud. It is this admission which confers on the journal its privileged status. By acknowledging the existence of hidden areas of her experience, and by declaring the need to voice them, Fanny Burney accords her journal an importance that it was to retain throughout her long and eventful life. For behind the comic, self-mocking tone of this opening entry, lurks anxiety, a dread of misbehaviour and of exposure. As one of Burney's most acute critics has pointed out, 'the story of her life, as the journals and letters tell it, dramatizes the freedoms and the restrictions of fear'.[2] This is especially true of the early sections. In creating for herself a correspondent who will not leave her, nor die, and who will be absolutely reliable, Burney reveals her own misgivings. She can find nobody who can be completely trusted to guard the confidences of her hidden life, and nobody who can be safe from the effects of time. She is scared of being ridiculed, of having her failings noticed and criticised. Much later in life she was to remark how 'the fear of doing wrong has been always the leading principle of my internal guidance'.[3] She is moreover, like the child she then was, terrified of having love withdrawn when admitting her faults – and it is for her secret, unspoken thoughts that she fears condemnation. When her uncle claimed a right to examine her step-sister's journal, Burney's immediate response was one of panic. 'I ran into my closet and lock'd myself up', she recounted, the threat of psychological invasion realised in terms of practical security.

This sense of a double identity – the public and the private persona – is central to the purpose of Fanny Burney's journal. She admits frankly that she leads two lives. The decorous surface, conformist and obedient, conceals subversive depths, and it is only in her journal that those depths can find expression. Burney's final point about the gender of her imaginary correspondent directs us, despite all her lightheartedness, towards her suspicion of men and her sense of a shared female understanding. Only a woman can elicit the sort of intimacy Fanny Burney has in mind, but even as she posits such a requirement, she neatly turns her terms on their heads in a quizzical self-irony. Yet the joke has a serious undercurrent, for Burney's journal, throughout its long history, centrally confronts the issue of what it means to be female in a world which conventionally denied women the means of overt self-expression.

The style of writing we find in this opening entry closely resembles the techniques and subject matter of Burney's first best-selling novel, *Evelina. Evelina*, subtitled *A Young Lady's Entrance into the World*, deals with the problems faced by the young heroine, fresh from the country, when she has to cope with London society for the first time. It is written in the form of letters, each encapsulating the naive and unspoiled quality of Evelina's perception as she comments on contemporary fashions and social mores, many of which seem to her to be ridiculous. Yet she does not allow this criticism to be voiced in public; instead she saves it for her private correspondence. In her teens, Fanny Burney had been forbidden to write romantic fiction and had turned for compensation to journal writing. *Evelina*, written in secret in her early twenties, shows the dividing line between the fiction and her own life as projected through her journal to be a very narrow one. In some ways the novel exactly duplicates Burney's own position in her journal, presenting a modest and quiet young lady, whose sharp critical intelligence manifests itself only in private. The epistolary method of the novel, its tone of spontaneity and its subjective format are taken directly from the journal style that Burney had spent nearly ten years in perfecting.

If we look again at the first journal entry we can see how, even at this early stage in her literary endeavours, Fanny Burney was writing as a conscious artist, formulating her ideas with more than half an eye on her non-existent audience. It is clear on the very first page that her need to exercise her fancy rests on the nature of that audience. Seeking her individual literary voice she tries to reproduce her natural speech patterns, and in this search for free expression paradoxically discloses her artistry. Right from the start of her literary career, she emerges as a writer who is exceptionally sensitive to tone, recognising that an act of imagination is required to give the impression of spontaneity. As she grew older Burney gradually exchanged Miss Nobody for real, living correspondents. One of these, her father's friend, Samuel Crisp, advised her to develop the immediacy of her written style. 'There is no fault in an epistolary correspondence like stiffness and study', he told her. 'Dash away whatever comes uppermost; the sudden sallies of the imagination clap'd down on paper, just as they arise.'[4] By the time she came to write *Evelina* Fanny Burney had profited from the advice, but we should recognise that the apparent artlessness of the novel was the result of the careful craftsmanship practised in her private writings.

The correlation between the private journal and the material presented for publication is not confined to technique alone. One of the motivating factors behind Evelina's behaviour is her fear of men and the consequent public suppression of her instinctive reactions, a recurrent theme of Burney's juvenile journal. We are made acutely aware in the novel of how Evelina discovers that the world she inhabits is dominated by a male power structure. Purely in order to survive, she has to cultivate a submissive feminine image, and to attract masculine approval she must suppress her inclinations to laughter and to independent action. Fanny Burney's early diary documents the same procedure. 'I do not consider my self an independant member of society', she told her journal in 1775 (p. 50) but the evidence of her astute judgement and talents of observation are there to contradict her on every page. Fanny Burney's early journal is full of such defences, offering a contrast between the social image she liked to project and the sharp, comic talents she exercised in private. 'Young, artless, open, sincere, unexperienced', was how Samuel Crisp perceived her, and it was a view which deeply influenced Burney's own self-image. Yet at the time this judgement was pronounced, she was already skilled in the art of wicked portraiture, unsparing in her attack on the ridiculous. Here for example is her description of Dr Shebbeare, 'who was once put actually in the pillory for libel'.

He absolutely ruined our evening; for he is the most morose, rude, gross and ill-mannered man I was ever in company with. He aims perpetually at wit, though he constantly stops short at rudeness. ... For he did, to the utmost of his power, *cut up* everybody on their most favourite subject; though what most excited his spleen was *Woman*, to whom he professes a fixed aversion; and next to her his greatest disgust is against the *Scotch*; and these two subjects he wore thread-bare; though indeed they were pretty much fatigued, before he attacked them; and all the *satire* which he levelled at them, consisted of trite and hackneyed abuse. The only novelty which they owed to him was from the extreme coarseness of language he made use of. (vol. I, p. 285)

The indignant writer of this acid little sketch does not seem to conform to the gentle, artless model envisaged by Mr Crisp. It is interesting to note that on the evening in question, Burney kept her thoughts to herself, remaining a silent observer. It was only on paper that her strong opinions were voiced. Her analysis of the uncongenial doctor is uncompromisingly direct. Despite her public persona of timidity, she is here confident, articulate and forceful, pulling no punches in her attack on pretentiousness and prejudice.

A recurrent theme expressed in the early diaries is the tension Burney felt between her domestic role and her desire to write. Describing the routine of a typical day at home she commended herself on her admirable self-control. 'I make a kind of rule, never to indulge myself in my two *most* favourite pursuits, reading and writing, in the morning', she wrote complacently, ' – no, like a very good girl I give that up wholly, accidental occasions and preventions excepted, to needle work, by which means my reading and writing in the afternoon is a pleasure I cannot be blamed for by my mother, as it does not take up the time I ought to spend otherwise.' (vol. I, p. 15) Literature for her was clearly a luxury and her personal writings reveal her consciousness that 'reading and writing' was not an approved form of employment for a young woman in the mid-eighteenth century. Even after the publication of *Evelina*, she was ashamed to be caught reading by an unexpected visitor and 'instantly put away my book, because I dreaded being thought studious and affected'.

The journal presents both the practical and the psychological problems besetting the literary woman. The whole production of

Burney's first novel was clandestine and the preparation of the manuscript for the publisher created innumerable difficulties. 'The fear of discovery, or of suspicion in the house, made the copying extremely laborious to me; for in the day time I could only take odd moments, so that I was obliged to sit up the greatest parts of many nights, in order to get it ready.' (vol. II, p. 162) *Evelina* was published anonymously, so nervous was Fanny Burney of putting herself forward, and she only confessed her authorship when she felt sure of her good reception. Her inner conflict between the modesty and self-effacement of conventional femininity and the bold self-assertion involved in the act of publication caused her no little anxiety. In July 1778, she commented on *Evelina*'s publication that 'I have been in a kind of twitter ever since, for there seems something very formidable in the idea of appearing as an authoress! I ever dreaded it.' And at the very point of making her own appearance into the world of letters, she tried to deprecate her achievement. 'I have not pretended to show the world what it actually *is*, but what it *appears* to a girl of seventeen: – and so far as that, surely any girl who is *past* seventeen may safely do?', she wrote defensively in her journal. In suggesting that the book was never intended to be a critique of contemporary society, but merely the naive and therefore excusable vision of a young girl, she tried to deny her own responsibility for it, arguing against the evidence of the text, that Evelina (and thus her creator) was the butt of the novel's satire rather than its agent.

Burney's concern about the act of writing dominates her early diaries. Although her initial entries are characterised by a tone of spontaneous schoolgirl merriment, this is often modified by more sombre reflections on the propriety of journal-keeping itself. In July 1768, after 'a long conversation with Miss Young', she was advised that keeping a journal was 'the most dangerous employment young persons can have – that it makes them often record things which ought *not* to be recorded, but instantly forgot'. (vol. I, p. 20) Yet one of Fanny Burney's main sources of enjoyment was her sense of herself as privileged observer, reporting covertly on daily events. Mock-heroically she commented on the Burney household that 'But for my pen, all the adventures of this noble family might sink to oblivion! I am amazed when I consider the greatness of my importance, the dignity of my task, and the novelty of my pursuits!' (vol. I, p. 283) This playfulness does not tell the whole story, however. In part the journal was for her own future pleasure, anticipating the time when she could look back and remember long-gone events. More seriously though, writing helped her to visualise her own identity. 'I cannot express the pleasure I have in writing down my thoughts at the very moment – my opinion of people when I first see them, and how I alter or confirm myself in it', she confided to Miss Nobody. (vol. I, p. 15) It was a crucial statement. The journal, for Fanny Burney, was a chronicle of her personal growth, providing a means of measuring herself against some definite proof of her own past experience. The twin acts of recollection and creativity were later to prove life-saving when at Court she found herself in an environment which discounted her personal identity as worthless.

The upshot of Burney's conversation with the disapproving Miss Young was to offer a part of her journal for inspection, 'though I own I shall show it with shame and fear, for such nonsense is *so* unworthy her perusal'. Continually her journal illustrates how her instinctive pleasure in her own performance could be marred by the thought of censure from the outside world. Her description of family theatricals gives some insight into her terror of exposure. Enchanted by the idea of a play, she threw herself wholeheartedly into rehearsal and preparation until the moment of the actual performance itself when she was overcome by panic. 'To tell you how *infinitely*, how beyond measure I was terrified at my situation, I really cannot; but my fright was such as I should have suffered, had I made my appearance upon a public theatre.' (vol. II, p. 167) Fanny Burney's journal gives us plenty of evidence of her acuity of observation, her intelligent grasp of situations and her ability to discriminate and form an independent assessment. But it also reveals her lack of self-confidence as soon as she remembered how far she was departing from the conventional mould of female reticence. Yet, at fifteen years old, Fanny Burney had a natural penchant for scholarship: her appetite for reading was both prodigious and eclectic. One diary entry describes her rapturous responses to reading Plutarch and her strong views on Lycurgus, significantly finding herself 'as much *pleased* with all his publick Laws, as *displeased* with his private ones.' This is, however, immediately followed by a contrite apology for her forward opinions, for 'you must consider how very, very, very bad a judge I am, as I read with nobody, and consequently have nobody to correct or guide my opinion: nevertheless I cannot forbear sometimes writing what it is . . .' (vol. I, p. 22) The portrait that emerges in Burney's

early journal is of a confused personality, both sure and unsure of
how she ought to behave, her instinctive reactions and inclinations
often in conflict with what others expect from her. In 1775 she
received a marriage proposal from a young man whom she barely
knew. Determined not to marry without love, she was nevertheless fearful of how she would react to the pressures placed on her
by her family and friends. Her father's interest in the affair
unnerved her completely, and in an interview with him,

> I scarce made any answer; I was terrified to death. I felt the
> impossibility of resisting not merely my father's *persuasion* but
> even his *advice*. I felt too, that I had no argumentative objections
> to make to Mr Barlow, his character – disposition – situation – I
> know nothing against; but, O! I felt he was no companion for my
> heart! I wept like an infant when alone; eat nothing; *seemed as if
> already married* [my italics], and passed the whole day in more
> misery than, merely on my own account, I ever did before in my
> life. (vol. II, p. 69)

Her silence is significant, and although on this occasion she was
able to pluck up sufficient courage ultimately to challenge her
father's pressure, subsequently her inability to speak out against
his wishes was to prove almost fatal.

For in 1786 Fanny Burney, having published two sparkling and
successful novels, *Evelina* and *Cecilia*, was offered a place at the
Court of George III to be Second Keeper of the Robes to Queen
Charlotte. Largely because of her father's insistence, she accepted,
but only with the utmost reluctance, fearing, rightly, that her
independence was about to be extinguished, possibly for ever. For
one who relied for her security on the support of her family, and
who so delighted in gossip, the thought of being removed from
their companionship was deeply unnerving. On the morning of
taking up her post, she approached the Queen's Lodge on her
father's arm.

> In what agony of mind did I obey the summons! . . . I was now
> on the point of entering – probably for ever – into an entire new
> way of life, and of forgoing by it all my most favourite schemes,
> and every dear expectation my fancy had ever indulged of
> happiness adapted to its taste – as now all was to be given up – I
> could disguise my trepidation no longer – Indeed I had never
> disguised, I had only forborne proclaiming it. (17 July 1786)

Why did she do it? Once again her outward demeanour was defined by her silence. Fully aware of the self-denial involved in the court post, she nonetheless felt obliged to put others' interests before her own, and refused to voice her misgivings. It was only in her journal that she could articulate her true feelings. Her fears about the court life she was embarking on were to be fully realised, and the journal covering the five years she spent there gives a picture of increasing restriction and emotional repression. The lively, gay, witty girl of the early diaries gradually disappears, to be replaced by a more sombre and subdued young woman, who found herself in a regime which allowed her no time for self-expression. Her initial pictures of the minutiae of court life are still written in her early satiric style, such as her delightfully irreverent *Directions for coughing, sneezing, or moving before the King and Queen* in 1785:

> In the first place, you must not cough. If you find a cough tickling in your throat, you must arrest it from making any sound; if you find yourself choking with the forbearance, you must choke – but not cough.
>
> In the second place, you must not sneeze. if you have a vehement cold, you must take no notice of it; if your nose membranes feel a great irritation, you must hold your breath; if a sneeze still insists upon making its way, you must oppose it, by keeping your teeth grinding together; if the violence of the repulse breaks some blood-vessel, you must break the blood-vessel – but not sneeze. (17 December 1785)

A year later, however, she had become ground down by this sort of pettiness. On a visit to Oxford as part of the royal retinue she described how she and others of similar status found the insistence on ceremony almost unendurable. Denied food from six in the morning until seven at night, they were forced to stand for hours on end and, faint with hunger and exhaustion, had then to manoeuvre themselves backwards down steps because of the rules which forbade them to turn away from the royal presence. In general Fanny Burney's days were days of fatigue, boredom and wearisome routine. She rose at six and was never allowed to bed until well after midnight. During that time she had only two hours to herself, hours which she employed in writing, an activity she grasped like a life line. Her journal of these years – 'this dead and tame life' as she described it – seldom recaptures the playfulness of spirit that marked her earlier writings. A letter to her sister Susan reveals the conflict that was taking place within her. 'If to you alone I show myself in these dark colours', she wrote pitifully from Windsor, 'can you blame the plan that I have intentionally been forming – namely to wean myself from myself – to lessen all my affections – to curb all my wishes – to deaden all my sensations?' (20 August 1786) Her only solution to the constraints on her existence was to imagine a form of psychological split; to deny even to herself the presence of her inner life, to repress her individuality so absolutely that she would not be troubled by its demands.

Writing was her only means of emotional release. 'In mere desperation for employment, I have just begun a tragedy', she told her journal in October 1788. 'We are now in so spiritless a situation that my mind would bend to nothing less sad, even in fiction.' Her imaginative output reflected her inner condition, and however miserable her subject, writing provided some relief from the oppressive atmosphere of the Court. 'Had not this composition fit seized me, societyless, and bookless, and viewless as I am, I know not how I could have whiled away my being; but my tragedy goes on, and fills up all vacancies.' (19 October 1788) Even writing, however, could not rescue Fanny Burney from the depressive effects of her stagnant and gloomy way of life. Gradually 'the slavery of five years' took its toll,[5] both psychologically and physically. In 1790, weakened by the drudgery, the long hours, the hardships and the querulous company, Fanny Burney became ill, but, reluctant to push her claims to personal freedom, she remained silent until the desperate nature of her condition impelled her to speak out. Even then she first sought her father's permission to be released from her situation, at last telling him the truth that she had kept hidden from all except her journal. When she explained that at Court 'I was lost to all private comfort, dead to all domestic endearment; I was worn out with want of rest, and fatigued with laborious watchfulness and attendance', he agreed to her handing in her resignation, but it was more than a year later before the Queen allowed her to leave, 'though I was frequently so ill in her presence that I could hardly stand, I saw that she concluded me, while life remained, inevitably hers.' (November 1790)

As well as the sense of personal suffering they communicate,

Burney's court journals offer us a view of British royalty at the end of the eighteenth century which is almost totally domestic. The writer's perception to some extent forms an intuitive lens for her own values and cultural circumstances. Yet the journals provide a unique account of the patterns of daily life at the palaces of Windsor and Kew, the familial relationships, the staff hierarchy, the minutiae of protocol. They also give us an insider's view of the progress of King George III's illness and its effect on the royal household. Essentially the journal accounts confirm a bourgeois image of royalty. In Burney's journal, neither the King nor the Queen emerges with personal distinction, although Burney is careful to avoid overt criticism and rarely does she volunteer any political comment. An ardent royalist, she became deeply attached to the family during her time with them, despite their shortcomings. It is through her experience, rather than her analysis, that their insensitivity and callousness to those in their service comes to light. It is perhaps a sign of Burney's own spiritual oppression during those five years that she paints her life at Court almost completely without bitterness. Her talent for biting comic caricature that was such a feature of her early journal and her novels had become deadened by the stultifying routine she was forced to endure. Even the hideous Mrs Schwellenberg, the German Keeper of the Robes who was Burney's immediate superior, and who made her life a misery with her jealousies, petty cruelties and her hierarchical attitudes, is depicted with sadness rather than with viciousness. It is as if the life at Court had killed Fanny Burney's intellectual energy and sharpness. Surveying her career shortly after her death, Thomas Babington Macaulay remarked that already by 1788 'the fine understanding of Frances Burney was beginning to feel the pernicious influence of a mode of life which is as incompatible with health of mind as the air of the Pomptine marshes with health and body'.[6] Her powers of discrimination and her judiciousness were weakened by being 'too long at Court. She was sinking into a slavery worse than that of the body. The iron was beginning to enter into the soul.'[7] Certainly Burney's journals of this period tell a dismal story of tedium and personal suffering. She forced herself to observe and to comment on events around her, having 'weaned myself from myself', but the source of her emotional and imaginative life was missing, and her eventual collapse was a result of the inward stress as much as the physical hardships.

At Court Fanny Burney began the method of composition that she was to employ to full effect in later life. Instead of writing up her journals in their finished form on a day to day basis, she jotted down notes about each day's events in a pocket memorandum book or on erasable ivory tablets[8] and then used these notes as a basis to compose lengthy journal packets which she sent to her sister Susan or her other correspondents each month. Usually she made her notes at breakfast time and from these, with the aid of her astonishing memory she was able to recall scenes and recreate conversations in specific detail, despite delays often of several weeks between the event and the writing. Many of the entries in her later journals were not then the spontaneous effusions of fresh experience such as we might expect to find in a day to day diary, but were highly wrought and finished pieces of composition.

The most substantial section of Fanny Burney's diary which employs this method to full effect is that covering the years 1791–1825. Mixed in with the journal letters and the personal confidences are more formal set pieces, carefully organised accounts of events written in retrospect, such as Burney's harrowing experiences of Waterloo or her descriptions of her adventures during Napoleon's Hundred Days. Of particular note are the diverse forms of writing she employed to suit her varying purposes. During this period, Fanny Burney published two further novels, *Camilla* (1796) and *The Wanderer* (1814), but if we compare these with her journal writings of the same period, a striking difference is apparent. The journal entries of Fanny Burney's maturity increase in power and in dramatic intensity. They regain the intimacy of tone of her early writing, and consequently its immediacy, and frequently, in her engagement with the lengthy narrative tasks she set herself, show a development in artistic control. Her novels, however, written to appeal to a market with which their author had lost touch, lack the freshness of personal involvement. They are stilted in manner and conventional in sentiment, as Burney (or Mme D'Arblay as she then was) changed her style from the subjective narrative she had exploited with such success in *Evelina*, to adopt a more formal and didactic approach.

'The experience which teaches the lesson of truth, and the blessings of tranquillity, comes not in the shape of warning or wisdom;' preaches the narrator of *Camilla* solemnly. 'From such they turn aside, defying or disbelieving. 'Tis in the bitterness of personal proof alone, in suffering and in feeling, in erring and in repenting, that experience comes home with conviction, or impresses to any use'.[9] It is ironic that Fanny Burney could not put this understanding to use in her fiction. This sort of pompous rhetorical delivery is unfortunately typical of the novel's prevailing tone, and despite the possibilities of its subject matter, *Camilla* is a heavy-handed work. Yet both Fanny Burney's later novels continue to address issues which parallel the experiences dramatised in her journal. *Camilla or A Picture of Youth* focuses on the moral and social education of its eponymous heroine as she grows to learn the harsh nature of the world around her, where men appear as the 'Animals of Prey – All men are cats, all young girls mice –'[10] which she had been warned about in her youth. Similarly, *The Wanderer*, subtitled *Female Difficulties*, follows the struggles for survival of its penniless heroine who tries to earn her living in a hostile patriarchal society. Potentially these are adventurous subjects, but in her published texts, Burney evades their radical implications. Instead the main thrust of the narratives of both novels concentrates on a conformist message, while the real force of their themes lies latent in their subtext. In her journal, however, through her rendering of personal experience, Fanny Burney presents a dynamic story of emotional action and resistance to inimical forces. It is here that we find her literary themes most tellingly communicated with her insistence on female isolation, on the enforced passivity of women's roles and on the strength of women's friendship. On 28 August 1798, for instance, she heard that her sister Susan's long projected visit to England, from her home in Ireland, had been peremptorily cancelled by her husband, Major Phillips. Burney's spontaneous reaction recreates the impact of the moment more graphically than any episode from her fiction. It demonstrates too the importance of writing in her life. Although she acknowledges that language is woefully deficient as a means of expression, it remains the only tool of communication available to her:

If I could find words – but the language does not afford any – any – My dearest – dearest Susan – to tell what this final blow has been to me, I am sure I should be a brute to make use of them – but after so much of hope – of fear, of doubt, of terror, – to be lifted up, at length, to real expectation – & only to be hurled down to disappointment – – & You – sweetest soul! – that can think of anybody else in such a situation! – for though your neighbours are so good, Ireland is so unsettled, in *our* estimation, that I believe there is hardly one amongst us would not at least have parted with a little finger by the Hatchet to have possessed you for a few Months in England –

I write because I MUST write, but I am not yet fit for it – I can offer no fortitude to my Susan, & it is wrong to offer anything else – but I must write because I must let her see my hand, to tempt a quicker sight again of her own to Eyes which yearn after it incessantly,[11]

Interestingly it is the very incoherence of the passage that creates its impact, the deliberate breakdown of logical syntax that carries meaning. Impressionistic and direct, the entry also shows the emotional range Burney was capable of in her writing, a range which barely registers in the often forced sentimentality of *Camilla* and *The Wanderer*. As Macaulay remarked, Mme D'Arblay's last two novels and the *Memoirs* of her father (1832) 'are very bad; but they are so, as it seems to us, not from a decay of power, but from a total perversion of power'.[12] It is as if the division in self that Burney had practised while at Court and that had developed in her first diary had now come to dominate her own sense of identity. Throughout, Burney's journal is filled with a sense of role playing, as she describes tense social encounters, formal visits to the Palace or even lively family parties. She was continually sensitive to the presence of an audience, literary or non-literary. Her awareness of the dichotomy between public and private roles had been intensified by her years at Court. The fear of criticism and the weight of protocol she encountered there impaired, as Macaulay suggested, not her judgement itself, but the operation of her independence of mind in a public situation. Her novels were obviously public works, written for an unknown audience, to whom Burney dared not expose her true feelings. Her journal, written for herself and her family, was inhibited by none of these controls. Within it her true artistic voice had liberty to expand and to find itself. It is in her journal then that the real message underlying Burney's fiction makes itself heard. Burney herself is the heroine of this history, her experience incorporating her favourite fictioral subjects of solitude, struggle, anxiety and the nature of female heroism. One of the most powerful examples of this occurs in Burney's moving account of her mastectomy, undergone without anaesthetic in 1811. The operation took place in her own home in Paris on 30 September of that year, but she could not begin to write about it until six months later, and even then the composition took her four months to complete. Burney justified her account as a warning to her sisters and nieces against false modesty in submitting to intimate medical examination, for her own reluctance to seek professional help had clearly endangered her life. It cannot be read, however, merely as an argument for early cancer screening. Indeed Fanny Burney found the details so frightful to recount that she could not bring herself to re-read the manuscript for revision. The precision which she brings to the report of the initial consultations, her personal preparations for the operation and her reactions to the surgery itself turn the experience into a chilling story of outstanding courage. Given only a few hours notice of the doctor's arrival, she is then shocked into silence when without warning her chamber door opens and seven black-robed men enter her room:

> I was now awakened from my stupor – & by a sort of indignation – Why so many? & without leave? – But I could not utter a syllable. M. Dubois acted as Commander in Chief. Dr Larry kept out of sight; M. Dubois ordered a Bed stead into the middle of the room. Astonished, I turned to Dr Larry, who had promised that an Arm Chair would suffice; but he hung his head, & would not look at me. Two *old mattrasses* M. Dubois then demanded, & an old Sheet. I now began to tremble violently, more with distaste & horrour of the preparations even than of the pain. These arranged to his liking, he desired me to mount the Bed stead. I stood suspended for a moment, whether I should not abruptly escape – I looked at the door, the windows – I felt desperate – but it was only for a moment, my reason then took command, & my fears & feelings struggled vainly against it. I called to my maid – she was crying, & the two Nurses stood, transfixed, at the door. Let those women all go! cried M. Dubois. This order recovered me my voice – No, I cried, let them stay! *qu'elles restent!* This occasioned a little dispute, that re-animated me – The maid, however, & one of the nurses ran off – I charged to other to approach, & she obeyed me.[13]

Burney depicts herself trapped in a living nightmare. Surrounded by danger, penned in with no means of escape, her privacy is invaded and her body mutilated by men. Stunned into silence she is bereft of all means of self-protection. Yet she survives to tell the tale to other women, the sex whose support is denied her when she is most in need of female comfort. In her description of the ensuing operation, Burney spares her readers none of the gruesome details, but the horror of the scene comes not from the anatomical information but from the awareness and responsiveness of the central character in the drama. Unusually, for a medical report, it is the perception of the patient rather than that of the doctor which dominates, and which consequently transforms the account into a powerful metaphor of female helplessness, as well as making it a unique contribution to clinical history.

This view of herself as isolated in the midst of hostile circumstances is central to Burney's self-image. Looking back over episodes of stress in her life, she presents herself as a woman powerless in a male world and her survival finds its source in her belief in the value of her own identity. In 1823 she wrote a gripping account of her travels through France and Belgium in 1815, when she had desperately sought her husband, separated from him by the vicissitudes of war. In her account of this journey to Trèves, Burney describes herself as moving from one crisis to another, fighting through the obstacles placed in her way, and succeeding by virtue of her own persistence. She is helpless when faced with officials who deny the validity of her passport, and who impound her possessions and documents. She goes for a walk, only to lose her bearings in a strange city and (almost) to miss the carriage that will take her on the next stage of her journey. Panic, fear and potential disaster constantly surround her. Her own story as told through her journals becomes a paradigm of the female social condition, continually under threat; resilient despite hostile circumstances.

It is in her later journal-writing then that Burney's literary genius comes to fruition. Her scope widens. She began to treat subjects that were not purely domestic, but she always retained the personal lens as a means of presenting the wider movements of history. In 1802 she had accompanied her husband Alexandre D'Arblay to France, and she was still there in 1815 when the Battle of Waterloo took place. Her lengthy journal accounts of this period were written at her husband's instigation, for before his death in 1818, D'Arblay had urged his wife to provide some record of their life together for their heirs. Consequently in 1823, with her son Alexander in mind, she began to write her memoir of the events surrounding Waterloo. It was a massive task. She began by using her private letters of the period as a basis, but found that she could not continue to copy them out directly because 'the risings of my memory so interlard every other sentence, that I shall take my Letters but as outlines, to be filled up by my recollections'.[14] The difficulties involved in this sort of evocation were enormous. As she explained in September 1824, 'It is now Two Years since I *began this beginning*! – but my unhappiness so swells my breast, & so disorders my faculties when I try, when I even think of trying at committing to senseless paper those circumstances, anecdotes or traits that ... the contrast of this dead letter detail with the animating charm of living discussion, dispirits every attempt, & casts me, with augmented oppression of mind, into a species of inertness that borders upon incapacity.' It was the attempt to order the tumbling, painful memories that she found so arduous, but despite this she was able to transmit vividly the sense of chaos and the scenes of desolation that surrounded her. Alone in Brussels, her husband still away at the battlefield, she observed the devastation in the city.

For more than a week from this time, I never approached my Window but to witness sights of wretchedness. Maimed, wounded, bleeding, mutilated, tortured victims of this exterminating contest, passed by every minute: – the fainting, the sick, the dying & the Dead, on Brancards, in Carts, in Waggons, succeeded one another without intermission. There seemed to be a whole, & a large Army of disabled – or lifeless – soldiers! – ... for the Bonapartian prisoners, who were now pouring into the City by Hundreds, had a mien of such ferocious desperation, where they were marched on, in open vehicles, the helpless victims of gushing wounds or horrible dislocations; that to see them without commiseration for their direful sufferings, or admiration for the heroick, however misled enthusiasm to which they were martyrs, must have demanded an apathy dead to all feeling but what is personal, or a rancour too ungenerous to yield even to the view of Defeat. Both the one set & the other of these unhappy Warriors endured their calamities with a haughty forbearance of any species of complaint. The maimed & lacerated, while their ghastly visages spoke torture & Death, bit their own Cloaths, – perhaps their Flesh! – to save the loud emission of their groans; while those of their Comrades who had escaped these corporeal inflictions, seemed to be smitten with something between Remorse & Madness, that they had not forced themselves on to destruction ere this, in full muscular vigour, their towering height, & martial Uniform, were exhibited in dreadful parade, through the streets of that City they had been sent forth to Conquer. Their Countenance, grim & gloomy, depicted concentrated Vengeance & rage, as much against themselves that they yet lived, as against their Victors, that they were captured. . . . Everybody was wandering from home; all Brussels seemed living in the streets.

Despite the attempts evident in this passage to adapt her style to an unknown audience – the lengthy sentences, the occasionally awkward constructions, the inflated diction – Burney yet manages to convey a vivid picture of the appalling aftermath of battle. Although she faced problems with the massive time-lapse, she presents no impersonal overview. Rather she portrays Brussels in terms of a series of graphic scenes, a moving pageant of individual dramas, seen from the vantage point of her chamber window. Her focus is not on abstract generalisations but on the particular human predicament, on the visual detail, the sights, sounds and tumults of war, and it is her rigorous adherence to the truth of her own perception that gives authenticity to the whole. Burney is an exacting historian of the great adventures of her times, determined to remain faithful to her memory. More than any objective observer she is thus able to transmit an impression of direct participation in events that brings them alive for the reader. One problem for the female autobiographer, as critic Barbara Johnson has identified it, is, 'on the one hand to resist the pressure of masculine autobiography as the only literary genre available for her enterprise, and, on the other, to describe a difficulty in conforming to a female ideal which is largely a fantasy of the masculine, not the feminine, imagination.'[15] In her diary, Fanny Burney manages to address and to overcome this problem. Through a deliberate act of conscious evocation, Burney forces her experiences into a meaningful order and by so doing she is able to affirm her belief in her own identity, threatened on all sides by adverse circumstance. Her diary is thus both a highly individual and a distinctively female chronicle, reinforcing at every stage the tensions between the private demand to articulate feeling and the public demands of suppression. Despite the span of years involved in the writing of the journal, it emerges as a remarkably coherent document, telling a story of isolation, anxiety and the need to affirm identity through a construction of self. It is also the record of a writer's development, emphasising not only the the significance of articulation in a world that required female silence, but the effect of this on that writer's modes of expression. As Burney's own voice progressively declined in the works she presented for public consumption, she was yet able to use her journal to foreground her personal experience as a tangible and vital concern. However painful her memories, they did not need to be hidden from an audience that was known and therefore tolerant. When seen in the context of her journal, the palimpsestic nature of her novels becomes more apparent, the decorous surface concealing non-conformist elements, based on her own experience of suffering and oppression.

3

Self and Shadow:
The Journal
of Dorothy Wordsworth

It is a glorious wild solitude under that lofty purple crag. It stood upright by itself, its own self and shadow below, one mass – all else was sunshine.

— Dorothy Wordsworth's Grasmere Journal, 1802

On Saturday 29 May 1802, Dorothy Wordsworth wrote in her journal, 'I made bread and a wee Rhubarb Tart and batter pudding for William. We sate in the orchard after dinner. William finished his poem on Going for Mary. I wrote it out. I wrote to Mary H., having received a letter from her in the evening. A sweet day. We nailed up the honeysuckles and hoed the scarlet beans.'[1] Here, as elsewhere in the journal, she offers us a seductive image of genius at work. The great poet is portrayed composing his verse in a setting of modest domesticity and rural calm, succoured by the love and the practical help of his sister. Dorothy's precision is childlike in its simplicity, framing the act of literary creation in the prosaic fabric of living, rhubarb tart and hoeing the vegetable patch.

The notebooks which Dorothy kept during 1798 and 1800–3, the years when she and her brother William lived alone together, give a unique insight into the life of a major Romantic figure, his working methods and the sources of his creativity. It is for this that they have become famous. Yet the journals are also inevitably an account of Dorothy's life. As well as showing the Romantic temperament in action, and allowing glimpses of the raw material from which visionary poetry sprang, they expose a life which frequently consisted of more pain and self-denial than fulfilment, a life where the pastoral ideal became subordinated to tough practicalities, a life above all characterised by a fierce emotional hunger that was rarely satisfied.

In many ways Dorothy Wordsworth is one of the most unusual

40

of the diarists in this collection. Since her death, her journals have become celebrated as a classic work, but she herself never wrote for publication. Indeed, 'I should detest the idea of setting myself up as an Author', she stated vehemently in 1810, in response to a friend's suggestion that she publish a story from her diary.[2] Horrified at the thought of pushing herself forward into print, she insisted on the essentially private nature of her writings. By 1810 writing was no longer as disreputable a profession for women as it had been thirty years earlier when Fanny Burney worked on *Evelina*. Yet Dorothy Wordsworth, harbouring many of the prejudices of an earlier generation, still thought of the woman author in stereotypic terms, as aggressive, pretentious and unfeminine. As late as 1820, when she met Joanna Baillie, the Scottish poet and playwright, she was surprised to discover her a charming, unspoiled personality 'without the least mixture of the literary lady'.[3] Surprisingly perhaps, living in a household which was centred around literary production seems to have been for Dorothy counteractive, rather than constructive. Always in her brother's shadow, with a poor self-image that resulted in virtual self-effacement, she devoted her energies to promoting William's talents rather than fostering any of her own. Her efforts inevitably resulted in the depreciation of her real achievement by later readers of her journals, all too ready to take Dorothy's estimate of herself as definitive. 'While her Grasmere journal is of great interest as an account of how her life in the English Lake District affected her own receptive sensibility,' wrote Thomas Mallon dismissively in a book devoted to diary analysis, 'it is also the most complete record we have of her brother's reading and movements in his most creative years.'[4] Mallon's shift of interest away from the author of the text to its alleged subject is typical of the critical tendency to neglect the evidence of a work which continually suggests contradictions and confusions in its author's sense of self.

Dorothy Wordsworth was born in 1771 at Cockermouth in the English Lake District, and was orphaned at an early age. After her mother's death, when she was six, the young Dorothy was farmed out to live with relatives in Yorkshire. At fifteen she moved back to her grandparents' house in the Lakes and it was here that she made her first real contact with the four brothers whom she had left behind in childhood. During William's holidays from Cambridge where he was studying, the bond between brother and sister was formed that was to be the mainstay of Dorothy's life.

'Neither absence nor Distance nor Time can ever break the chain that links me to my Brothers,'[5] she confided to a friend in 1793. She felt strongly that 'love will never bind me closer to any human Being than Friendship binds me to . . . William, my earliest and my dearest Male Friend',[6] and to live with her brother in a home of their own became her supreme desire. Her ambition was realised when, in 1795, William was left a legacy which enabled him to have a small but independent income. In September that year he and Dorothy moved to Dorset where they had been offered a house, Racedown Lodge, by a friend of William's from his Cambridge days. It was here that the extraordinary poetic partnership between Wordsworth and Samuel Taylor Coleridge took root, a relationship in which Dorothy was an active participant. It is possible that she started writing a journal shortly after their removal to Racedown. In one of her letters she refers to buying a diary, but such a notebook has never been discovered. The only diary from this period which has survived is that which she began just before the Wordsworths left their idyllic existence in the south of England for ever.

In his memoirs, Thomas De Quincey presents a portrait of Dorothy which gives a clue as to how we might read her journals. 'Her manner was warm and even ardent', he wrote. 'Her sensibility seemed constitutionally deep; and some subtle fire of impassioned intellect apparently burned within her.'[7] Warmth, sensibility and passion, all these qualities shine through Dorothy's writing in the intensity of her response to the world around her, her sympathy for her fellow creatures, and her keen fluctuation between joy and despondency. De Quincey's account, however, goes on to suggest another side to the coin, as he tells how that 'subtle fire . . . being alternately pushed forward into a conspicuous expression by the irrepressible instincts of her temperament, and then immediately checked, in obedience to the decorum of her sex and age, and her maidenly condition, give to her whole demeanour, and to her conversation, an air of embarrassment, and even of self-conflict, that was most distressing to witness.' 'Self-conflict' is surely the key term here. The spontaneous impulses of Dorothy's nature were to be kept in check by her sense of what was appropriate for a woman of her situation. Her sublimation of her own sexuality, together with her negation of her literary talent, was largely determined by her sense of propriety. It is this sort of attitude, seen by De Quincey as characterising 'her whole demeanour' which provides a clue to explaining the tension we find in Dorothy's journals between the impetus to self-expression and the accompanying and equally strong tendency towards self-effacement.

Dorothy Wordsworth began her first journal when she was twenty-six. It covered a specific brief period in her life, the near-perfect four months that she spent with William in Alfoxden in Somerset, where they had rented a house to be near Coleridge, whose company had become virtually indispensable to them both. Her subsequent journals span similarly finite periods, mostly of a few months at a time when she wrote about holidays taken away from home, visits to Europe, to Scotland and to different parts of the Lake District. The only other journal which was kept on a daily basis was that written at Grasmere in the years just before William's marriage. The travel writings belong to a separate category, mostly written up from memory after the journeys they described were completed. It is the two domestic diaries which Dorothy wrote in her twenties that are the more significant and revealing. Each unconsciously celebrates a time of creative excitement – but in each case that creative excitement primarily belongs to someone else, her brother William. Dorothy's part in the great poetic enterprise of the *Lyrical Ballads* and the poems which were to follow remains subdued, essentially supportive rather than generative. As she tells us, she acted as her brother's secretary, faithfully copying out his manuscripts; as his critic, offering her opinions on work in progress and trying to find solutions to subtle problems of composition; and, more importantly perhaps, as his inspiration, her journals functioning as a storehouse of experiences which he could transform into some of the most profound poetry of the age. As readers of Wordsworth's work have noticed, there are numerous and by no means casual correspondences between his verse and her prose writings. The connection then between private and public writing, the daily journal and the finished art form acquires here a new and provocative dimension, for in Dorothy Wordsworth's work we find a diary which acts in many instances as a source of creativity in another, and a woman whose unquestionable literary gifts are put into service for a man's eminence.

The Alfoxden journal begins abruptly and dramatically on 20 January 1798:

The green paths down the hill-sides are channels for streams.

The young wheat is streaked by silver lines of water running between the ridges, the sheep are gathered together on the slopes. After the wet dark days, the country seems more populous. It peoples itself in the sunbeams. The garden, mimic of spring, is gay with flowers. The purple-starred hepatica spreads itself in the sun, and the clustering snow-drops put forth their white heads, at first upright, tipped with green, and like a rosebud when completely opened, hanging their heads downwards, but slowly lengthening their slender stems. The slanting woods of an unvarying brown, showing the light through the thin network of their upper boughs. Upon the highest ridge of that round hill covered with planted oaks, the shafts of the trees show in the light like the columns of a ruin.

There are hints of self-consciousness in this description, certain formal constructions and conventional expressions that do not recur as Dorothy learns to relax into her medium in the later entries. The main impression is visual, the colours of nature blending with the shades of light and dark in a detailed and carefully composed arrangement to provide a full appreciation of the pastoral landscape. But where in all of this – the streams, the sheep, the sunshine, the flowers, the trees – is Dorothy? The Alfoxden journal, with its focus on the changes in the weather, the plants and trees, and the approach of spring is also a journal characterised by the absence of its author. In this it is exceptional, for conventionally we think of a diary as first and foremost a means of self-projection. Here, however, the reverse is true, for throughout the Alfoxden journal Dorothy Wordsworth remains the hidden observer, deliberately refusing to let her personality intrude into the final picture.

Certainly nowhere in this early journal does she allow her own discomforts to surface. When she and William unexpectedly find themselves caught in a 'violent' storm one January evening, forced to take shelter beneath some holly bushes, 'The sound of the pattering shower and the gusts of wind, very grand', reported Dorothy. '. . . The hawthorn hedges black and pointed, glittering with millions of diamond drops; the hollies shining with broader patches of light'. (31 January 1798) To be out on a winter's night, with 'the wind high' and 'a violent storm of hail and rain', cannot have been pleasant. Yet Dorothy's feelings are all directed towards her admiration of the grandeur of the natural spectacle and the beauty of its effects. Nature never ceases to be a wondrous phenomenon for her: it is never uncomfortable, never uncongenial. Even the murky English fog has something to recommend it, obscuring 'the distant prospect entirely, but the shapes of the nearer trees and the dome of the wood dimly seen and dilated ... The shapes of the mist slowly moving along, exquisitely beautiful, passing over the sheep they almost seemed to have more of life than those quiet creatures. The unseen birds singing in the mist.' (1 March 1798)

The Alfoxden journal is an open air journal. It contains no interiors and no domestic scenes. Only occasionally does mundane detail break into the pastoral atmosphere. 'Hung out the linen' is her bald entry for 28 March. 'Walked to the bakers and shoemakers', she reported on the 5th. But it is the weather which is the journal's central subject, active, dynamic, and imbued with personality. In its continual movement and its capacity for change, it was for Dorothy undoubtedly more fascinating than any human life. Perhaps this is why she never quotes conversations that have taken place, nor comments on social gatherings, other than Coleridge's visits. When she notes, as she often does, that she and William have spent 'an uninteresting evening', it soon becomes apparent that her definition of what is 'uninteresting' relates to the particular climatic or scenic conditions that evening. There have been no curiously shaped branches to capture the attention, no distant views to admire, and no moonlight to give character to vistas that by day would seem nondescript. Always we find Dorothy seeking for the original and the picturesque in nature to remark upon, such as the singularity in an otherwise blank evening of 'the one only leaf upon the top of a tree – the sole remaining leaf – [that] danced round and round like a rag blown by the wind'.

Apart from her brother and Coleridge, human figures are mentioned only when they merge into the landscape. 'We passed the morning in sauntering about the park and gardens, the children playing about, the old man at the top of the hill gathering furze', she recorded on 10 March 1798. 'Interesting groups of human creatures, the young frisking and dancing in the sun, the elder quietly drinking in the life and soul of the sun and air.' Emanations of nature, the 'creatures' are only incidentally human, devoid of individuality. In Dorothy's Alfoxden journal we can see the fundamental elements of the Romantic vision that we also find in Wordsworth's early poetry, in the significance attached to pictorial detail and the sense of harmonious landscape that it produces.

The journal describes walks taken with William and Coleridge each morning and evening, the rising of the moon and its particular appearance each night. As the three tramped through the local countryside, sharing their thoughts about the scenery and the effect of the seasons upon it, a literary division was established, which was to be maintained for the rest of their lives. While Wordsworth and Coleridge threw themselves into the poetic composition which was to result in the publication of the *Lyrical Ballads* later that year, Dorothy recorded her responses in her Grasmere diary, open to no one but herself and William, unassuming and unpublicised.

The Wordsworths left Somerset in the summer of 1798, shortly after the conclusion of Dorothy's Alfoxden journal. They spent most of the following year in Germany, a country which she found cheerless, cold and dull. She was homesick for England, and the December after their return home in 1799 they settled in Dove Cottage, a small stone Lakeland house in Grasmere. That spring, Dorothy took up her journal again.

The Grasmere journal, written between May 1800 and January 1803, is a more complicated document than the notebook she kept at Alfoxden. It covers a time of turmoil in Dorothy's life, a time both of intense happiness and extreme, if covert, anxiety. It is a testament to her twin passions for William and for the Lake District. On 14 May 1800 William and John Wordsworth set off on a visit to the Hutchinsons, their close friends in Yorkshire. Two years later, it was Mary Hutchinson who was to become William's wife. The moment of parting from her brothers launches Dorothy's journal. 'I left them at the turning of the Low-wood bay under the trees', she recounted. 'My heart was so full that I could hardly speak to W. when I gave him a farewell kiss. I sate a long time upon a stone at the margin of the lake, and after a flood of tears my heart was easier. The lake looked to me I knew not why dull and melancholy, and the weltering on the shores seemed a heavy sound.'

How different from the entries of two years earlier! The image of isolation with which the journal begins is never totally absent from Dorothy's account of her life during this period, even in the moments of intimacy with William that illuminate her days. She turned to Nature as a solace, sympathetic in its reflection of her misery and therapeutic in its effects. Indeed it was primarily in order to alleviate her depression that, 'I resolved to write a journal of the time till W. and J. return, and I set about keeping my resolve because I will not quarrel with myself, and because I shall give Wm pleasure by it when he comes home again'. Just as throughout the journals disharmony is perceived as a threat to Dorothy's ordered universe, so here the impulse to write seems to spring from a desire to keep psychological fracture at bay. Significantly she shows herself aware of the dangers of introspection, the tensions that lurk beneath the fragile surface. Yet, although writing was begun as a solitary activity, it was sustained by thoughts of William. This first entry ends with a cry from the heart – 'Oh! that I had a letter from William!' – that reveals something of the loneliness she was so valiantly trying to keep under control.

Dorothy did not share the current eighteenth-century fashion for sentimental musing. Despite her obvious misery during her brothers' absence, she was determined to avoid brooding on her feelings. On 19 May, 'I strolled on, gathered mosses etc. The quietness and still seclusion of the valley affected me even to producing the deepest melancholy. I forced myself from it'. Yet she could not prevent her thoughts from dwelling on William. Twice she walked eight miles to meet the post in the hope of finding a letter from him, only to be disappointed. For the five days before his return she was in a state of febrile excitement, waiting for him. 'I lingered out of doors in the hope of hearing my Brothers tread', she confessed on Wednesday 4 June, and the next day 'would not go far from home, expecting my Brothers'. On the Friday, 'I slackened my pace as I came near home fearing to hear that he was not come', and when he eventually arrived at 11 o'clock at night on Saturday 7th, they did not go to bed until four in the morning, 'so he had an opportunity of seeing all our improvements' in the house and garden. Such psychological strain inevitably produced sharp physical symptoms. 'I went to bed soon with a bad head-ache', she noted on 24 May and three days later, again not finding her longed-for letter, 'had a bad head-ache – went to bed after dinner, and lay till after 5 – not well after tea'. Dorothy's headaches recur throughout the journals, as subsequently do references to severe bowel complaints, both conditions often induced by anxiety states, and occurring at times of particular tension. She suffered particularly severe attacks, for instance, in the summer of 1802, the months preceding William's marriage and indeed did herself recognise that her illnesses had a psychological source. 'I had a woful headache, and was ill in stomach from agitation of mind', she wrote on 18 June of that year. Her absorption in William had become for her literally unhealthy.

Dorothy's utter devotion to her brother is a central feature of the Grasmere journal. Often she mentions his activities before her own in describing a day's events. Entries begin 'William had slept well', 'William slept badly', or by way of variety, 'William had slept very ill'. (June 1802) She protected his interests at the expense of her own. One night when she could not sleep from cold, she would not go into the pantry to get extra bedding 'for fear of waking William'. It is worth noting that she made a point of telling her journal about her self-sacrifice. Ironically she worried that he was overworking. 'I was oppressed and sick at heart for he wearied himself to death', she wrote in May 1802. 'He will be tired out I am sure. My heart fails in me'. William's poetry was the main focus of the household, and Dorothy's energies were directed towards sustaining her brother's acknowledged art. 'All the morning I was busy copying poems' or 'Writing all the morning for William', are typical entries, recording tasks that took up much of her time. Her journal on the contrary was often written in a rush, when she could find a few minutes to spare from the onerous household duties. For Dove Cottage was a hive of domestic activity. On 2 August 1800 Dorothy papered William's room before tea, and after tea 'worked my shifts in the orchard'. During the next few days she made pies, baked bread, stuffed the pike that John had caught, pulled peas, worked in the garden nailing up honeysuckle and tying beans, spread out linen, did the laundry, ironed, sewed, picked and boiled gooseberries, '2 lbs of sugar in the first panfull, 3 quarts all good measure – 3 lbs in the 2nd 4 quarts – 2½ lbs in the 3rd'. Meanwhile William was 'composing in the wood'. This is by no means an isolated example of the division of labour at Dove Cottage. Three weeks later we find Dorothy busy 'baking in the morning, gathered pea seeds and took up – lighted a fire upstairs ... mended stockings', ... 'I shelled peas, gathered beans, and worked in the garden till ½ past 12 ... got tea ... mended stockings'. William was 'walking in the wood all morning' or 'composing'. Coleridge was later to remark how Dorothy had spoiled William, who was 'living among *Devotees* – having every the minutest Thing, almost his very Eating and Drinking, done for him by his Sister or Wife.'[8]

Dorothy's own acute sensibilities were not fostered by her brother. The passionate nature that De Quincey had noticed was given little encouragement to develop in the domestic atmosphere at Dove Cottage. If anything, Wordsworth seems to have been dismissive of his sister's finer feelings. 'I was melancholy and could not talk', she confessed to her journal, mourning Coleridge's departure after an extended visit in October 1801. 'But at last I eased my heart by weeping – nervous blubbering says William. It is not so. O how many, many reasons have I to be anxious for him.' Forbidden to express her emotions in public, she turned to her journal for comfort. She also directed all her love towards the one available object who was not averse to receiving it, her talented, if unsympathetic brother.

During their time together at Dove Cottage, Dorothy's feelings towards her brother are often expressed more in the language of romantic desire than of sisterly affection. She presents a picture of their life together as one of perfect empathy. In the spring of 1802, one of the rare periods when Dove Cottage had no visitors, the days passed for Dorothy in a blissful intimacy. After dinner on 17 March, 'we made a pillow of my shoulder, I read to him and my Beloved slept', and again on 23rd 'it is about 10 o'clock, a quiet night. The fire flutters and the watch ticks I hear nothing else save the Breathing of my Beloved'.

When William left her to visit Coleridge, she was sick at heart. 'Since he has left me (at ½ past 11) it is now 2 I have been putting the Drawers into order, laid by his clothes which he had thrown here and there and everywhere, filed two months' newspapers and got my dinner 2 boiled eggs and 2 apple tarts. I have set Molly on to clear the garden a little, and I myself have helped. I transplanted some snowdrops – The Bees are busy – Wm has a nice bright day. It was hard frost in the night. The Robins are singing sweetly. Now for my walk. I *will* be busy, I *will* look well and be well when he comes back to me. O the Darling! Here is one of his bitten apples! I can hardly find it in my heart to throw it into the fire. I must wash myself, then off – I walked round the two Lakes crossed the stepping stones at Ryedale Foot. Sate down where we always sit. I was full of thoughts about my darling. Blessings on him. I came home at the foot of our own hill under Loughrigg. They are making sad ravages in the woods. Benson's Wood is going and the wood above the River. The wind has blown down a small fir tree on the Rock that terminates John's path – I suppose the wind of Wednesday night. I read German after my return till tea time. After tea I worked and read the LB, enchanted with the Idiot Boy. Wrote to Wm then went to bed. It snowed when I went to Bed.' (4 March 1802)

It is a revealing entry. Dorothy's frenzy of activity can be interpreted as an attempt to subdue and gain control over her depression, but she cannot control her thoughts. William is everywhere – in the litter he has left behind him, in the weather, in the Lakeland hills and in the poetry he has left for her to read. Significantly she is determined to suppress signs of her own misery, knowing that any open display of her inner feelings would only displease him, but the effort of such a task is clearly apparent here. The journal entry is a conglomeration of small domestic details, observations on the natural surroundings and her own emotional investment in them. The brief phrases, darting from one topic to another and the movement between present and past tenses suggest a mental agitation quite different from the calmer tone that dominates most of the entries written up at the end of each day. This is dramatised thought, hurried and haphazard, not the steady stocktaking of daily life. In her solitude it could well have seemed to Dorothy that the journal was her only confidante.

Whatever the psychological inferences we read into the pages of Dorothy's journal, we need also to recognise its value as a distinctive work of art in its own right. The Grasmere journal is an outstanding prose poem on the beauty of nature and its spiritual significance. But more than this it places natural phenomena in a context of everyday activity that invests them with a personal message. Whereas Wordsworth extracted a 'universal' and transcendent philosophy from the natural world, Dorothy's world is one where rhubarb tarts carry as much significance as do crooked thornbushes. Reading Dorothy's journal is an object lesson in the sources and conditions of literary production. It makes us realise why we should not find it surprising that William Wordsworth was so easily able to isolate and refine the elements of his experience for the purposes of poetry, for he had always someone in the background to provide his meals, mend his stockings and pick up his apple cores. What is so remarkable about Dorothy's journal is her ability to integrate the domestic and the natural surroundings, the interior and exterior settings of her life, so as to construct a unique vision of the transforming power of the locality on a life whose substance relied upon it. The Lake District was to her both a source of literal food – the runner beans, the plump fish, the wheat

– and a source of imaginative sustenance, woven into the fabric of female existence. Just as William ransacked Dorothy's journals for material he could use as a basis for his poetry, so he could similarly select from experience what he needed for his art. For her, such selectivity, in her writing as in her life, was impossible. When Margaret Homans, in general a most astute reader of Dorothy Wordsworth's work, suggests that 'It is as if she wished literally to bound or enclose her vision, to domesticate it by putting the eternal in the context of the daily',[9] she rather misses the point. For in Dorothy Wordsworth's journal we read how, as a woman and as an author, the luxury of artistic choice was denied her. What we see in its place is how she managed to produce a literary master-piece despite that deprivation.

The Romantic ideology which inspired Wordsworth's poetry also informs Dorothy's humanisation of natural objects in her journal. 'Our favourite Birch tree', seen in a November gale acquires for Dorothy a spiritual dimension.

> It was yielding to the gusty wind with all its tender twigs, the sun shone upon it and it glanced in the wind like a flying sunshiny shower. It was a tree in shape with stem and branches but it was like a Spirit of water. The sun went in and it resumed its purplish appearance the twigs still yielding to the wind but not so visibly to us. The other Birch trees that were near it looked bright and cheerful, but it was a creature by its own self among them. (November 1801)

In many ways, Dorothy's response to the natural surroundings was largely reliant on conventional picturesque taste for the dramatic, uncultivated and unusual. 'It was a wild scene of crag and mountain', she observed of Easedale in the winter of 1801. 'One craggy point rose above the rest irregular and ragged and very impressive it was.' She did, however, bring to her apprecia-tion a sensitive awareness of the invisible elements in nature, and their suggestive power. Stopping to admire 'Churn Milk force like a broad stream of snow. . . . it was a valley of streams and Islands with that great waterfall at the head and lesser falls in different parts of the mountains coming down to these Rivers. We could hear the sound of these lesser falls but we could not *see* them. We walked backwards and forwards till all distant objects except the white shape of the waterfall, and the lines of the mountains were gone.'

The pictorial images here combine with the dynamic perception of the observers to create the impression of a world where the visual retreats, to be replaced by the aural. As Margaret Homans has noted, 'at every point Dorothy causes her readers to wonder why she never became a competent or ready poet, at the very least, if not a great poet.'[10] Her perspective and her style of writing verged continually on the poetic. In the Grasmere journal, her appraisal of the natural surroundings is instinctively metaphoric. Trees are 'beautiful, Red brown and glittering – the ashes glittering spears with their upright stems'. The moon is 'like a gold ring snapped in two and shaven off at the ends' or 'a perfect Boat, a silver boat'. A star 'appeared for a moment in a lake of pale blue sky' and a rivulet is 'a ghostly white serpent line'.

Her diary is a burst of vivid colour, Grasmere in January 1802 is 'a rich purple, the fields of soft yellow, the Island yellowish-green, the copses Red Brown the mountains purple', while in April there are 'Primroses by the roadside, pile wort that shone like stars of gold in the Sun, violets, strawberries, retired and half buried among the grass. . . . the snow in patches at the top of the highest hills, yellow palms, purple and green twigs on the Birches, ashes with their glittering spikes quite bare. The hawthorn a bright green with black stems under the oak. The moss of the oak glossy'. Simultaneously, as 'the island pushed itself upwards', inanimate nature is imbued with an active spirit. The journal communicates a permanent sense of wonder at the magical quality of the mercurial English landscape, where normal, mundane sights become transformed, such as the sheep with a 'glittering silver line on the ridges of the Backs . . . – which made them look beautiful, but with something of a strangeness, like animals of another kind – as if belonging to a more splendid world'.

Yet Dorothy could not recognise her own artistic skill. Watching, transfixed, by Rydal Water in that Spring of 1802, she realised how 'with that bright soft light upon it, it made me more than half a poet.' Yet, moved to literary composition, she was conscious only of how far she fell short of her brother's achievement. Sadly she noted that she 'tried to write verses but alas!', was forced to abandon the task. Striving after the male medium, she could think of prose writing only as an inferior species of literature, unaware of its effectiveness and her talent for exploiting it. 'I have no command of language, no power of expressing my ideas, and no one was ever more inapt at modeling words into regular metre',[11] she confided miserably (and inaccurately) in a letter to Lady Beaumont. In a poem unpublished in her lifetime, she revealed the inhibiting effect of comparison with the masculine literary tradition.

> I *reverenced* the Poet's skill,
> And *might have* nursed a mounting Will
> To imitate the tender Lays
> Of them who sang in Nature's praise;
> But bashfulnes, a struggling shame
> A fear that elder heads might blame
> – Or something worse – a lurking pride
> Whispering my playmates would deride
> Stifled ambition, checked the aim
> If e'er by chance "the numbers came."[12]

Does the second line include a punning reference to her brother? Certainly the poem presents forcefully her fear of failure and of public censure, not just for what might have proved unsuccessful, but for the boldness implicit in the attempt. The sense of audience reaction is clearly a determining factor in her decision to remain silent, and the verse is packed with references to concealed levels of experience. 'Struggling', 'lurking', 'stifled', 'checked' all point to latent potential, unvoiced and consequently clandestine. With no confidence in her own gifts of expression, she suggests that any literary triumph of hers can only be a fluke. In her journal of 1802 she remarked the beauty of the Columbine, 'a solitary plant . . . a graceful, slender creature', and compared it to 'a female seeking retirement and growing freest and most graceful where it is alone.' For Dorothy, women flourished only in solitude, their natural environment, away from intrusive or critical eyes.

Dorothy's diaries show, however, not just an incipient poetic ability but a spontaneous and sure narrative touch. Unlike the earlier Alfoxden Journal which was devoted almost entirely to landscape pictures, some of them heavily reliant on convention, the Grasmere Journals are filled with stories which have no formal literary counterparts, but find their source in an older oral tradition. Dorothy tells numerous tales of beggars, pathetic solitary figures whose histories she recounts in simple detail. Meeting these cold, half-starved creatures on the road, or finding them supplicant at the door of Dove Cottage, she never failed to respond to their misery, both practically, with gifts of food and money, and imaginatively as we see in her analysis of their plight in her journal. On 12 February 1802 she described a beggar-woman and her child, 'poor creatures!', who came to beg for rags and food, noting that 'This woman's was but a *common* case'. That same evening, a second incident demonstrated just how common it was. 'The snow still lies upon the ground', she wrote. 'Just at the closing in of the Day I heard a cart pass the door, and at the same time the dismal sound of a crying Infant. I went to the window and had light enough to see that a man was driving the cart which seemed not to be very full, and that a woman with an infant in her arms was following close behind and a dog close to her. It was a wild and melancholy sight.'

Whereas for Wordsworth such figures stand as timeless symbols, conveying eternal truths, for Dorothy they carry local and particular meaning, often forming a comment on the appalling poverty of the times and the harshness of the English climate. Wherever possible she provides her cast of characters with a personal past, seeing their present situation as a part of a chain of events often conditioned by circumstances beyond their control. The 'great wind' blows the slates from a roof, exposing the family within to the bitter winter weather; women are widowed or abandoned by their dissolute menfolk, left struggling to support young children, by wandering from village to village in search of food and shelter; the old leech-gatherer has 'been hurt in driving a cart, his leg broke and his body driven over, his skull fractured'. The children who figure prominently in these accounts are often resilient, like the little girl with 'a wildness in her whole figure, not the wildness of a Mountain lass, but a *Road* lass, a traveller from her Birth, who had wanted neither food nor clothes'. If Dorothy had a tendency to romanticise these children as free spirits, she also responded genuinely to the real suffering they encountered.

The story of Alice Fell is a case in point, told without sentimentality, but with evident compassion. In February 1802, Dorothy recorded the story told the Wordsworths by their friend, Mr Graham, of how 'he was riding in a post chaise and he heard a strange cry that he could not understand, the sound continued and he called to the chaise driver to stop. It was a little girl that was crying as if her heart would burst. She had got up behind the chaise and her cloak had been caught by the wheel and was jammed in it and it hung there. She was crying after it. Poor thing.

Mr Graham took her into the chaise and the cloak was released from the wheel but the child's misery did not cease for the cloak was torn to rags; it had been a miserable cloak before, but she had no other and it was the greatest sorrow that could befal her. Her name was Alice Fell. She had no parents, and belonged to the next Town. At the next Town Mr G. left money with some respectable people in the town to buy her a new cloak'.

It is interesting to compare this account with the poem Wordsworth based on the incident, written a month later. Whereas Dorothy gives the main part in the drama to the child, Wordsworth places himself as the protagonist; Alice becomes the object which generates his sympathy and his humanitarian response. Subtitled 'Poverty', the poem exalts the reactions of the poet from his first hearing the sound of the child's cry, through his questioning and rescue of the little girl to his benevolent action in donating money to ease her misery. This shift of focus, however, is if anything reductive, for Wordsworth ends with a somewhat facile vision of Alice in her new clothes, effortlessly restored to health and happiness by the gift.

> "And let it be of duffil grey,
> As warm a cloak as man can sell!"
> Proud creature was she the next day,
> The little orphan, Alice Fell![13]

Dorothy's version, the base material on which Wordsworth drew, does not patronise Alice in the same way. Rather its simplicity, the straightforward narrative progression and the sense of artistic distance help to retain the child's dignity. The loss of Alice's cloak is a serious matter, and Dorothy does not attempt to trivialise it. Dorothy too was not one to project herself into second-hand experiences. That was her brother's forte.

Frequently the experiences he relied upon were hers. On Saturday 13 March 1802 he began work on the poem that was ultimately to be titled 'Beggars'. The story of the beggar woman and her children, who ask shamelessly for alms, inventing false stories of misery to inspire pity, was taken from Dorothy's journal entry of nearly two years before. Wordsworth himself was away from Grasmere at the time the incident happened. His only source for the poem was his sister's description. As Dorothy tells the story, 'a very tall woman, tall much beyond the measure of tall women, called at the door. She had on a very long brown cloak, and a very white cap without Bonnet – her face was excessively brown, but it had plainly once been fair. She had a little bare-footed child about 2 years old by the hand and said her husband who was a tinker was gone before her with the other children. I gave her a piece of Bread.' For William, the woman

> had a tall man's height or more;
> Her face from summer's noontide heat
> No bonnet shaded, but she wore
> A mantle, to her very feet
> Descending with a graceful flow,
> And on her head a cap as white as new-fallen snow.[14]

She becomes for him an Amazonian Queen or a 'ruling Bandit's wife'. For Dorothy she is no one but herself, carrying her history with her. Yet it was during the composition of this poem that William was compelled to recognise the power of Dorothy's journal writing. After tea on 13 February, she read aloud to him the account she had written 'of the little boys belonging to the tall woman and an unlucky thing it was for he could not escape from those very words and so could not write the poem.' In assessing this incident, one critic has suggested that in this instance Wordsworth ultimately and rather reluctantly wrote Dorothy's poem rather than his own. 'The aggressions of conscious fictionalisation would have aggravated the problem', for according to him, Wordsworth's 'problem' was a psychological one: his relation to Dorothy that of guilty son to a mother figure on whom he relies but from whom he needs to break free.[15] It is a speculative reading of the relationship, although Dorothy's journal entry does go some way to support it. For, interestingly, neither Wordsworth nor Dorothy can perceive the poet's dilemma in anything other than negative terms. Dorothy's writing was seen by them both only as a nuisance, an impediment to Wordsworth's creativity, not a welcome source of inspiration. Certainly it seems clear that the poet did not want to acknowledge his debt to his sister's gift for expression. Caught, however, by the force of her language, he could not re-think the experience in other words. So, the later verses are almost a direct transcription of her diary. Dorothy's children for instance are 'wild figures, not very ragged, but without shoes and stockings; the hat of the elder was wreathed round with yellow flowers, the younger whose hat was only a rimless crown, had stuck it round with laurel leaves'. Wordsworth visualises them as

> The taller followed with his hat in hand,
> Wreathed round with yellow flowers the gayest of the land.
>   . . .
> The other wore a rimless crown
> With leaves of laurel stuck about;[16]

Although Dorothy's diary suggests that in the writing of 'Beggars', Wordsworth felt uncomfortably aware of the effect of her language, there are other occasions when his reliance on her journal produced some of his finest work. In April 1802 she described a walk they took together in Gowbarrow Park, where

> we saw a few daffodils close to the water side. We fancied that the lake had floated the seeds ashore and that the little colony had so sprung up. But as we went along there were more and yet more and at last under the boughs of the trees we saw that there was a long belt of them along the shore, about the breadth of a country turnpike road. I never saw daffodils so beautiful they grew upon the mossy stones about and about them, some rested their heads upon these stones as on a pillow for weariness and the rest tossed and reeled and danced and seemed as if they verily laughed with the wind that blew upon them over the lake, they looked so gay ever glancing ever changing.

Wordsworth's poem, in itself an apotheosis of the retrospective vision, was written two years later. It relies heavily on Dorothy's journal, but the opening line, 'I wandered lonely as a cloud', effectively dismisses her, both as a companion and as a source of literary evocation. Whereas Dorothy's emotional involvement in her brother's life and work was total, his need of her often went unacknowledged and ignored.

Her self-denial was both personal and artistic. Underrating her writing, she similarly belittled her life. Her journal, remarkable partly for the absence of self-analysis, also displays her extraordinary lack of personal pride. So low was her opinion of herself that when a strange man to whom she had given alms responded by saying '"You're a fine woman!"', she brushed the praise aside. 'I could not help smiling. I suppose he meant "You're a kind woman".' (June 1802) Transferring the force of the compliment, she used the incident to provide a self-deprecating comment on her own appearance. Despite her energy she had, according to De Quincey, an 'ungraceful even unsexual character to her appearance'.[17] While she was still in her twenties, her teeth had begun to fall out, creating the impression of a woman old beyond her years, with sunken cheeks, so thin and drawn that her aunt and cousin visiting her in 1804 could scarcely recognise her.[18] Her loss of youth and beauty was an occurrence she accepted as resignedly as she accepted her relegation in the Wordsworth household. On 31 May 1802, she observed that 'My tooth broke today. They will soon be gone. Let that pass I shall be beloved – I want no more.' Two days later her journal entry seems to justify her confidence as she described a perfect evening spent alone with her brother, sitting together 'in deep silence at the window – I on a chair and William with his hand on my shoulder. We were deep in Silence and Love, a blessed hour.' But the rapport between them, the ultimate sign of fulfilment in Dorothy's life, was soon to be shattered.

On Monday 4 October 1802 William married Mary Hutchinson at a small church in Brompton-on-Swale. Dorothy, having travelled to Yorkshire for the wedding, could not, at the last minute, bring herself to attend the ceremony. Writing in her journal after their return to Dove Cottage, she gave, unusually, a full and detailed account of her feelings on the occasion.

I slept a good deal of the night and rose fresh and well in the morning. At a little after 8 o'clock I saw them go down the avenue towards the Church. William had parted from me upstairs. I gave him the wedding ring – with how deep a blessing! I took it from my forefinger where I had worn it the whole of the night before – he slipped it again onto my finger and blessed me fervently. When they were absent my dear little Sara prepared the breakfast. I kept myself as quiet as I could, but when I saw the two men running up the walk, coming to tell us it was over, I could stand it no longer and threw myself on the bed where I lay in stillness, neither hearing or seeing anything, till Sara came upstairs to me and said 'They are coming'. This forced me from the bed where I lay and I moved I know not how straight forward, faster than my strength could carry me till I met

my beloved William and fell upon his bosom. He and John
Hutchinson led me to the house and there I stayed to welcome
my dear Mary.

The deeply traumatic nature of the episode is not glossed over
here, either by Dorothy herself or by the family, who were so
sensitive to her condition that they virtually neglected the bride in
the attention they paid to her sister-in-law. Dorothy depicts herself
as abandoned, her position as William's beloved about to be
usurped. Both she and her brother recognised the significance of
the ring that she had worn throughout the night, an emblem of the
unbroken spiritual intimacy they had shared until that day. The
strain she was under while the ceremony was taking place manifests itself in her description of a hypnotic-like trance, culminating
in her almost magnetised movement towards William as he
approached the house from the church. It is a psychologically
fraught description, not least in its choice of vocabulary, indicating
the conflict present in Dorothy between her overpowering sense of
suffering and the loving duty she knew she must display towards
Mary.

After William's marriage, Dorothy's journal entries became more
sporadic until finally they stopped altogether at the beginning of
January 1803, four months after the wedding. The harmony of her
life with William had been radically disturbed, to be replaced by
another lifestyle in which she was superseded. No longer could
Dorothy claim to be the centre of her brother's life, the one person,
most necessary both to his domestic comfort and his artistic
survival. It is not clear how far the marriage represented too a
disruption of her creative energies. Ironically, the Grasmere Journal concludes with a resolution for the future 'to write regularly
and if I can legibly', but nothing ever materialised. It could be that
she no longer had time for writing, for by the beginning of 1803
Mary was pregnant and the supervision of the growing Wordsworth household became Dorothy's responsibility. A bleak note
towards the end of the journal – 'It is today Christmas day
Saturday 25th December 1802. I am 31 years of age. – It is a dull
frosty day' – could be taken as an image of her future, the
emotional climate of her life exposed in the sparse entry.

Dorothy Wordsworth died in January 1855, after a long illness.
She had succumbed to a form of senile dementia while still in her
fifties, and in the last twenty years of her life experienced only

occasional moments of lucidity. Although she produced journals recording travels taken with friends and with her family during the period 1803–28, she never again wrote of life in the Lake District with the same pleasure or keenness that had inspired her earlier work. In fact, much of her travel writing is obscured by her insistence on retrospective comparison with the landscape she had been so closely involved with around Grasmere. The Alfoxden and Grasmere journals both show her literary skill in their evocation of a rural lifestyle in all its manifestations. They gain a further critical interest from the association with Wordsworth's poetry, the light they shed not just on the origins of his verse and his methods of working, but on the part played by the journal as a necessary ingredient in the process of production.

The relationship between brother and sister, while providing a sustaining framework for Dorothy's life, simultaneously inhibited her. The journal became a substitute for the poetry she felt prevented from writing, offering an unpretentious medium of expression, which allowed her to present the material of Romantic poetry with a different slant. Is one literary form 'better' than another? Dorothy certainly thought so, undervaluing her prose writing because it was not verse. Her journal bears witness to the literary problems she encountered, those problems facing many women diarists; of inadequate time for writing – her longest entries are often written during her brother's absence; of the pressures of household duties; and of the lowly status of her output. On the other hand, the private nature of her writing gave her confidence to express herself without fear of criticism. She did not try to mould her style according to any literary criteria, and consequently was able to recreate the substance of her life in its entirety, both as historical record and as imaginative vision. As she wrote of the Columbine that 'I observed that the more shaded plants were always the tallest', so we can see that Dorothy's journal, private and unassuming, was nourished by the protection from the public glare of appreciation that might, as happened with Fanny Burney's fictional career, have distorted its natural development.

4

Dark Imagery:
The Journal
of Mary Shelley

*Well, then, now I am reduced to these white pages which I am to blot with
dark imagery.*

—Mary Shelley, Journal, 5 October 1822

Mary Shelley's journal is an enigmatic document. Despite its
private character, it fails signally to tell us what we want to hear
about the feelings of the writer at some of the sensational moments
of her extraordinary career. Certainly there are occasions when she
gives us full and vivid accounts of events and impressions. During
Mary's travels with Shelley through Europe in 1816, for instance,
she used her diary to record her responses to the dramatic natural
landscape as well as to comment more mundanely on the discomforts of the journey, such as the filthy French beds that she could
not bear to sleep in. And some months after Shelley's death in
1822, we find a harrowing account of her sense of despair as she
attempted to come to terms with her loss. But this sort of charged
emotion is a rare occurrence in her early journal. Rather the main
impression left by Mary Shelley's diary from her most creative
period is that it frequently withholds more than it imparts, with
tantalisingly brief entries occurring at moments of the greatest
passion and intrigue. It is an uneven text in its patchy taciturnity
and its occasional fulsome passages, but its very unevenness, the
silences and spaces it contains, are what provide much of its critical
interest. Recent feminist literary theory has located the specifically
'feminine' in writing in 'the gaps, the absences, the unsayable or
unrepresentable of discourse and representation'. As one critic has
paradoxically suggested, 'If the woman in the text is 'there', she is
also 'not there'.'[1] Mary Shelley's work is full of such contradictions
which relate her writing to a scheme where 'the unsayable', in its
various forms, dominates. Once her journal is read in the light of

her letters and of information about her activities from other sources, its reticence on salient issues becomes transmuted into eloquence, expressing its author's confusions concerning her sense of identity and her creativity, and providing insight into the strategies she adopted in learning to express herself.

Mary Shelley's extant journal runs from 1814 to 1844. The most regular entries were made during the dramatic and often fraught years 1814–22, the period covering Mary's elopement with Shelley, their marriage, their travels together, the writing and publication of *Frankenstein*, and Shelley's tragic death by drowning. The journal was begun on 28 July 1814, the date of Mary and Shelley's elopement, and was originally intended to be a shared journal. The first entries were in fact divided between Shelley and Mary, but when Shelley became preoccupied with his poetry, it was left to Mary to keep up the journal on a regular basis, along with other routine chores. At the same time she was involved in a mass of correspondence, especially when she was living abroad, and frequently a journal entry is helpfully amplified for us by a letter written on the same subject – she in fact spoke of her letters as 'a journal kind of writing'.[2] These tended to be intimate in tone and often contain the sort of emotional profusion we might look for in vain in her diary. For in her correspondence Mary showed no reticence in her passionate declarations of love for Shelley, and her most casual letters to friends are dominated by references to her moods and states of mind. 'A year ago I remember my private hours were all made bitter by reflection on the certainty of death – and how the flight of time has the same power over me', she wrote to Leigh Hunt in 1817. 'Everything passes and one is hardly conscious of enjoying the present before it becomes the past . . . I will not indulge this gloomy feeling . . . I had a dream tonight of the dead being alive which has affected my spirits'.[3] Whereas the letters allowed her licence for such philosophising, she thought of the journal, on the contrary, as a factual record only. As she declared to a friend after Shelley's death, 'While the dayly occurrences of my life were at all interesting to me I kept a kind of journal – more for the sake of dates than anything else'.[4] Yet implicit in her disclaimer is an acknowledgement of the diary's value, attributing meaning to the 'dayly occurrences' which lost all sense of significance when the pivotal focus of her life was removed. Journal-writing for Mary Shelley, whether she was aware of it or not, clearly bore a direct relation to the intrinsic interest and direction of her life overall. Routine events in themselves, however banal, were recorded and valued for the contribution they could make to the total pattern of her experience.

For indubitably we can identify a pattern. As her most recent journal editors point out, the extant journal, 1814–44, seems to divide naturally into three discrete stages, each with its own distinctive style. The first section, covering the early months of Mary's life with Shelley up to May 1815, is open and often ingenuous in tone. For instance:

> Tuesday October 25th 1814. Write to Shelley. Jane goes to Fanny. Read *Elements of Morality*. Grow alarmed. Send to Marshall. Hear that Jane is coming home – she returns – they want her to go into a family – learn the account of Fanny in Wales & that Charles knew of the treachery of the Hookhams & did not tell Jane when she asked him – this is very bad. Hear of Patrickson killing himself – Flather is the true assassin. This is another of those cold-blooded murders that, like Maria Schooning, we may put down to the world.
>
> Call at Peacock's – go to the hotel – Shelley is not there. Go back to Peacock's. Peacock goes to Shelley. Meet Shelley in Holborn. Walk up & down Bartlett's Buildings. Shelley is much shocked at hearing of Patrickson's death. Come with him to Peacock's – talk with him till 10 – return to St Pancras without him. Jane in the dumps all evening about going away.

Mary here is concise but not secretive. Inconsequential details, comments on her feelings and those of her family, plus the rather naive political opinions advanced, give this a gossipy flavour, simple, straightforward and undirected. The diary of the following year from May 1815–16 (the time of *Frankenstein*'s invention) is lost, and the subsequent section from 1816 to 1822 shows a decided change in style, more guarded than the easy, youthful first part, and mostly confined to brief jottings on domestic matters. The sentences are short. Sometimes a whole day's events will be compressed into a single line referring to the weather or to note the book she was currently reading. The third section, after Shelley's death in 1822, changes again to become more emotional, a source of comfort to Mary in her loneliness. 'My thoughts are a sealed treasure which I can confide to none', she wrote in October 1822, her first entry since Shelley's drowning three months earlier.

'White paper – wilt thou be my confident? I will trust thee fully, for none shall see what I write.'[5] It is in the journal of these years too that we can see Mary beginning to salvage something of her own identity, a difficult task after she had lived in the shadow of Shelley's acknowledged genius for so long.

Despite the laconic nature of so many of the early entries, Mary Shelley's diary has much to relate. It tells an essentially feminine story, a personal tale of recurrent loneliness, periodic illnesses, difficult pregnancies, and of a woman's constant anxieties about her family's health. It also reveals a pattern of domestic instability, with repeated images of Mary packing, travelling, moving house. The entries for the years 1816–22, though regular, are terse, mostly written in note form. In January 1820, Mary prefaced her journal with the words 'I now begin a new year – may it be a happier one than the last unhappy one', but the contents are as succinct as any:

Monday 24. – Walk with Shelley – Work – Pack &c.
Tuesday 25. – Pack – Percy Florence baptized – Shelley unwell.
Wednesday 26. – Go to Empoli very uncomfortably in a boat – & the rest of the way much jolted in a carriage – arrive at Pisa.
   Pisa
Thursday 27. – Spend the day with Mrs Mason – read *Travels Before the Flood*.
Friday 28. – A rainy day – look for lodgings – Finish *Travels Before the Flood*. Shelley calls on Mrs Mason & Signor G . . . o. Read Pamphlets.
Saturday 29. – Spend the day at Mrs Mason's. – Go into our lodgings – Read Pamphlets.
Sunday 30. – Finish the Pamphlets – after dinner, go to Mrs Mason's – drink tea there – Begin *Julie*.

This is typical of the curt tone of the journal of this period. Commonplace remarks about the weather are mixed with notes of domestic discomforts and the daily round of visits paid and received. The diary is practical. The absence of opinions, personal details, or analysis would seem to bear out Mary's earlier assessment of its purpose as a factual record, an *aide memoire* only. Edward Trelawney, a friend of Shelley's, commented after his first meeting with Mary that 'she brought us back from the ideal world Shelley had left us in, to the real world'.[6] It could be argued that the catalogue of everyday events that we find throughout the journal

was one method Mary Shelley employed to maintain a sense of
order and normality in an existence that was shifting and uncer-
tain. In the face of her own and Shelley's constant ill-health, her
worries over her children, the continual changes of lodgings, the
financial difficulties in which they frequently found themselves, to
say nothing of the tensions and psychological dramas that were
played out between the Shelleys and their friends, Mary's concentration on objective fact provided something of an anchor for her to
hold on to in a world where emotions were at their height. This is
not, however, a completely satisfying explanation for what ultimately emerge as deliberate omissions and coded messages, designed to subvert and conceal meaning. The very brevity itself is
highly charged. Some of the most telling entries for instance are
those that baldly record moments of crisis in Mary's life with no
expatiation. Even in the apparently innocuous entry quoted above,
she notes, as if in passing, the baptism of her baby son on 25
January, a momentous family event typically understated. We
should bear in mind the fact that at the same time as she was
making this sparse synopsis of her life, Mary was also involved in
writing fictions of the most outrageous kind, works which dealt
with taboo subjects, disturbing in the intensity with which they
explored dangerous subliminal areas of consciousness. *Frankenstein*, the story of a monstrous creation, was written in 1817;
Mathilde, taking incest and death as its central subjects, in 1819; and
Valperga, a Gothic novel based on the life of a demonic Renaissance
prince, in 1820. It is this curious triangular relationship between
the taciturn style of Mary Shelley's journal, the bizarre circumstances of the events surrounding her, told in the letters and
commentaries of her contemporaries, and the extravagant nature
of the novels' subjects and style that is finally so provocative.

Until recently, interest in Mary Shelley's journal was confined to
information it could provide about her celebrated husband, Percy
Bysshe Shelley. Mary was largely ignored as a writer of merit. 'All
Mrs Shelley did was to provide a passive reflection of some of the
wild fantasies which were living in the air around her',[7] suggests
the influential critic Mario Praz, exemplifying the general view and
dismissing Mary with the 'Mrs' merely as the poet's wife, surrounded by greatness but unable to contribute anything original of
her own. Partly this was a view encouraged by Mary herself. In her
introduction to the 1831 edition of *Frankenstein*, she presented
herself as an imitator 'rather doing as others had done, than

putting down the suggestions of my own mind'. Offering an image
of herself as both modest and conventional, she tried to play down
the idea of an authorship which might undermine the model of
conformist femininity she cultivated. She later spoke of how her
'incapacity and timidity always prevented my mingling in the
nightly conversations of Diodati'[8] between Shelley and Byron, and
vehemently rejected any suggestion that she had 'a masculine
understanding'.[9] Edward Trelawney was later to describe her as
'the most conventional slave I have ever met ... devoid of
imagination and Poetry'.[10] The text of *Frankenstein* alone is sufficient to challenge such a judgement, but in addition Mary
Shelley's journal provides irrefutable evidence of her commitment
to her art and the seriousness with which she took herself as a
writer. Trelawney, deceived by the wifely exterior that Mary chose
to project, conveniently ignored the novels she had produced in
his assessment of her, for Mary, 'very averse to bringing myself
forward in print', had in public allowed her husband to take the
limelight, content to remain in his shadow.

Yet Mary Shelley, the daughter of two famous and talented
parents, was forecast a career of brilliance virtually from the
moment of her birth. She was, as a contemporary noted, 'the only
offspring of a union that will certainly be matchless in the present
generation'.[11] Her mother, the pioneering feminist Mary Woll-
stonecraft, died from puerperal fever eleven days after Mary's
birth. Her father was the renowned radical writer William Godwin,
and Mary's troubled relationship with him figures in much of her
writing. She was brought up with her half-sister, Fanny Imlay, her
mother's daughter, and her half-brother, William Godwin, the son
of Godwin's second marriage, as well as a step-brother and sister,
Charles and Jane Clairmont, but despite this extended family, she
was often alone, denied the sympathy and understanding she
needed. When she left home to spend some time in Scotland on
account of her health, Godwin admitted his own 'incompetence for
the education of daughters' and described his relations with Mary
as distant and strained.[12]

Mary was only sixteen when she fell in love with Shelley, whom
she had met on his visits to Godwin. For the next eight years, her
life was to be filled with passion and incident. A synopsis of it
reads rather like the incredible plot of a sensational novel. In July
1814, despite the fact that he was already married, Shelley and
Mary eloped, taking Mary's step-sister Claire Clairmont (the name

by which Jane came to be known) with them. After two months abroad, they returned to England, estranged from their families and beset with legal and financial difficulties. They were constantly in debt and several entries in Mary's early journal refer to demands for money, to visits from bailiffs, and to the couple's struggles to find lodgings where they would be safe from creditors. There were personal problems too, not the least of which was the presence in London of Shelley's wife, Harriet, who was pregnant with their second child. Much of the time Mary and Shelley were forced to live apart as he desperately tried to avoid being arrested for debt. Claire Clairmont was an extra complication. Throughout her journal, Mary steadfastly refuses to expand on the subject of Claire's often awkward position in their household, although the tensions between them emerge in brief but pointed comments and in a private system of symbols she later adopted to refer to Claire. Her reticence suggests her unease about Claire's relations with Shelley, who had notoriously liberal views on the subject of sexual experiment and whose intimacy with Claire became increasingly marked. Subsequently, Mary was to make no reference to Claire's more public liaison with Lord Byron, nor to the birth of Claire's daughter by Byron, Allegra, in 1817. Throughout the diary, Mary's reserve on sexual matters forms an acute contrast to the violent passions and unconventional behaviour of those around her, as documented by Byron, Trelawney and others. Her journal for January 1817, for example, refers only obliquely to the events of the household.

> *Saturday 12.* – Charles Clairmont – Four days of idleness. Letters from Shelley, he is obliged to stay in London. Read *Comus*, *Knights of the Swan*, 1st volume of Goldsmith's *Citizen of the World*.
> *Thursday 16.* Read Cumberland's *Memoirs*; work.
> *Friday 17.* Read *Memoirs*, walk out and work.
> *Saturday 18.* Read *Memoirs* and work.
> *Sunday 19.* Finish the *Memoirs of Cumberland* – read *The Rambler*.

Yet on that Saturday, 12 January, Claire's baby had been born. Although the confinement took place under her roof, Mary's journal comment remains cryptic, her 'Four days of idleness' being her only reference to the fact that more pressing domestic matters caused her to neglect her writing during this period. We can only infer that her journal was written with extreme care, perhaps to avoid any suggestion of irregularity. Despite – or perhaps because of – the unorthodox circumstances of her life, she tried to preserve the decorous image that she felt was incumbent upon her position. 'All I ask is obscurity', she was later to assert,[13] fearing exposure to the world's censure. Although she occasionally gave vent to her feelings, both in the journal and, more freely, in her long, intimate letters, it was primarily in her novels that she allowed her emotional turmoil to surface: those strange, fantastic fictions which unleashed the fears and anxieties of their author to the full.

For there is a direct relationship to be traced between Mary Shelley's published writings and her personal journal. As Virginia Woolf pointed out, 'The extraordinary woman depends on the ordinary woman. . . . it is only when we can measure the way of life and the experience of life made possible to the ordinary woman that we can account for the success or failure of the extraordinary woman as writer'.[14] Although Woolf was referring to different women in her distinction between 'ordinary' and 'extraordinary' here, her comment might aptly be applied to the separate elements in a single personality. Mary Shelley's *Frankenstein* gives us the extraordinary woman. Her journal gives us the ordinary one. But the two documents are interdependent. The separate parts form the whole, both simultaneous products of the same mind. It is in the journal that we find the genesis of *Frankenstein*, in the day-to-day concerns of Mary Shelley's own life, as she wandered from place to place, establishing homes only to have them disbanded. Motherless, isolated from her family and much of the time exiled from her native land, she was dependent on Shelley's rather erratic love for her succour and support. So does Frankenstein's monster parallel Mary's daily life in his fugitive and nomadic existence, searching for love, for a stable home and a normal family life, unable to accept his own difference from the human society he sees around him. As Mary admitted in her later introduction to the novel, writing was an activity which meant that 'I was not confined to my own identity'. Rather it allowed her access to her other self, to explore the regions of her psyche that she was unwilling to probe too deeply in her diary. 'Above all', she wrote in her journal, 'let me fearlessly descend into the remotest cavern of my own mind – carry the torch of self-knowledge into its dimmest recesses – but too happy if I dislodge any evil spirit or enshrine any new deity in some hitherto uninhabited nook.' (25 February 1822) Mary's fiction indeed dislodged the 'evil spirit', the anger, hatred, vengefulness, aggression and pain which define her monster, but which lay dormant in the quiet, reserved persona she presented to the world. As one critic has commented, the subsequent defensive introduction to the novel reiterates the thematic emphasis of the text itself as Mary Shelley 'expresses the tension she feels between the self-denial demanded by domestic activity and the self-assertiveness essential to the act of artistic creation'.[15] In developing the twin characters of Victor Frankenstein and the monster, Mary was able to project aspects of her divided personality which in her journal she controlled and thus contained.

In that 1831 preface to *Frankenstein*, Mary asked the question which has intrigued critics ever since. 'How I, then a young girl, came to think of, and to dilate upon, so very hideous an idea?' Much of the answer lies in that bleak, spare chronicle, her journal. In the spring of 1816, Mary, Shelley and Claire had left England for Europe and were settled in a cottage on the shores of Lake Geneva, where they became neighbours of the poet, Lord Byron, in his Villa Diodati. Shelley was occupied with Byron, and Mary, isolated from her husband and bereft of the intellectual companionship she valued, was left much to her own reflections. In June 1816 she began work on *Frankenstein*. Just over a year later, after some months spent in England, the Shelleys were back in Italy again where they lived until Shelley's death. It was during this period that Mary wrote *Mathilda* and *Valperga*, Gothic fictions of the most extreme kind, dealing with ungovernable passion and tormented, destructive relationships, and permeated by an overriding sense of gloom. The experience of unhappiness and rejection which pervades *Frankenstein* and the later works covertly speaks to us on virtually every page of the journal of this time, however subdued its expression. The three novels emanated from feelings of wretchedness that consumed Mary Shelley in the turbulent, difficult and often lonely days that her diary records. All employed a personal narrative format. The private letter, the memoir and the journal, the subjective literary forms which were most familiar to her, were used to full effect in her fiction, allowing her to adopt a variety of personae to convey submerged areas of her experience. In an essay on Emily Dickinson, the feminist critic Adrienne Rich has commented that 'it is always what is under pressure in us, especially under pressure of concealment – that explodes in poetry.'[16] If *Frankenstein* is the poetic explosion, the pressure that produced it is on full display in Mary Shelley's journal.

Five years after she had eloped with Shelley, Mary wrote that 'if all the events of the five years were blotted out, I might be happy – but to have won & then cruelly to have lost the associations of four years is not an accident to which the human mind can bend without much suffering'. (4 August 1819) She was writing after the death of her adored son William, aged three, a calamity so dreadful that it was two months before she could bear to return to her journal, with its last pathetic clutch at hope on 3 June 1819, 'William is very ill, but gets better towards the evening'. William had caught malaria, and the deterioration of his condition was noted meticulously if concisely by his mother. He was the third and most cherished of her children to die. Later she described how 'after my William's death this world seemed only a quicksand sinking beneath my feet'. (19 October 1822) The previous year, in Venice, she had witnessed the death of her little girl Clara, just a year old, who had been born in September 1817. Characteristically Mary's journal dismisses the event in a sentence. 'We go to Venice with my poor Clara who dies the moment we get there'. (24 September 1818) It is important not to confuse such brevity with callousness. Rather, as Mary grew older she learned how to suppress her feelings more effectively. Her laconic treatment of Clara's death and her utter silence about William's indicate a more withdrawn woman than the girl who had given birth to her first baby in February 1815, only to discover it dead in bed beside her twelve days later. One of the most moving sections in Mary Shelley's early journal is that which deals with this ordeal. On Monday 6 March 1815, Mary recorded in her journal, 'Find my baby dead. Send for Hogg. Talk. A miserable day.' It is the very simplicity and restraint of her language that helps to lay bare the anguish beneath. But although she tried to repress her grief in her writing, Mary could not maintain the same degree of control over her subconscious mind. Three days later, we find the entry, 'Still think about my little baby – 'tis hard, indeed, for a mother to lose a child', and on 13 March, when Shelley and Claire had gone to town, Mary stayed at home and brooded silently on her loss. 'Think of my little dead baby', she confided to her journal. 'This is foolish, I suppose; yet, whenever I am left alone to my own thoughts, and do not read to divert them, they always come back to the same point – that I was a mother, and am so no longer'. A fortnight after the death, her journal shows that she had not been able to eradicate the trauma from her consciousness. On 19 March she noted sadly, 'Dream that my little baby came to life again; that it had only been cold, and that we rubbed it before the fire, and it lived. Awake and find no baby. I think about the little thing all day. Not in good spirits'. The following day, Monday 20 March, 'Dream again about my baby'. Haunted by the dual associated images of birth and death, of discovery and loss, of hopeful dream and harsh reality, Mary had already found in her own experience the elements that were to provide the bedrock of *Frankenstein*.

Not unnaturally, motherhood obsessed her. During the eight years that she lived with Shelley, Mary was almost continually pregnant or nursing, and references to her health during pregnancy and worries about her children's welfare fill her journal. In 1816, when she began writing *Frankenstein*, her second child William was a few months old. By the end of the year, she was pregnant again. Later she was to suffer a near-fatal miscarriage. Only one of her children, her son, Percy Florence, born in November 1819, was to survive. Given the context of the journal, it is easy to read *Frankenstein* as a birth trauma.[17] Mary's nightmare about re-animating a corpse contains both the hopes and the fears of such a terrifying possibility, re-enacting the experience of birth and delineating what had been for Mary its accompanying terrors of infant mortality. In this, Mary's journal directly anticipates the ambitions and the dreadful actuality of Victor Frankenstein's creation. In Chapter 20 of the novel, Mary describes Frankenstein looking at the half-completed female counterpart to his male monster. 'The remains of the half-finished creature, whom I had destroyed, lay scattered on the floor, and I almost felt as if I had mangled the living flesh of a human being'.[18] The image of miscarriage mingles with a sense of slaughter as the creator assumes responsibility for the aborted being, so physically realised. The repeated acts of creation and death had penetrated deep into Mary's consciousness. The mirage of her past experience reappears to unnerve Frankenstein as he begins again on a project the thought of which had once delighted him. 'Three years before I had created a fiend whose unparalleled barbarity had desolated my heart, and filled it for ever with the bitterest remorse. I was now about to form another being, of whose dispositions I was alike ignorant'.[19] The innocence of Mary's youth and her careless passion for Shelley had led her to a chilling understanding of what her future, with its unseen possibilities, could bring. In *Frankenstein*'s unnamed monster we find the realisation of a parent's nightmare. Like Mary's own babies, what originated with self-seeking pleasure turned out to be an image of death.

But although we can be in no doubt about the powerful effect such closeness to death had on her, Mary Shelley did not allow her grief or her horror to be voiced explicitly through the medium of her journal. Her letters and her imaginative writings, pervaded by a sense of loss, reveal her morbid fascination with death and bereavement. The journal, however, remained tight-lipped. In October 1816, Mary's half-sister, Fanny Imlay committed suicide by taking an overdose of laudanum. Mary's journal notes only that after 'a very alarming letter from Fanny, Shelley goes immediately to Bristol; we sit up for him till 2 in the morning, when he returns but brings no particular news.' Three days later, she reported that 'He returns with the worst account. A miserable day. Two letters from Papa. Buy mourning and work in the evening'. In December of the same year, she recounted the suicide of Shelley's wife, whose body was found in the River Serpentine, with no sign of visible emotion. 'A letter from Hookham', she noted, 'with the news of the death of Harriet Shelley. Walk out with Shelley. He goes to town after dinner – read Chesterfield.' There the entry for the day ends, the startling and the mundane, the horrific and the normal, placed side by side. The complications surrounding these events are passed over: that Fanny Imlay's depression was possibly a result of her hopeless love for Shelley; that Harriet, abandoned by Shelley, was pregnant with an unknown man's child when she died. The next entry in Mary's journal, written about a fortnight later, notes another fateful event. 'I have omitted writing my journal for some time', she apologised. 'Shelley goes to London & returns – I go with him – spend the time between Leigh Hunts and the Godwins – a marriage takes place on the 29th – draw – read Lord Chesterfield and Locke'. The marriage she was referring to was her own.

The secretive nature of much of the journal finds its complement in the dark emanations of the imaginative fictions. But whether private or public, the act of writing formed a central feature of Mary Shelley's daily experience. Together with her reading, it is the most frequently mentioned activity in the journal. Repeatedly we find the single word 'write' in the description of a day's events. The diary tells us of projects started and never completed – a work significantly entitled *Hate* for example – as well as her concern over the publishing fortunes of her novels. She was a conscious artist, intensely aware of the problems of composition. Referring in a letter to the reception of her novel *The Last Man* in 1826 she commented in a letter, 'You can form no idea of the difficulty of the subject – the necessity of making the scene (general) universal to all mankind and of combining this with a particular interest which must constitute the novel – If I had at the commencement foreseen the excessive trouble & then (much worse) the state of imperfection in which partly for want of time I was obliged to leave it – I should never have had the courage to begin.'[20] Like other Romantic writers, she was keenly interested in the way in which the creative imagination operated, yet apart from the evidence of the methodical approach to writing that the journal provides, we find little analysis of her own performance.

Once again we are faced with her silence on an important issue, a silence that would seem to reinforce the idea that Mary Shelley was determined to isolate the different areas of her personality. The private woman, immersed in domestic affairs, mother, wife and social being, was kept distinct from the independent, forceful writer, whose thoughts and fantasies soared beyond everyday routine. 'The most contemptible of all lives', she wrote in one of her more expansive moments, 'is where you live in the world & none of your passions or affections are called into action – I am convinced I could not live thus'. (25 February 1822) Undoubtedly she was aware of the division in her self. 'Sometimes I awaken from my ordinary monotony & my thoughts flow', she noted, 'until as it is exquisite pain to stop the flowing of the blood, so it is painful to check expression & make the overflowing mind return to its usual channel'. (18 February 1822) For Mary, it was a daily routine which resembled the dreamlike state, as she moved mechanically through her everyday tasks. It was in her visionary imagination that her real life functioned. A great deal of recent critical commentary on *Frankenstein* has emphasised the metaphoric dimensions of the novel, focusing on the monster as the embodiment of a freed imagination, a vehicle for the author's untamed spirit, angry, threatening and destructive.[21] Certainly the style of Mary Shelley's early journal provides the counterpart to the wild terrors of the fiction. Her unnatural discretion, the avoidance of mention of pain and anguish, the elaborate system of signs she concocted to refer to Claire, and to unpleasant episodes, such as a blackmail attempt on Shelley, give every indication of a repressed sensibility, intent on maintaining silence. In addition they show us a writer determined to distinguish between the two areas of her literary experience.

The journal also offers us a portrait of a woman bound by domestic ties. The images of liberty, flight and open spaces which *Frankenstein* incorporates are offset by the claustrophobic quality of much of the journal. Despite the nomadic existence led by the Shelleys, Mary's picture of her days as communicated to her diary is one of confinement (often literal), her restriction intensified by illness. While Shelley travelled to see to their business affairs, went sailing round Lake Geneva with Lord Byron, or visited Claire, Mary remained in a variety of rented rooms, whether in England or in Italy, waiting for his return and for his instructions on where to go next. In August 1816 her diary entries record somewhat grimly what was gradually becoming a routine.

> *Friday 2nd.* – I go to the town with Shelley, to buy a telescope for his birthday present. In the evening Lord Byron and he go out in the boat, and, after their return, Shelley and Clare go up to Diodati; I do not, for Lord Byron did not seem to wish it.
>
> *Wednesday 14th.* Read *Le Vieux de la Montagne* – translate. Shelley reads Tacitus and goes out with Lord Byron before, and after dinner. Lewis comes to Diodati. Shelley goes up there, and Clare goes up to copy. Remain at home and read *Le Vieux de la Montagne*.
>
> *Tuesday 27th* ... Shelley dines at Diodati, and remains there all evening. They go out a short time in the boat.

Images of imprisonment pervade her journal 'It would be pleasant enough living in Pisa if one had a carriage & could escape from one's house to the country', she grumbled privately (12 November 1820). After Shelley's death, this develops a more metaphoric strain. It was life itself that seemed to Mary to be 'a painful prison' (19 October 1822), where 'my active thoughts beat against the bars of their cage' (17 November 1822), while her son was 'the only chain that links me to time – but for you I should be free' (5 October 1822). Given these conditions of enforced passivity, recourse to her imagination was perhaps inevitable. As she told her journal, 'People must know little of me who think that, abstractedly, I am content with my present mode of life – Activity of spirit is my sphere'. (11 November 1822)

One of the few constants in the diary is Mary's record of her diet of reading. She made a point of listing all books currently under review in the household, not only in her jottings for individual days, but in a table at the end of each year, which catalogued all books read in the preceding twelve months. She was immersed in an intellectual and imaginative world which ran parallel to her domestic one. Elsewhere she noted that reading took her out of herself and helped to alleviate the morbid introspection to which she was prone. It was by no means a casual pursuit, but became a crucial point of reference in marking her intellectual progress. Her reading was a natural corollary of her creative output. The history books, travel literature, romances and poetry she devoured were used to inform her own writing. She was meticulous in her research for her novels. In 1820, for instance, we find her reading up contemporary sources for information about Castruccio, Prince of Lucca, for *Valperga*, her novel based on his life story. Amidst the domestic turmoil, she craved mental stimulation, working hard at the classics, philosophy, science, and studying English literature in foreign translations in order to extend her literary range. 'I must be more industrious, especially in learning Latin which I neglected shamefully last summer', she rebuked herself in the winter of *Frankenstein*'s composition.

Yet there is a definite tension between Mary Shelley's determination to discipline her mind and her natural tendency towards freer inspirational writing. 'I am busy writing an Article for the London', she wrote to a friend in 1815, ' – after which I shall begin a Novel – not *Alfred* – more wild & imaginative & I think more in my way ... as I listen to music (especially instrumental) new ideas raise and develope themselves, with greater energy & truth than at any other time – thus I am becoming very fond of instrumental music of which before I was more careless – singing confines one's thoughts to the words – in mere playing they form a song for themselves which if it be not more in harmony with the notes at least is more so with one's tone of mind'.[22] Even at this early stage in her literary career she was finding the structures of language themselves prohibitive. Groping for a personal literary voice, she needed to reject what she felt were the imposed restraints of logic and systematic thought. Her sense of the inadequacy of language – 'I have long accustomed myself to the study of my own heart, and have sought and found in its recesses that which cannot embody itself in words – hardly in feelings', she wrote in her diary in May 1823 – could help to explain further the sparse nature of her journal style when dealing with a life of emotional intensity. As a twentieth-century literary theorist has commented, 'the feminine takes its place with the absence, silence, or incoherence that discourse represses'.[23] Mary Shelley, identifying herself strongly with her sex ('most women I believe wish that they had been men – so do not I', she wrote in her journal on 3 December 1824) perhaps sought recourse in silence, a precondition of her femininity. Women, she noted 'are all alike – we live by detail – & feel too sensibly every passing incident' (23 April 1830). In such circumstances, language, with its reliance on logic and externalisation, was clearly useless.

Occasionally Mary used the journal as a direct source for her fiction. The Romantic interest in landscape which had occupied Shelley's attention during much of the 1814 journey through Europe surfaces in Mary's description of their trip to Chamonix in July 1816, the time when she was composing *Frankenstein*.

> *Wednesday 24th.* Today is rainy therefore we cannot go to Col du Baume – About ten the weather appears clearing up – Shelley and I begin our journey to Montanverd – Nothing can be more desolate than the ascent of this mountain – the trees in many places have been torn away by avalanches and some half leaning over others intermingled with stones present the appearance of vast & dreadful desolation – It began to rain almost as soon as we left our inn – when we had mounted considerably we turned to look on the scene – a dense white mist covered the vale & tops of the scattered pines peeping above were the only objects that presented themselves – The rain continued in torrents – we were wetted to the skin so that when we has ascended more than half way we resolved to turn back – As we descended Shelley went before and tripping he fell upon his knee – this added to the weakness occasioned by a blow on his ascent – he fainted & was for some minutes incapacitated from continuing his route.
>
> We arrived wet to the skin – I read nouvelle nouvelles and write my story – Shelley writes part of letter.
> *Thursday 25th* This day promises to be fine & we set out at nine for Montanvert *Beaucoup de Monde* go also – we get to the top at twelve and behold *le mer de Glace*. This is the most desolate place in the world – iced mountains surround it – no sign of vegetation appears except on the place from which we view the scene – we went on the ice – It is traversed by irregular crevices whose sides of ice appear blue while the surface is of a dirty white – We dine on the mountain – the air is very cold yet many flowers grow

here & among other the *rhododendron* or *Rose des Alps* in great profusion – We descend leisurely – Shelley goes to see the mine of Amianthe but finds nothing worth seeing.

We arrive at the inn at six fatigued by our days journey but pleased and astonished by the world of ice that was opened to our view – .

This extract is worth quoting in full because of the use Mary Shelley made of it in Chapter 10 of *Frankenstein* when she chose the *mer de glace* as the setting for the encounter between Frankenstein and the monster. Filtered through the subjective consciousness of the writer, the scenery both in the journal and in the novel becomes imbued with personality. The landscape is perceived in terms of its effect upon the travellers, its emotional power to instil awe and the sense of desolation it conveys, as well as the practical dangers it affords. It exhibits perfectly the qualities noted by *Frankenstein*'s reviewer that 'There never was a wilder story imagined; yet like most of the fictions of this age, it has an air of reality attached to it'.[24] Shelley and Mary are wet, uncomfortable, miserable. Shelley falls, faints and is incapacitated. So does Victor Frankenstein, amidst torrential rain and thick mists, find his path to the summit exhausting and fraught with danger. We should note too the sense of frustration the expedition elicits, a frustration that we find recurring in the journal as a whole, with its continuum of dashed hopes and thwarted plans. Here, at Chamonix, the first day's climb has to be abandoned and even on the second day, after they have achieved the summit, Shelley's expectations of the mine of Amianthe are disappointed, an unwitting paradigm of the pattern of their lives, reverberating throughout Mary's fictions of failed aspirations.

The journal description of Chamonix is one of contrasts, a strange combination of beauty and devastation, of barrenness and wild vegetation. On the *mer de glace* nothing can survive, but Mary's scientific eye notes and classifies the unfamiliar Alpine vegetation growing on the lower mountain side. In the earlier accounts of her European travels, Mary had concentrated mainly on personal, factual remarks about the dirt, the beds, the food, the rudeness of the natives. On 11 August 1814, for instance, she described with disgust an overnight stop in France at 'a kind of an *auberge* where having in some degree satisfied our hunger by milk and sour bread we retired to a wretched apartment to bed – But first let me observe that we here discovered that the inhabitants were not in the habit of washing themselves either when they rose or went to bed'. It was Shelley who expounded upon the sublime qualities of the surroundings, the forests and mountains that Mary barely registered. Two years later, however, Mary's response to her journey shows her exposure to the conversation and values of Shelley and Byron. Her sensibilities had become attuned to the power of the natural spectacle. When mingled with her natural pragmatism, this resulted in the depiction of a landscape that was both realistic and unearthly, a combination that she exploited to the full in the psychological landscape of *Frankenstein* where the alien territory of the glacier was recreated as essentially life-denying.

It is in the journal too that stories of the supernatural were recorded for further use. Matthew Lewis, the author of the sensational Gothic novel, *The Monk* (1796), visited Shelley and Mary in August 1816, just when Mary was in the throes of writing *Frankenstein*. He told them four ghost stories which Shelley included in the journal, and which Mary later transcribed for publication. They all focused on death, on visions that could not be explained by rational means, and on the sensations of fear experienced by the protagonists, elements which have clear links with the fiction that Mary was then absorbed in. In October 1818 she related several more tales of horror, again concerned with the walking dead, with unaccountable occurrences, and with the limitations of human perception. Like the stories that Lewis had told them, these were carefully sifted and some chosen for inclusion in Mary's essay 'On Ghosts', in the *London Magazine*. Her keen interest in the unexplored regions of the mind is manifested elsewhere in the journal. We hear of Shelley's experiments with 'magnetism' (15 December 1820), the name then given to hypnosis, in an attempt to relieve pain by allowing himself to relinquish control over his conscious responses. Mary's constant state of apprehension, occasioned by her bitter experiences of disaster over the years, determined much of the tone of the journal as fearful and foreboding. 'Babe unwell – We are unhappy & discontented', was the sum of her entry for 17 June 1820, as she recognised some symptoms in Percy Florence that recalled to her the onset of William's fatal illness. Like the characters in the ghost stories that had gripped her imagination, she was beset by premonitions of doom, several of which were to be realised. On 4 August 1821,

Shelley's birthday, she was unable to survey her present situation without looking both to the past and the future, 'S birthday – 7 years are now gone – what changes what a life – we now appear tranquil – yet who knows what wind – I will not prognosticate evil – We have had enough of it – when I came to Italy – I said all is well if it were permanent – it was more passing than an Italian twilight – I now say the same – May it be a polar day – Yet that too has an end.' Her broken sentences mirror her uncertainties; the retreat from language allows her latent fear and the ephemerality of her hopes to be exposed. On 11 January 1822, Shelley and his friend Edward Williams discussed plans for building a boat on the model of an American schooner. Mary noted later that 'on that night – one of gaiety and thoughtlessness – Jane's and my miserable destiny was decided. We then said laughing each to the other, 'Our husbands decide without asking our consent, or having our concurrence: for to tell you the truth, I hate this boat, though I say nothing'.[25] Characteristically, Mary's public silence belied her inner feelings. On the first of July, Shelley and Edward Williams set sail in the boat bound for Leghorn. On the eighth they began their return journey despite a storm that was already brewing. Their bodies, water-logged and half-eaten by fish, were washed ashore ten days later. From 8 July to 2 October, Mary's journal is blank. When she took up her pen again, it was to pour out her feelings of inconsolable despair after three months of widowhood.

October 2 – Genoa
On the 8th July I finished my journal. This is a curious coincidence – the date still remains, the fatal 8th – a monument to show that all ended then. And I begin again? – oh. never! But several motives induce me, when the day has gone down, and all is silent around me, steeped in sleep, to pen, as occasion wills, my reflexions & feelings. First; I have now no friend. For eight years I communicated with unlimited freedom with one whose genius, far transcending mine, awakened & guided my thoughts; I conversed with him; rectified my errors of judgement, obtained new lights from him, & my mind was satisfied. Now I am alone! Oh, how alone!'

From this moment on her journal changes its character. No longer is it a repository for brief facts about the weather, daily visits, books read etc. Instead Mary focuses on her personal condition, giving full utterance to her melancholy. Maintaining her practised role of female inadequacy, she adopts in the journal the unguarded, intimate tone that she had previously reserved for letter-writing, and indeed some of the first entries of this period are written as if directly addressing Shelley himself. 'You will be with me in all my studies, dearest love!' she wrote with desperate assurance on 7 October. 'Your voice will no longer applaud me, but in spirit you will visit & encourage me. I know you will. What were I if I did not believe that you still existed?' Her closing question reveals her lack of confidence in her own independent identity, and indeed she felt deeply the instability of the present moment. 'So may it be said of me that I am nothing', she wrote despondently on 17 November 1822, 'but I was something and still I cling to what I was'. For her it was the past which provided the only sense of reality.

Feeling herself abandoned and isolated, she consciously acknowledged the existence of the separate worlds which she inhabited, the actual and the visionary. 'Entirely & despotically engrossed' by her personal feelings, she now altered her priorities, trying to convince herself that she could lead 'as it were an *internal* life, quite different from the outward & apparent one'. (7 October 1822) Significantly she noted how her exterior demeanour, quiet, restrained and apparently calm, belied her inner tumult, and brought accusations of coldness from her critics. 'No one seems to understand or to sympathize with me. They all seem to look on me as one without affections – without any sensibility – my sufferings are thought a cypher – & I feel myself degraded before them; knowing that in their hearts they degrade me from the rank which I deserve to possess. – I feel dejected & cowed before them, feeling as if I might be the senseless person they appear to consider me. But I am not. I am much given to self examination, & this does not add to my confidence before my judges – for so I consider all who behold me . . .' (21 October 1822).

Mary's sense of isolation was profound. The inability to express herself in public, coupled with the removal of the one person in whom she had been able to confide unreservedly, results in a corresponding alteration in the function and shape of her journal. The loneliness and despondency which had formed an undercurrent to the journal of the past eight years, now became the explicit subject of her private writings. Consequently, writing itself was converted into a form of therapy, going some way towards alleviating her inner confusions. 'I have made my first probation in writing & it has done me great good, & I get more calm', she found in November 1822, referring to the preparation of her story 'A Tale of the Passions, or the Death of Despina' for the *Liberal*. Yet at the same time as she was spurred on to articulacy, she was made acutely aware of the deficiencies of language as an effective medium of expression. Denied any other outlet, she turned to her journal for support. 'But can I express all I feel? Can I give words to thoughts and feelings that, as a tempest, hurry me along? ... Beneath all this my imagination never flags. Literary labours, the improvement of my mind, and the enlargement of my idea, are the only occupations that elevate me from my lethargy.' (2 October 1822) The style of her entries had changed radically. Where before her control had produced compression, now her indulgence in emotion led to diffuseness. Her phrasing became extravagant, drawing on overblown literary conventions. It is not surprising, so sensitive as she was to the nuances of language, that she was dissatisfied with the effect.

In the years 1822–44, Mary Shelley's journal became a record of her unfailing devotion to Shelley's memory and her commitment to their son, Percy. Financially matters were not easy for her, and much of the later sections of the journal record her struggles to make ends meet. Shelley's father refused to see her, threatened to deprive her of her son, and made numerous difficulties over Percy's allowance. Mary was forced to become reliant on her writing to bring in an income. In 1823 she returned to England where she lived until her death in 1851. She spent a great deal of time in her journal moaning about the English climate and its effect on her creative abilities. In retrospect she felt that despite the misery of her Italian years, her writing then had been effortless, inspired by the Italian culture and by the dramatic local scenery. 'Then I could think, and my imagination could invent and combine, and self become absorbed in the grandeur of the universe I created' (15 May 1824), she wrote, ground down by the chill of her first London spring for six years. Perhaps she was right. Although she threw herself with enthusiasm into her novel, *The Last Man*, a futuristic fantasy modelled on Shelley's iconoclastic personality, she never achieved the dynamism that had permeated *Franken-stein*. Her later works were more conventional, historical novels, travelogues, essays and editions of Shelley's works. Her journal entries of this last period, although infrequent, were more substantial than before. They present an initial picture of virtually unrelieved gloom, of monotony and of emotional starvation, a picture which gradually changes to one of resolve and quiet acceptance. In 1840 she wrote about the change that time had effected, 'Years have – how much! – cooled the ardent and swift spirit that at such hours bore me freely along. Yet, although I no longer soar, I repose. Though I no longer deem all things attainable, I enjoy what is, and while I feel that whatever I have lost of youth and hope I have the enduring affection of a noble heart, and Percy shows such excellent dispositions that I feel that I am much the gainer in life.' (1 June 1840) Her comment forms an astute analysis of the aspirations of her earlier years when her imaginative powers were at their height.

Ironically, the immersion in personal feeling and recollection that we find in the later journal is often less informative than the reticence of previous volumes, offering such telling evidence of emotional restraint. 'The weight of social imagination rests in denial, repression, concealment',[26] says Patricia Meyer Spacks, while Adrienne Rich has pointed out that 'Lying is done with words and also with silences'.[27] In its silent, social lies, Mary Shelley's journal forms the natural corollary to her published writing. Through consistent, controlled daily entries, she created the access for her fiction to disrupt and release deep-seated anxieties and emotions which touched a collective consciousness in *Frankenstein*.

5

Behind the Scenes:
The Early Diary of
Elizabeth Barrett Browning

My diary is not meant to be read by any person except myself: but she
deserves to be let behind the scenes.

—Elizabeth Barrett. *Diary* 1831

Elizabeth Barrett kept a journal for one year only, 1831–2, the year
she was twenty-five. For that year she kept it faithfully, writing up
her long entries daily, with hardly any omissions. It was a year that
was full of tensions and uncertainties in her life, all of which
surface in the pages of her diary to give us a picture of a lonely and
frustrated woman. For Elizabeth Barrett's journal, with its
wholehearted immersion in feeling, bears witness to her intensely
passionate nature, its daily entries spilling anger, doubt, resentment and bewilderment onto the empty pages. At a time when
other women of her age were managing households and bearing
children, Elizabeth Barrett had neither lover, husband nor family
responsibility to occupy her attention. Her days were spent in
solitary reading, in teaching Greek to her small brothers, and in
trying to avoid the desultory engagements which were the bedrock
of mid-nineteenth century leisured society. Her journal, recording
her empty hours, is packed with obsessive dissection of minute
events and her own profoundly felt reactions to the trivia of
existence. Acutely aware of her own displaced situation, she
aggravated her maladjustment by escaping family commitments
whenever she could, and turned instead for consolation to the
writers of the past with whom she could share a world of
imaginative sympathy. Yet her diary, written in a year when she
produced little else of artistic merit, is of much more than mere
biographical interest. It contains crucial features, both of content
and style, that illuminate her later position as a poet and social
commentator, intent on maintaining her distinctively female

identity and exceptionally sensitive to her literary isolation.

In 1831 Elizabeth Barrett was living at her family home, Hope End in Ledbury, Herefordshire, with her younger brothers and sisters, in the care of their Aunt Arabella, 'Bummy' of the journal. Her mother had died just over two years previously, causing Elizabeth to withdraw into a despair from which she had not fully recovered. Her father, Edward Moulton Barrett, had found himself in grave financial difficulties after the failure of his Jamaican estates which had been the basis of the family fortunes. Forced to sell Hope End, he spent much of that year away from home, arranging the sale of the house from a distance and trying to find alternative accommodation for his large family. His absence was sorely felt by his eldest daughter, who had relied on his notice and commendation for her well-being, and who was consequently thrown on her own resources, with some disquieting results. Her journal, begun in a spirit of playfulness, became a site for the uncovering of feelings and psychological revelations that she might well have preferred not to confront. As she commented much later in a letter to a friend,

> Once indeed, for one year, I kept a diary in detail and largely, at the end of the twelve months, was in such a crisis of self-disgust that there was nothing for me but to leave off the diary. Did you ever try the effect of a diary upon your own mind? It is curious, especially where elastic spirits and fancies work upon a fixity of character and situation.[1]

More than any other of the diarists treated in this study, Elizabeth Barrett used her diary for continuous and concentrated emotional analysis. 'Let me be honest if I cant be wise!', she pleaded with herself only a week after she had launched on her intense chronicle of feeling. Familiar with the works of sentimental and Romantic writers, she adopted their methods of immediate recall to capture the sensations of the moment, loading the most casual action with heavy significance. Recording, and thus re-living, the anxieties, hopes, passions and petty jealousies of her otherwise blank days became a way of magnifying their importance, as well as operating as a form of self-torture. 'Oh I never never should have begun this journal!', she wrote distractedly on 16 June 1831. 'Noone should write journals, who is not wiser, on a hundred points, than I am! & stronger, on a thousand!' It is a mark of her resilience and her inner courage that she persevered, and did not shrink from the truth as her diary gradually revealed it to her. As well as its personal value, however, the diary had a deeper literary function, for it marked Elizabeth Barrett's first serious experiment in writing in a non-poetic mode. In her journal, for the first time, she composed a sequential narrative, a story that had no precedent in the great literature of the past but took its foundation in her own unmediated experience.

In the summer of 1831, the date when the *Diary* begins, Elizabeth Barrett was a forlorn figure, lacking real companionship within her family circle. She had been ill during her teens, an illness which had never been properly diagnosed, but which had been serious enough for her to be prescribed enforced rest for a year. From that time on she accepted, and some would say exploited, the role of invalid, and as a result had never taken up the duties which might have been expected of the eldest daughter in a pre-Victorian household, never acted as hostess nor managed household affairs. Instead, with her social development arrested at the age of fifteen, she was treated by the other members of her family as delicate and unconventional. Effectively relieved then of all domestic responsibility, her position at home had become somewhat anomalous. At the age of twenty-five, mature in body but sexually unawakened, she was in situation a child, needing to ask permission if she wanted to go out, scolded for having dirty shoes, sulking in her room at cross words from her aunt, who once said 'that I required more looking after than my squirrel, & that I ought to have a cage made for me!'.[2] Others too took up this view of her. She records how a neighbour 'called me her pet today, & "could not help treating me still as a child"'. (25 October 1831) Tellingly she reported these comments with relish. In itself her position was not of course remarkable, for all single women in mid-nineteenth century England were legally and politically considered to be minors. It was only to be expected that they should be regarded as such socially. What is striking, however, is Elizabeth Barrett's own ambivalence towards this juvenile condition, for her journal reveals her both as attracted to the childlike image and struggling to free herself from it. Indeed the whole tenor of her diary with its curious combination of intellectual restlessness and emotional immaturity smacks of adolescence. As she admitted, 'I am very extravagant with my expectations & feelings!' (p. 167) This extravagance characterises much of the content and style of her journal,

and makes it a sharp contrast to the formal verse she had produced
in her poetic apprenticeship. As she grew older, she learned to
regulate its expression, but her impulsiveness remained a part of
her personality and informed her writing throughout her adult life.

In addition to this excess of feeling, which seemed in 1831 to
have little outlet for expression other than in the pages of her diary,
Elizabeth was denied the intellectual stimulation she required.
Diffident in company, she felt isolated in the active local scene of
the county with its constant visiting and entertaining, greatly
preferring to stay at home reading the works of Greek poets and
philosophers than to go out to dinner. Her younger sister, Henrietta, was a natural social butterfly, who leapt at every invitation, but
the round of parties and calls from neighbours that so fascinated
her sisters only irritated Elizabeth, involving as it did, 'Curling hair
& dressing to meet a crowd of people whom I know nothing of, &
care for less than I know'. (p. 232) She found the company
frivolous and tiresome, fodder only for her wit. 'The outside of Mrs
Watson's head, larger a very great deal, than the inside. Does she
plume herself upon that?' she commented caustically on a neighbour. 'What a pity it is that some people shd. take more pains about
covering their intellects than their shoulders!' She could find little
in common with the local gentry, whose conversation she was
determined to despise. 'What is called "going out" should be
called "the greatest bore in the world"', she sighed after one
particularly dull evening. Her retreat into scholarship could be
interpreted as a defence against the awkwardness she undoubtedly felt in a crowd, 'frightened' as she confessed herself by 'the sight
of the tremendous assembly in the Barton Court drawing room, of
Biddulphs, Brights, Cliffes, Peytons!' (p. 185) Whatever its psychological source, it is in her diary that this retreat is most consciously
articulated and it was through her journal-writings that Elizabeth
Barrett was able to some degree to establish her difference from
others and work her way towards the discovery of her evolving
self.

In seeking something more than the light-minded social life
which surrounded her, she required both intellectual and emotional fulfilment, and struggled to alight on some activity that would
occupy her days so as to satisfy her as yet indefinable demands.
She had already gained modest success as a poet and felt convinced that literature 'was the star which in prospect illuminated
my future days'.[3] Yet at the beginning of 1831 she seemed to have

reached a standstill, with no obvious literary direction. Her work at this time was still immature. Reading widely in Greek and Latin, she used the classics as models for her poems, and clearly lacked the confidence to develop an artistic voice of her own. As she acknowledged later in *Aurora Leigh*:

> And so, like most young poets, in a flush
> Of individual life I poured myself
> Along the veins of others, and achieved
> Mere lifeless imitations of live verse.
> And made the living answer for the dead,
> Profaning nature. (Book I, lines 71–6)[4]

It is significant that she turned to journal-writing as a mode of creative self-discovery, however unsettling this process ultimately proved to be. The journal as a literary form had no inbuilt constraints. Through it she could experiment with alternative voices which reflected her fluctuating moods, sentimental, morose, quizzical, or reasoning. These variant voices illustrate corresponding literary confusions that beset her as she tried to find her way through the maze of tradition. But instead of being contained in separate poetic utterances, lyric, epic or dramatic, as had been her habit, they were now mingled in one continuous composition, a composition moreover that related her personal experiences directly, without any modulating or masking poetic filter. In such a context, the year 1831–2 can be seen as a crucial period in Elizabeth Barrett's growth both as a poet and as an independent personality.

The opening entry in Elizabeth Barrett's journal, written on Saturday 4 June 1831, demonstrates the enquiring mind of the girl who was eventually to take on board a series of social and political issues in her poetry. It also shows her egoism. As a piece of supposedly informal writing, it is supremely self-conscious and even defensive in tone. Yet it also contains a degree of self-knowledge and the same honesty of approach that we find in her mature autobiographical verse. Characteristically it begins with a speculation.

I wonder if I shall burn this sheet of paper like most others I have begun in the same way. To write a diary, I have thought of very often at far & near distances of time: but how could I write a diary without throwing upon paper my thoughts all my

thoughts – the thoughts of my heart as well as of my head? – &
then how could I bear to look on *them* after they were written?
Adam made fig leaves necessary for the mind, as well as for the
body. And such *a* mind as I have! – So very exacting & exclusive
& eager & headlong – & *strong* – & so very very often *wrong!* –
Well! but I will write: I must write – & the oftener wrong I know
myself to be, the less wrong I shall be in one thing – the less vain
I shall be!

From the beginning Elizabeth Barrett shows herself aware of the
dangers lurking in the fraught world of introspection that journal-
writing invited her into. If anything, such danger was a challenge
to her sense of adventure into the self. The diary was to be a mirror
of her personality and as such she identified what she saw as her
distinguishing marks, her impulsiveness, her emotional integrity
and her unusual mental power. Her style is dynamic and fresh in
its attempt to reproduce her thought processes. The rhetorical
questions that we find here are a stylistic feature of the journal as a
whole as she worked through her conflicting impulses and analysed her own behaviour in minute detail. For Elizabeth Barrett her
personal writing became a means of dissecting her own life and
relationships, with its endless interrogation of her own behaviour,
her minute reworking of the days' events and the construction of
scenarios for the future that might never happen.

For her days during this period were all fraught with uncertainty. Throughout the summer of 1831 rumours circulated about the
sale of Hope End, and the family waited anxiously for news about
their future. Mr Barrett kept his children in suspense, telling them
nothing of his plans. Elizabeth's insecurity was confided to her
journal. 'Suppose we should go after all: – Oh, I *will* not think of it!'
she wrote on 6 June, trying to guess from the activity on the estate
and from her father's moods what the outcome would be. 'How
unhappy I seem on the brink of being!' she admitted tentatively
four days later. 'While Eliza, Bummy & I were sitting in the
drawing room, talking & singing, in came Lane. He wished to
speak with Bummy. She went out; & I felt breathless – dreading to
hear something past supporting'. As prospective purchasers came
to view the property, she sat rigid, praying for deliverance from
such misery. Yet she and the others remained largely in ignorance
as to the business that was being conducted around them, their
only information coming from second-hand gossip. 'Their servant

spoke to ours of having seen Hope End advertised to be sold this month. How is it to be? Are we really to go? I am sick at heart about it; but will hope on still. Something may be doing, still', she wrote nervously on 10 June and the following day learned from her brother that 'Hope End is advertised in the Sun newspaper, to be sold in August – no name but a full description. He & Bro heard it yesterday from Henry Trant.'

It is hardly surprising that Elizabeth Barrett's journal reflects an immature personality if she and the rest of the family were neither consulted nor kept informed about how their future was to be decided. Encouraged to remain in a childlike dependence, she retreated into the turbulent world of her private emotions. In a house where secrecy flourished, she too was trained to be secretive, keeping her thoughts to herself, and watching for signs that would confirm or refute her suspicions. 'Papa was in very good spirits today at breakfast, most undoubtedly', she reported with delight on 16 June. 'He told Bro to put the clock half an hour more forward; & this sent my hopes forward . . . a little way. Would he think about altering the clock if it were likely to strike so seldom before we are removed for ever from its sound?' But she was not to be enlightened one way or the other. When Mr Barrett left them at the end of the month, the family were none the wiser, and waited frantically for letters that would give them something definite to go on. 'No letters today', ran Elizabeth's entry for 30 June, typical of many. 'What can be the reason? Bummy says she looks on the bright side. I look *for* it, but cannot do more. What miserable suspence we have suffered on this subject – & no let-out from it, even now!' The thought of being torn from the only home she could remember and of being far removed from familiar places and friends was agony to her. To her dismay a letter arrived from Mr Barrett postmarked the Isle of Wight. 'He seems pleased with it', wrote Elizabeth, horrified. 'Delighted with the scenery & Mr Sipthorpe. Oh, if we shd. intend to settle there – if we shd. be separated from England by the sea! . . . I hope, I hope, this dungeon in the air, will fall into ruins. Hastings, Eastbourne, Brighton – Portsmouth – any place but the isle of Wight!' (p. 154) Although this awful prospect passed, her father still refused to communicate any definite news, throwing family arrangements into chaos. At Hope End it was impossible to plan ahead for even the simplest occasions, such as entertaining prospective guests, without any solid information to rely on. In October Bummy wrote to Mr Barrett to tell him of their quandary, but still he remained silent on the issue. 'When will his answer come?', wondered Elizabeth vainly on 27 October. The next day, 'We got home at about four. A letter from Papa to Henrietta – & not *a word* in it! – How extraordinary! Poor Bummy does not know what to do.' In this context of anxiety, the background to the journal as a whole, Elizabeth did the only thing she could and turned to her work for consolation.

Elizabeth Barrett's early journal gives us a record of a poet in embryo. Its author emerges as a young woman of great literary potential, starved of intellectual and emotional sustenance, and seeking outlets for her inner frustration. The diary contains her search for a voice that would accurately reflect the self she was struggling to define. Its textual confusions, the mixture of tones and styles, indicate her debt to other literary forms and her attempt to break away from her reliance on them. In order to read her diary as informing her work, it is important to understand something of her peculiar situation at that time. As the eldest daughter in the Barrett family she had, thoughout her childhood and teens, been both exceptionally privileged and remarkably deprived. The privilege lay in the special relationship she enjoyed with her father, who encouraged her penchant for scholarship and her writing. His pride in her precocity was first made evident when he had her version of *The Battle of Marathon* privately printed for her fourteenth birthday, an action which only fostered her subsequent need for an appreciative audience. Her writing helped to secure her father's notice, and his admiration spurred her on. At the same time as she was encouraged to pursue academic attainment, however, she was denied the education and the freedom of movement enjoyed by her brother Bro, only a year younger than she was, who by virtue of his sex was allowed schooling from which she was barred. It was a denial that she felt fiercely, and she sought to make up the deficiency by her absorption in classical studies at home, alone. The development of her undeniable intellectual gifts singled her out, both from her brothers and sisters and from other young women of her day. Her journal is full of references to her current reading. When on 14 July a parcel of books arrived for her by carrier, she unpacked it eagerly and with growing excitement 'read the title pages of Barnes's Euripedes, Marcus Antoninus, Callimachus, the Anthologia, Epictetus, Isocrates, & Da Vinci's Painting', (14 July 1831) moving on quickly to 'read some of the Alcestis' as a treat she had been looking forward to.

Her erudition did not stop with the classics. She was informed about current philosophical and religious debates, and much of her diary consists of commentary on these issues. 'I have been hard at work all day, reading & meditating on the first eleven chapters of Romans', she reported on 8 September.

> Dr Adam Clarke is wrong, I think, about 'the whole creation', & wrong about 'who shall separate us from the love of Christ'.
>
> The close of the 5th chapter, strikes me strongly as it has done before, as favoring the doctrine of general redemption. Why should any body of Christians struggle to deny it? Is it not enough that redemption is by *free grace*, – & *only* of God who showeth mercy? I cannot believe that the Christian church will ever have a united opinion of some passages of Romans; and if my opinion of those passages shd. ever become clearer & more decided than it now is, I could not look upon Christians who differed from me, less as brethren than I do now. (p. 165)

Elizabeth Barrett took such issues seriously and her independence of thinking is evident both in her careful reading of the text in question and in her challenging of contemporary theorists. Her argument springs from her own humanitarian impulses, and her warmth does not inhibit her ability to reason logically. Her diary frequently shows her grappling with problems where her personal instincts are at variance with conservative doctrine. The same fervour that we find in this entry is apparent in her approach to practical matters. She involved herself in local religious politics, and landed in trouble when she arranged the baptism of a neighbouring young lady without her parents' knowledge.

In addition, she took a keen interest in national affairs, an interest which was to expand and which fired much of her later verse. Her diary registers her shock at hearing of the failure of the Reform Bill in October 1831. 'The bill is thrown out! majority 41!!!', she noted, fully alive to the implications of such an event. 'What will the people do! – What will the king do? What will Lord Grey do? Resign – or make the Lords resign . . . I am afraid there will be a change of ministry . . . But on the other hand, what Tory administration *can* carry on the government against such a House of Commons?' In an atmosphere of general political upheaval, she contributed to discussions on political and social matters. 'Mr &

Miss Peyton, Mr Deane, H, & I have settled the English form of government for next year. It is to be a parthenocracy. For Universal suffrage will include our sex, – the married people will neutralize each others votes by voting pro & con; & then how can the young men be uninfluenced by the young ladies? Impossible!' The playful tone does not totally disguise the seriousness of the subject of social revolution. More materially, the arguments she conducted with herself in the pages of her diary were to find expression in her poetry. In January 1832 her strong social conscience instigated the composition of 'my poem on the cholera', to send to *The Times* as part of a symposium on the epidemic which had devastated many areas of the country.

The public face of the poetry then found its corollary in the pages of the journal and the uncertainties she uncovered in this most private form of writing were to reappear in verse. Her 1833 volume contained several poems which explored her doubts about the self in the guise of religious subjects. 'Idols', 'The Image of God' and 'The Tempest', all written about this time, suggest that her only means of presenting her personal fears and psychological dilemmas was through the medium of theological debate. As Angela Leighton has remarked about 'The Tempest', 'It is impossible to separate the poem's intriguingly private and autobiographical elements from its public and literary ostenation.'[5] 'The Tempest' was based on an actual storm which took place near Hope End in 1826, when two young women died after being struck by lightning. In Elizabeth's version, the victim of the storm is a man, and one well known to the poem's narrator. The poem begins with a description of the poet welcoming the approaching tempest, identifying with the violence and finding a voice to match it.

> Yea! and I lifted up my glorying voice
> In an "All hail"; when, wildly resonant,
> As brazen chariots rushing from the war,
> As passioned waters gushing from the rock,
> As thousand crashed woods, the thunder cried:
> And at his cry the forest tops were shook
> As by the woodman's axe; and far and near
> Staggered the mountains with a muttered dread.[6]

The power she greets with such enthusiasm proves to be as destructive as the imagery predicts. Her recognition of the dead man gives rise to contradictory emotions, and the second part of the poem dwells on her troubled response to his death, ending with a disquisition on the implications of death itself. It is a disturbing poem to read, and has been variously interpreted, many recent critics seeing it as a reflection of Elizabeth Barrett's fraught relationship with her father, whose death she both longs for and dreads.[7] Certainly her diary, more prosaically, discloses the ambivalent nature of her feelings for him. Receiving a parcel from him in the summer of 1831 she 'opened it in a fright' to find six pairs of stockings. 'My own dear kind Papa!' she gasped with relief. 'How very kind to think of me & my pedestals at such a time! – How I ought to love him! – *ought*! – how I *do*!' Her quick self-correction does not hide the fact that her initial reaction was fear, nor that love was perhaps a conditioned response only.

In 'The Tempest' it is surely significant that the strength of the poet's voice contributes centrally to the disaster, and the atmosphere of noise and energy which colours the first half of the poem changes to one of silence and stillness towards the close. Does this suggest a recognition of the dangers of explicit articulation, which could promote a psychic split, moving towards a self-confidence that incorporates a move away from male protection? Whatever meaning we ascribe to it, 'The Tempest' shows Elizabeth Barrett employing a conventional subject which serves to act out her own confusions. The poem's language may be derivative and stylised, but the personal undercurrents, however unconsciously realised, spring from the sort of troubled experience which is at the heart of her diary.

As well as pursuing her enthusiasm for the classics, Elizabeth Barrett in 1831 immersed herself in contemporary literature. She read novels rapturously, although she was forced to admit that they 'lead the mind to expect more in life than can be met in life'. Still, she strongly defended the escapist value of fiction. 'Well! – allow that they do!' she declared. 'The expectation brings more happiness than any reality, – as realities go, – cd. do. Romance of spirit is a far rarer fault than worldliness of spirit.' (p. 248) Her journal mentions Mary Brunton's *Self Control*, Mme de Staël's *Corinne*, Mary Shelley's *The Last Man*, Mrs Radcliffe's *The Mysteries of Udolpho*, Susan Ferrier's *Destiny* and *The Inheritance* as being among the 'thousands of novels' that she had read, enjoyed and judged on their merits. Significantly they were all written by women. When she subsequently wrote, 'I look everywhere for

grandmothers and see none', Elizabeth Barrett Browning was
referring most specifically to her role as woman poet in a patriarchal poetic line. The female fictional tradition offered her plenty of
reminders of a literary inheritance with which she could identify,
and the various modes these novelists employed – romantic,
sentimental, Gothic, ironic – all have their impact on the tones of
her diary. As one critic has suggested, Elizabeth Barrett Browning's
later work can be seen as 'an overlapping sequence of dialogues
with other texts, other writers'.[8] Already this sense of literary
enquiry is apparent in her journal-writing. Echoes of sentimental
novelists can be heard in her extravagance or in her protestations
of excessive sensibility. Her heart, she declared, 'is itself far too
affectionate! – Far too affectionate! Oh I feel *that* whenever I feel
pain: & almost *ever* when I feel pleasure.' (p. 168)

A Romantic strain too is evident, more carefully modulated, in
her studied reflections on her situation at Hope End, appropriately
timed to coincide with the approach of autumn.

> I may have to leave this place where I have walked & talked &
> dreamt in much joy; & where I have heard most beloved voices
> which I can no more hear, & clasped beloved hands which I can
> no more clasp: where I have read immortal books, & written
> pleasant thoughts, & known at least one very dear friend – I may
> have to do this; & it will be sorrow to me! (p. 149)

This is perhaps all too reminiscent of Marianne Dashwood's
parodic leavetaking of Norland in Jane Austen's *Sense and Sensibility*. Certainly the balanced and controlled melancholy prose with
its suggestive generalisations is a far cry from the impassioned
outpourings we find in the journal at moments of real misery. Yet
these too betray their literary antecedents. Sitting by herself in her
bedroom in June, 'I heard what I used to hear in the summer of
1828, & only *then* the *deathwatch*. I grew sick & pale & dizzy – &
slept miserably all night . . . I have mentioned it to nobody & don't
much like mentioning it here.' (p. 107) Superstitiously she was
recalling the summer of her mother's death, and, hardly coin-
cidentally, she turned to *The Mysteries of Udolpho*, 'by way of
quieting my imagination?', as she remarked with wry self-
awareness. The confusions of identity explored so centrally by
Gothic writers reappear again as the subjects of her dreams, as her
entry for 8 January 1832 records:

Dreamt about Adolphe & Endymion, & a lady who was by turns Emily & Amalthea, & of her murdering Endymion, whose soul was infused into Adolphe. Papa reproached her. But she held up her beautiful face, & said, 'I am yet very fair'. 'Clay Walls', said Papa!

The fusion in this dream of mutant identity, death and violence, culminating in a confrontation with her father, indicate the degree of empathy she found in the works of Mrs Radcliffe and Mary Shelley, novels which operated as locations for her own deep-seated Gothic fears. The language of the final sentence here suggests too Elizabeth Barrett's uneasiness about gender in its presentation of opposing discourses, a clash between the feminine emphasis on romantic beauty and the masculine emphasis on prosaic rationality and judgement.

The contradictions that many readers have found within Barrett Browning's poetry can therefore be partially explained by reference to her early diary, and the division between feminine and masculine forms of writing it discloses. In contrast to the women novelists with their immediate appeal to her sensibilities, the poets she mentions, often critically, were all male, from Homer and Xenophon to Victor Hugo, Lamartine, Byron, Shelley and Keats. 'I finished the Endymion today', she wrote on 19 August:

I do not admire it as a poem, but I do admire many passages of it as being very fine poetry. As a whole, it is cumbrous & unwieldy. Your imagination is confused by it: & your feelings uninterested. And yet a poet wrote it. When I had done with Keats, I took up Theophrastus. Theophrastus has a great deal of vivacity, & power of portraiture about him; & uplifts that veil of distance ... veiling the old Greeks with such sublime mistiness; & shows you how they used to spit & take physic & wear nailed shoes tout comme un autre.

Interestingly it is Theophratus' 'spirited' and 'amusing' style that attracts her, and a few days later we find her proposing to copy it, for 'Something in his manner might catch the popular ear, at least as well as the tinkling of certain fools' bells! Shall I try? There is time enough to think of it.' (p. 149)

Never do we find her consciously attempting to model her writing on fiction in this way. Novels were for casual reading.

Poetry, on the other hand, was for serious consideration, an attitude promoted by her father and by other scholars of her acquaintance. Her consequent sensitivity to verse forms and to the possibilities of the genre led her to be stern in her poetic judgements. 'It is not in my opinion, written in the highest vein of poetry; & it is dull and heavy' (p. 180), she commented on Shelley's 'Queen Mab' and after sampling 'The Revolt of Islam', she noted that Shelley 'is a great poet; but we acknowledge him to be a great poet as we acknowledge Spenser to be so, & do not love him for it. He resembles Spenser in one thing, & one thing only, that his poetry is too immaterial for our sympathies to enclasp it firmly. It reverses the lot of human plants: its roots are in the air, not earth!' (p. 149)

Poetry had already become of major importance in her life. To her it was the ultimate artistic form, prestigious in a way that novels were not. When a neighbour confessed to her that 'she had lost all her taste for poetry', Elizabeth's reaction was acid. 'Lost! Did she ever possess it? Can anyone *lose* his taste for poetry? Can any one lose his life, & yet live?' (p. 134). As early as 1831, she had come to think of herself primarily as a poet and her own future as firmly literary. It is tempting to read the diary as an experiment in literary method, picked up and then discarded for reasons which she did not want to probe too deeply. Perhaps it brought about an uncomfortably close confrontation with aspects of her personality that she would have preferred to keep hidden. Certainly it provided an opportunity for her to articulate her ideas in an informal mode free from the artistic controls she exercised in verse. Subsequently her most successful poetry was to exploit subjective forms, establishing a variety of dramatic voices, such as we find in the diary. The love lyrics to Browning published as *Sonnets From the Portugese* and *Aurora Leigh* both rely on the forms of personal address for much of their impact, the latter in particular utilising a retrospective format in its recollection of many of the events of this crucial period in her life. The inbuilt constraints of the verse form helped to negotiate what was probably a vital distance for Elizabeth Barrett between the raw experience and its literary expression.

There is, however, another aspect of Elizabeth Barrett's early diary which is essential to any consideration of its formative significance. This is the story of her friendship with her neighbour, the blind classical scholar, Hugh Stuart Boyd, and it forms the most central single narrative strand in the journal. After the publication in 1826 of her *Essay on Mind* (again at her family's expense), Elizabeth Barrett had received a fan letter from Boyd, a middle-aged man, who was living with his family close to Hope End. Despite his blindness he was an accomplished student of Greek with a prodigious capacity for memorising huge quantities of verse. Ultimately pedantic in his manner and opinions, he was nonetheless mentally alert and could debate vigorously on theological and literary subjects. Married to a woman who did not share his interests, he, like Elizabeth, was eager to find opportunities for intellectual stimulus beyond the home. After a long-drawn-out correspondence on scholarly matters, they met and from this bookish alliance a close bond developed between them.

Elizabeth Barrett's diary of 1831–2 tells the story of her love affair with Boyd, whether or not she was prepared to recognise it as such. He was in many ways a most unsuitable object for her devotion, but it was presumably precisely because of these qualifications that she found him so attractive. He was of her father's generation, married, with a daughter about the same age as herself. His respect for classical learning and his interest in poetry of all periods seemed to match her own. His blindness made him an intriguing figure, and the pathos of his situation seemed to increase as she imagined his unhappy marriage. Boyd tutored her, argued with her, appraised, and let her talk openly about her work. Her quest for a father-figure, who could take on the roles of teacher, critic and unattainable lover was satisfied in this curious liaison, which grew to its most intense while her actual father was away from home. While she clearly needed to have an emotional fixation outside her family, it is still revealing to note how often the language of Elizabeth Barrett's diary takes on childish nuances when it speaks of Boyd. In July, for instance, she became anxious at hearing that Boyd's sister was coming for an extended visit to Ruby Cottage, the Boyds' home, bringing with her a young girl whom she feared might replace her in Boyd's affections:

> The young lady is 16; & was, when she was 6, a clever child. Her father had amused himself by teaching her the Greek characters, & had made her read the Hecuba thro', without of course, her understanding a word. Mr Boyd does not think she understands Greek. I hope that she – – I hope he wont prefer her society to mine. I hope Miss Boyd will like me. I will take pains to please Mr Boyd's sister.

He asked me to talk to Mr Spowers at dinner: 'on *his* account, he thought I ought to do it.' I promised to do my best; and as I went out of the room, he said that I must remember what I had promised, & that he wd. ask Mrs Boyd if I had been 'naughty or good'.

A more moderate impression of their relationship is conveyed by her poem 'Wine of Cyprus', dedicated to Boyd in her 1844 collection of verse, when she recalls their intimacy as being one of perfect harmony, a union of minds, despite their difference of age and sex.

> Ah, my gossip! you were older,
> And more learned, and a man! –
> Yet that shadow – the enfolder
> Of your quiet eyelids – ran
> Both our spirits to one level;
> And I turned from hill and lea
> And the summer sun's green revel, –
> To your eyes that could not see. (Stanza xx)[9]

'Wine of Cyprus' perhaps reveals more than Elizabeth Barrett realised. On one level it is a straightforward tribute to the shared pleasure of the days spent with Boyd in classical study, but on another the stress on age and gender that we find in this stanza hints at an incompatibility between the poet's youth, energy and vision and Boyd's static blind scholarship. In Sonnet XXVI of *Sonnets From The Portugese*, she acknowledged that:

> I lived with visions for my company
> Instead of men and women, years ago.[10]

In 'Wine of Cyprus', there is a strong suggestion that her innate respect for masculine learning finally becomes an inhibiting factor in her creative development, as she turns from the light and the natural world outside to the darker realms of the past that Boyd invites her into. Elizabeth Barrett's diary, continually reminding us of her insatiable desire to soak up the works of the masters, reinforces this image. As she commented twelve years later in *Aurora Leigh*,

> For me, I wrote
> False poems, like the rest, and thought them true
> Because myself was true in writing them.
> I peradventure have writ true ones since
> With less complacence. (Book I, 1022–5)[11]

By the summer of 1831, Elizabeth had known Boyd for four years. His initial appreciation of her as a classicist had developed into a mutual dependency, based on the intellectual kinship which had first brought them together. Elizabeth's diary describes her visits, sometimes for days at a time, to the Boyd household, visits which were made ostensibly in order to improve her Greek and to read to the blind man. Yet the entries affirm that her interest in him was much more romantic than she was prepared to admit openly. 'If he knew how much it gratifies me to assist him in any way (I wish . . . I cd. do so in *every* way)' she fantasised, while tortured with doubts about his commitment to the relationship. 'Oh I would give anything if I could *know* – not think, not guess – but *know*, what the feeling is there, with respect to me.' (p. 130) Her emotions were at a constant pitch of excitement. As she repeatedly acknowledged about herself, 'My disposition is far too exclusive & exacting' (p. 75) and, once inflamed, she was unable to rid herself of thoughts of Boyd. On the days she could not see him, she wrote and waited impatiently for his replies. Often she was disappointed. She wrote petulantly after receiving only a curt response to work she had sent him:

I suppose he means to neglect me altogether, never to write to me again! & expects that I should show my *gratitude!* by continuing to write as I have written, & feel as I have felt! Well! – I feel *bitterly* – – as I have felt – for some time at least. He has not written to me once since the 16th May; and this is the 29th of June. I may be exacting & irritable & inconsiderate & passionate – but I *cannot* feel satisfied or feel that I *ought* to feel satisfied. I wish I had half the regard for him, impressed on this paper, that I might erase it thus [ink blot]. Mrs Boyd may throw difficulties in the way of his writing. She may be busy & be out of the way, & he out of the humour for it – But if he wished it – oh if he really & indeed *wished* it, there could be no lasting obstacle – none!! How was it during the first year & a half of our intercourse? Did he ever even *delay* writing, *then*?

Well! It is better far better that I should go away; better in every way, & perhaps for everybody. Better for *me*, I dare say. I am not of a cold nature, & cannot bear to be treated coldly. When cold water is thrown upon hot iron, the iron *hisses*. I wish that water wd make my iron as cold as itself. Perhaps it may – *in time*.

The agonised, self-dramatising tone that we find in this entry recurs on almost every page of the diary, as Elizabeth Barrett recounts the fluctuations that each day brings in the relationship. She puts herself in the role of a martyr, 'lacerating myself and kissing the rod' for wishing so much 'to be with a person who certainly does not wish *so much* to be with me.' (p. 94) Yet three days later we find her ecstatic while reading Aeschylus to Boyd in the privacy of his room, so happy 'while I was reading it. A kind of happiness which cannot now last long!' Her obsession with Boyd dominates the journal, and the attempt to depict her feelings accurately becomes almost as important to her as the experience itself.

Witness what I have written today. I should erase every line of it, could I annihilate the *feelings*, together with the description of them; but, since I cannot, let the description pass! That Friendship should fade away before my eyes, as Fame did in my poetical vision, is too painful! And that the 'skeleton' of Friendship . . . but I am getting wrong again! (pp. 75–6)

As with her vain attempt to erase her problem with an ink blot, Elizabeth Barrett used her diary to provide herself with palpable evidence of intangible experience. In this entry, as she gradually gets carried away with her own rhetoric, she becomes aware that the primary sensation is also eluding her at the very moment she wishes to emphasise its importance. The diary thus constitutes an essential component in the recreation and revision of emotion. In her imperfect analysis of the relation between feeling and expression, we can find an anticipation of the mature poetic technique that was to find its most graphic formulation in *Sonnets From the Portugese*.

The act of diary writing also brought her a degree of insight into her situation. 'I am ashamed of writing down my own feelings & the causes of them', she confessed (p. 133), having broken off in mid-sentence while unburdening herself of a particularly unedifying thought. It was useful too as a means of boosting her confidence. When her friend, Eliza Cliffe, sent a letter to Boyd, Elizabeth was tormented by petty jealousies.

'What did she write to him about, I wonder! I sent a note from myself. Which will he read first? – There is no use in asking questions on this subject. It is *unquestionable*, that he prefers me to Eliza Cliffe.' (p. 102) Vehemently she affirmed her prominence in Boyd's life, as if the declaration was undeniable proof of the fact.

Although Mr Barrett did not immediately register his disapproval of the intimacy, Boyd was never invited to visit Hope End, not even to accompany his daughter, Annie, who had struck up a friendship with the Barrett girls. During 1831–2 her father's absence from home prevented him from witnessing the full force of Elizabeth's fascination with their neighbour. Her journal shows how each day that she could not see Boyd, she was thinking about him, planning how they might meet and how she could contrive visits to his house. Despite her reputation for fragility, and her possibly anorexic condition – 'Miss Commeline decides that half of me has vanished away in my thinness', she reported in October – she always discovered reserves of energy for visiting Boyd. On Monday 4 July, for example, she was so impatient to see him that 'I drove away at seven, after my having had a partial breakfast in the nursery.' Arriving at Ruby Cottage at eight o'clock in the morning, she not surprisingly found the family still in bed, and while waiting for them to be ready to receive her, as soon as the dining room door had shut on her, 'out of the window I jumped. My hat I left behind, & ran up thro' the grove to the hill where I let my hair blow about & my feet walk about ad libitum.' Yet only a fortnight later, she described her state of exhaustion when obliged to pay a social call on neighbours with her aunt.

> There I sate in the armchair more dead than alive – certainly more disagreeable than agreeable – until tea-time. The tea was a collation for the cricketers & sinecure visitors; & it was hardly over, before I fairly fainted away. They dragged me out of the room & packed me up on the sofa. (p. 115)

It is surely significant that this episode took place after an unsatisfactory visit to Boyd earlier in the day, when, through a misunderstanding, she was able to spend only a bare fifteen minutes in his company. The psychological sources of Elizabeth Barrett's illness make their presence felt in the journal, as her strength grew and waned with her enthusiasm, and her physical debility occurred most noticeably at moments of inner tension. She was to some extent aware of the link between her emotional and physical states. On 10 August she felt that Boyd was unusually cool to her. Miserably she noted 'What a weight there is on my heart today. It is like lead, only colder ... My energies felt dead within me', and the next day found that she was 'Unwell, very unwell all the evening! A strange nervous depressed feeling, as if I were both soulless & boneless'. The only cure for such a condition was to fix on a firm date for a visit to Boyd the following Tuesday. That done, 'I felt better, far better', in the certain knowledge of being with him again.

Elizabeth's infatuation with Boyd throws some light on the nature of the deprivation she was suffering, and shows also how she was able to use that deprivation to her own advantage. Her creation of an intellectual environment for herself, in which Boyd participated, incorporated an act of rebellion, however tacit, against her father's regime. She plotted for days, thinking of ways she could engineer further intimacy between herself and Boyd, and her diary charts the fluctuation of her emotions as she relived the moments they had spent together, or concocted fanciful scenarios to be acted out in the privacy of his room. Boyd encouraged her in her more morbid reflections, probably not thinking how faithfully his idle comments would be recorded. 'Mr Boyd observed that "if we remained at Hope End, & if I were *to die*, it was clear to him that my family wd. break off all intercourse with his''. If I were to die! – Not an improbable case; but supposed so coldly!' (p. 128). Such remarks only served to heighten her sense of isolation from her family and the romantic element in her adoration of the blind man. Melodramatically she represented her own case as hopeless. 'There is no use in it. Of one thing I am convinced; that if, from any change of circumstance, *one* of his visitors were forced to return home immediately, – he would feel more *sorrow*, – than if *I* were to leave this neighbourhood for ever. And this is the weight of human friendship! Ashes! *Dust* is too heavy!' (p. 128). In July, she related disturbing dreams, of her teeth 'tumbling out' and of a unicorn appearing to her, two classic Freudian manifestations of frustrated sexuality. For Elizabeth Barrett, as was to be shown in her later relationship with Robert Browning, romantic passion was generated by intellectual closeness. As with Browning, so too her relationship with Boyd began with letters on literary matters written over several months. In both cases, Elizabeth was able to express herself openly on paper and could allow her imagination to run riot before she actually met her correspondent.

Her entanglement with Boyd does mark, however, a crucial stage in Elizabeth Barrett's growth to independence, both of spirit and of mind. For the first time her days were spent away from her family's protection, and without her father's presence, she was free to follow her own dictates. However severely her aunt disapproved, she was not nearly as fearsome a figure as Mr Barrett, and although Elizabeth had qualms about incurring his censure, she was prepared to risk it in order to spend time with Boyd. Through her loosening of family ties and her closer engagement with literary matters in an atmosphere of scholarly encouragement, a further development occurred which was to have a lasting effect on her own future as a poet.

At the beginning of 1832, there is a remarkable change of direction in Elizabeth Barrett's journal as its author lighted upon a literary task that captured her concentration fully. In order to clarify certain linguistic points in their reading that she and Boyd were finding obscure, she translated a particularly difficult Greek oration. 'I have written as hard & fast as I cd. write', she noted on 27 January. '& therefore had no time for sentencerounding & polishing. . . . Mr Boyd meant to be a fortnight about it. I shd. be four days.' To her surprise, she then discovered that 'He does not mean to translate the oration. It is too much labour!' However assiduously Elizabeth asserted that 'the very act of seeming to compete with him . . . would diminish his regard for me' (p. 241), an element of rivalry had crept into their studies, with pupil outstripping master. Clearly she found both the work and the achievement of having performed a task that he shrank from stimulating. At once she launched into further translation, this time of the whole of Aeschylus' *Prometheus,* with the thought that she might publish it, together with 'a preliminary essay which might be made very critical & interesting'. (p. 243) Deeply absorbed in this demanding occupation, she had little time for diary writing. As she commented on 6 Febuary, 'Finished the translation of 130 lines, Who cd. write in a diary after that?' Gone are the lengthy, introspective passages of journalising that characterise the main part of her diary to be replaced by brief reports on work in progress.

Friday Feb 10th.
Writing – but not in my diary.
Saturday Feb 11th.
Intended to have finished the Prometheus today. Not possible.
Monday Feb 13
Writing hard.

She had visited Boyd only once in the past fortnight. Perhaps predictably, his reaction to her accomplishment was dismissive. He was not in favour of her plans for publication, and although he asked her to send him part of her translation, Elizabeth had become suspicious about the genuineness of his interest. 'What is his motive?', she wondered:

> Not, I am afraid, a wish of seeing my work. Perhaps he perceived that my manner of writing is not what it was. I sent the extracts, & wrote in my 'new style', – begging him not to read what I sent. Would I not a thousand & a thousand times *rather* have *his* work attended to than mine? (p. 247)

How different from her earlier effusions! In October, when Boyd 'confessed to me that he thought his translation of a part of the oration which we read today, translated at the age of 22, was well done', she saw the boastfulness only as a mark of trust. 'His confidence in me is really the confidence of a friends. He evidently *thinks* out loud before me!', she had reported delightedly, dazed by her infatuation into uncritical acceptance of his limitations. Now, however, her work and the distance from him that had been created during the two weeks of translation made her judgement sharper. Her comments reveal her sense of her own literary progression and her ability to manipulate her style of writing. Her evident confusion at the twist in the relationship is manifested in her final sentence. Like other women writers, she was beginning to perceive, however dimly, that her success could have a distorting effect on her personal relationships. The incident also marked for Elizabeth Barrett the beginning of a distinct break between her reliance on others' guidance and her independent artistic growth.

Elizabeth Barrett never kept a diary again. Convinced that poetry was her vocation, she confined her prose writings to letters, a form that combined personal elements with public demands in a way that she could handle more comfortably. As she wrote in 1832, 'My diary is not meant to be read by any person except myself'. Perhaps the inevitable confusion between roles of author and reader that had resulted from the experiment determined her to stick to a path more clearly defined in her later career. Leaving behind, however, that interior and perhaps more feminine narrative mode in favour of an established and approved public literary format was to create other problems. It was not until the composition of *Aurora Leigh*, published in 1856, that she confronted these in any sustained way and gave explicit articulation to the confusions that had dogged her earlier work and whose only previous arena for expression had been her private diary.

6

The Double Life:
The Journal
of Louisa May Alcott

This double life is trying, and my head will work as well as my hands

Louisa May Alcott. *Journal*, October 1882

In 1843 when she was ten, Louisa May Alcott described in her journal 'A Sample of our Lessons':

> 'What virtues do you wish more of?' asks Mr.L. I answer:–
> Patience, Love, Silence,
> Obedience, Generosity, Perseverance,
> Industry, Respect, Self-denial.
> 'What vices less of?'
> Idleness, Wilfulness, Vanity,
> Impatience, Impudence, Pride,
> Selfishnes, Activity, Love of cats.

On the next page, the interrogation continues:

> What are the most valuable kinds of self denial? Appetite, temper.
> How is self-denial of temper known? If I control my temper, I am respectful and gentle, and every one sees it.
> What is the result of this self-denial? Every one loves me, and I am happy.
> Why use self-denial? For the good of myself and others.
> How shall we learn this self-denial? By resolving, and then trying *hard*.
> What then do you mean to do? To resolve and try.[1]

This childish entry is dominated by abnegation of self, that apotheosis of Victorian womanhood and the bugbear of Louisa

May Alcott's adolescence. Alcott's most famous work, *Little Women*, exalts the abstract ideals of Puritanism, reflected in the ethical absolutes of the opening paragraph above and significantly including 'silence' among their number. It was these which helped her to define an image of womanly perfection and which became in her own life an unattainable goal towards which she strove unceasingly. We should note that her youthful list of vices, not without its hint of reductive humour, contains the sin of 'activity', that very unfeminine quality that throughout her life Alcott tried to repress or channel into the more acceptable 'industry'.

Reading Alcott's journal we get an overwhelming impression of suppressed energies. As an adult she tried, whenever possible, to go out for a run at sunset or first thing in the morning. It was the only moment in her daily routine that gave her body and spirit the release she longed for, and that housework, sewing or writing cramped almost unbearably. The diary entry quoted strikingly encapsulates the motives for Alcott's later *modus vivendi*. Like many other woman of her day, torn between her individual impulses and the demand to conform, she was desperate for others' approval. Perhaps naively, she saw happiness as the inevitable sequel to being loved, and if being loved was dependent on acquiring the virtues that did not come naturally to her, then she would change her personality to win the rewards she sought.

The habit of journal keeping was instilled into Louisa May Alcott at an early age. Both her parents kept diaries, and Louisa and her sisters were all expected to do the same. She began her first diary when she was seven, and its importance as a record of her inner thoughts – 'it helps you to express them and to understand your little self', said her mother – was firmly impressed upon her. The diary was seen as a spiritual record and the Alcott children had to ensure that their diaries were always available for their parents to read, hardly the most propitious circumstances for encouraging intimate revelations. As a birthday token on the 29th November 1843, Mrs Alcott wrote in Louisa's journal, 'Remember, dear girl, that a diary should be an epitome of your life. May it be a record of pure thought and good action'. But how honest could such a record be when it was open to the scrutiny of her parents' regular examination? While still a child, Alcott was being programmed to present herself for public inspection and she was made bitterly aware of her moral deficiencies. Her personal thoughts had to comply with the standards imposed by others, and although she later felt sufficiently confident to set down her opinions even when they differed from the prescribed mould, she never fully got rid of the feelings of guilt about her interest in self.

For it was not easy to conform, and in the Alcott family circle, her liveliness and enquiring mind did not always meet with her father's approval. When she was seventeen, she confessed sadly, 'In looking over my journals, Father says, 'Anna's is about other people, Louisa's about herself. That is true, for I dont *talk* about myself; yet must always think of the wilful, moody girl I try to manage, and in my journal I write of her to see how she gets on . . . I can't talk to anyone but mother about my troubles, and she has so many now to bear, I try not to add any more'. Forbidden to take the central place even in her own life, she retreated into silence, and as the journals develop, we can see a continual attempt to resist self-absorption and to turn her attention instead to the outside world. Her diary is telling evidence of the growth of Alcott's split self, as its subject and author become increasingly separated. Frequently Alcott writes of herself in the third person, as if trying to gain a detached perspective on her own behaviour. She baldly documents events, notes the problems of others, reports issues and concentrates on describing scenes of general interest rather than dwelling on personal feelings. Very rarely in Louisa May Alcott's diary do we find direct references to her own suffering. Yet the experience of unhappiness is ever present, referred to obliquely, but never expanded upon. As the above extract demonstrates, she was always uncomfortable with her unorthodox leanings and it is in the journal, rather than in her published writing, that this discomfort surfaces. Any reading of Louisa May Alcott's journal inevitably gives a new meaning to that classic novel, *Little Women*, the text which inspired a whole generation of American women, but which reflected a life style that its author could not privately commend.

Louisa May Alcott was born in New England on her father's birthday, 29 November 1832, and she always remained close to her roots, moving between the small town of Concord and the neighbouring city of Boston. Her father, Amos Bronson Alcott, was a well-known local figure, a writer, preacher and educationalist who spent most of his time and energy trying to attract converts to the futuristic philosophies of transcendentalism. But he lacked the intellect, vision and the charisma of his more distinguished contemporaries, Ralph Waldo Emerson, Nathaniel Hawthorne and

Henry David Thoreau and, although fervently committed to his cause, promoting it widely through schools, lecture halls and public platforms, Bronson Alcott never achieved their success or status. Despite his passionate idealism and his undoubted talents, he was constitutionally unable to provide for his family with any degree of stability, and Louisa May Alcott spent her early years in poverty, watching her mother struggle to support her children on hopelessly inadequate funds. Abba May Alcott, later to figure as that unreal image of maternal perfection, Marmee in *Little Women*, worked in a mission to bring in extra income for her four children, relying on occasional charitable gifts from her family and friends to stave off destitution, while unflaggingly bolstering her husband's sagging morale. Bronson Alcott's successive failures in virtually every activity he embarked upon had a deep impact on Louisa's own perception of gender roles. She developed a cynical attitude towards marriage, and her journal reveals her difficulties in accepting stereotyped notions of male and female behaviour when the examples before her of her father and mother were so markedly different from the idealised versions presented for her consumption. Repeatedly we find the journal expressing Alcott's frustration with the restrictions of her feminine role. 'I was born with a boy's spirit under my bib and tucker', she wrote disconsolately in 1865, and more passionately, resenting her enforced idleness at the outbreak of the Civil War, 'I long to be a man'. She had, however, recognised much earlier that she was something of a misfit, for 'I . . . don't care much for girl's things. People think I'm wild and queer, . . . I have not told anyone about my plan; but I'm going to *be* good'. Pathetically the journal exposes her determination to suppress her impulses and to acquire the moral perfection demanded of her by her parents.

In her early diary, some of which was written at Fruitlands, the experimental farm where Bronson Alcott subjected his family to the hardships of transcendentalism in action, Louisa's practical nature began to assert itself. Living according to idealist principles of vegetarianism, self-sufficiency, and communal brotherhood meant for Louisa and her sisters a monotonous diet of coarse bread and hard apples which had not been allowed to mellow (Bronson Alcott was not a good farmer!). The family shivered through the icy winter without proper fuel or light and they had to share their home with uncongenial strangers. Somewhat ironically, Louisa's mother, Abba, belied the implications of her public silence and made her bitterness about the enterprise known to *her* journal. For her, November 1842 was a period 'full of hardships, doubt, fears, adversities, struggles for my children, efforts to maintain cheerfulness and good discipline, under poverty and debt – misapprehension and disgrace'.[2] Such was the legacy she bequeathed to her daughter who watched her mother labouring away at domestic tasks while the men, better dreamers than agriculturalists, talked optimistically of the future. As Louisa gradually became aware of the burdens placed upon her mother (who noted how her own 'dislike for cooking [was] so great I would not consume that which cost me so much misery to prepare'),[3] her resentment refused to lie passively, and in her later writings it is always feminine strength which lies at the heart of any household. *Little Women* itself is pervaded by the spirit of Mr March, the absent father whose ideas on proper Christian feminine conduct dominate his wife and daughters, but whose actual presence is shadowy, even when he has returned from the war and is allowed to participate in the novel's action. This negative male figure who has a negligible impact on the reader but who claims rewards and status from his family plays a central role in *Little Women* and his type recurs in its sequels; as John Brooke in *Good Wives* and in *Little Men* as Professor Bhaer, significantly a father-figure cast as husband for Jo, Alcott's self-portrait. There is a revealing account in Alcott's journal of her father's return home late one winter's night after an abortive lecture tour. In the journal description, his wife and daughters, whom he has woken from sleep, greet him rapturously:

> We fed and warmed and brooded over him, longing to ask if he had made any money; but no one did till little May said, after he had told all the pleasant things, 'Well, did people pay you?' Then, with a queer look, he opened his pocket-book and showed one dollar, saying with a smile that made our eyes fill, 'Only that! My overcoat was stolen, and I had to buy a shawl. Many promises were not kept, and travelling is costly; but I have opened the way, and another year shall do better.'
> I shall never forget how beautifully Mother answered him, though the dear, hopeful soul had built much on his success; but with a beaming face she kissed him, saying, 'I call that doing *very well* Since you are safely home, dear, we don't ask anything more.' (p. 70)

This entry is a consummate example of the journal as fiction, as Alcott diffuses the unpleasant actuality with a soft focus effect. Family expectations are disappointed; the provider clearly is not going to provide. But, conditioned by her Puritan upbringing, Alcott sentimentalises the event, and turns it into a salutary tale of proper marital conduct. She does not, however, prevent the sense of her own frustration spilling over, and the overall impression is a sharply drawn picture of a family of women keeping their anger and sadness from the man who has let them down.

Not surprisingly, the main focus in all Alcott's writing is on the value of female bonding. Louisa May Alcott was exceptionally close to her three sisters, Anna, Elizabeth and May. Sanitised versions of their stories are told in *Little Women*. Anna, the eldest, married John Pratt in 1860. Describing the wedding-day, Louisa could not forgive her new brother-in-law for having broken up the family circle. Her own dress was 'gray thin stuff and roses, – sackcloth, I called it, and ashes of roses; for I mourn the loss of my Nan, and am not comforted' (p. 121). The imagery of death forms a sharp contrast with the description of Meg's wedding in *Good Wives*, when the March girls are clothed in 'suits of thin, silvery gray ... with blush roses in hair and bosom'.[4] Her second sister, Beth, died young in 1857. Only twenty-five, she was so ravaged by her illness that Louisa, shocked by her sister's appearance, reported in her journal that on her deathbed Beth looked more like a haggard middle-aged woman than a young girl at the pinnacle of her beauty. Once again it is interesting to compare this with the angelic description of Beth, 'like a tired but trustful child' emitting a 'beautiful serenity'[5] in the published text. The youngest Alcott, May, married a Swiss. She died in childbirth shortly afterwards, bequeathing her baby daughter to her sister Louisa's care. In all Alcott's work, sisterhood, a metaphorical as well as a literal source of support, is an enduring and unfailing emblem of shared female experience. Correspondingly throughout the journals, men are portrayed as unreliable figures: Bronson Alcott unable to give his family an income on which to live; John Pratt dying young, leaving his wife with two young children and no means of support; and May's foreign husband, kind and gentle, but ultimately responsible for her premature death. It is hardly surprising that Louisa herself never married, but preferred to find her own way to financial independence. 'Very sweet and pretty', she commented dismissively after her sister Anna's wedding, 'but I'd rather be a free spinster and paddle my own canoe'. Her pragmatism had surfaced in response to the circumstances of her childhood but it was at odds with the moral ideals her parents insisted she aim for.

Her frustrations and her sense of her own inadequacies are a continuous theme of Alcott's journals, running like a thread from her earliest entries to the years just before her death. Surrounded by the bustle of family life, in childhood she longed for a room of her own where 'I should want to be there about all the time, and I should go there and sing and think.' A perfect exemplar of Virginia Woolf's theories about female creativity, Alcott tried desperately to subdue her craving for solitude, for a space in which her imagination could run riot as it wished, but her dreams of mental freedom refused to go away. Her mother's rebukes and the instructions to 'go on "trying", my child; God will give you strength and courage, and help you fill each day with words and deeds of love' (p. 46) only confirmed her suspicions about her own imperfections. In May 1850, aged seventeen, she was forced to admit that 'every day is a battle', as she fought to control the natural energies that plagued her. Conscious that she did not conform to the expected model of feminine behaviour, behaviour which seemed to come so naturally to their father's favourite, her gentle, domesticated sister, Anna, Louisa felt continually guilty about her own dynamism. Two monthly entries for the summer of that year are pathetically revealing.

July 1850. – Anna is gone to L. after the varioloid. She is to help Mrs –– with her baby. I had to take A's school of twenty in Canton Street. I like it better than I thought, though it's very hard to be patient with the children sometimes. They seem happy, and learn fast; so I am encouraged, though at first it was very hard, and I missed Anna so much I used to cry over my dinner and be very blue. I guess this is the teaching I need; for as a *school-marm* I must behave myself and guard my tongue and temper carefully, and set an example of sweet manners.

I found one of mother's notes in my journal, so like those she used to write me when she had more time. It always encourages me; and I wish someone would write as helpfully to her, for she needs cheering up with all the care she has. I often think what a hard life she has had since she married, – so full of wandering and all sorts of worry! so different from her early easy days, the youngest and most petted of her family. I think she is a very

brave, good woman; and my dream is to have a lovely quiet
home, with no debts or troubles to burden her. But I'm afraid she
will be in heaven before I can do it. Anna, too, she is feeble and
homesick, and I miss her dreadfully; for she is my conscience,
always true and just and good. She must have a good time in a
nice little home of her own some day, as we often plan. But
waiting is so *hard!*

The raging unhappiness and the pitiful attempts to conquer it, the
hopes for the future, and the recognition of her mother's sufferings
were later to be dismissed by a more controlled Alcott as the
'sentimental musing' of adolescence. Reading over her journal
only five years afterwards, she did not want to acknowledge the
message of suffering that spoke so poignantly, claiming that it was
mere juvenile self-indulgence which she had now outgrown.
Nothing, however, can banish the impression of this lonely girl,
trying unsuccessfully to stifle her tears as she seeks to obey the
Christian tenets of her parents' teaching, a poor substitute for real,
human comfort. Comparing her own situation with her sister's
isolation and her mother's resilience, she suggests a pattern of
female hardship that is strengthened in her novels. In both the
journals and the fiction, she tries to elicit a moral message from the
inheritance of suppression. Marmee, the model of patience in *Little
Women*, tells her tomboy daughter Jo that she too has had to learn
the difficult lesson of emotional self-control, a requisite for social
acceptability and one she insists on passing on to her daughers.
The August entry in Louisa's journal for the year when she was
eighteen shows how the idea of moral inadequacy dominated her
behaviour.

August 1850. – School is hard work, and I feel as though I should
like to run away from it. But my children get on; so I travel up
every day, and do my best.

I get very little time to write or think; for my working days
have begun, and when school is over Anna wants me; so I have
no quiet. I think a little solitude every day is good for me. In the
quiet I see my faults, and try to mend them; but, deary me, I
don't get on at all.

I used to imagine my mind a room in confusion, and I was to
put it in order; so I swept out useless thoughts and dusted
foolish fancies away, and furnished it with good resolutions and

began again. But cobwebs get in. I am not a good housekeeper, and never get my room in any order. I once wrote a poem about it when I was fourteen and called it 'My Little Kingdom'. It is still hard to rule it, and always will be I think.

Reading Miss Bremer and Hawthorne. The 'Scarlet Letter' is my favourite. Mother likes Miss B. better, as more wholesome. I fancy 'lurid' things, if true and strong also.

Anna wants to be an actress, and so do I. We could make plenty of money perhaps, and it is a very gay life. Mother says we are too young and must wait. A. acts often splendidly. I like tragic plays, and shall be a Siddons if I can. We get up fine ones, and make harps, castles, armor, dresses, water-falls, and thunder, and have great fun.

The dichotomy between on the one hand the rigorous duties of her life as a school-marm and obedient daughter and on the other the attractions of her mental life is evident. The tension between order and confusion, so neatly expressed in Alcott's image of the room that needs tidying, reflects the division of her two realms of experience. Alcott is dogged by guilt and frustration. She needs 'a little time' and 'a little solitude' to be her own person, but on all sides these are denied her. Significantly her favourite novel is Hawthorne's symbolist narrative, the story of an outsider, a woman who defies her society. The idea of the heroic misfit held obvious imaginative appeal. Another entry of the same period cites *Hamlet* as her favourite play. Although Alcott was not at this stage of her life writing for her mother's inspection, the above extract reads as if it is still overlooked by that stringent moral mentor, watching for signs of deviance and waiting to correct them. The 'wholesome' books of Miss Bremer and the sensible rebukes about theatrical ambitions stand as awful reminders of the conventional strictures that young women were supposed to abide by.

In spite of all attempts to repress them, Alcott's imaginative energies refused to be stilled, and her journal gives a unique insight into the fantasy world that her mature novels only hint at. In 1852, a list of her favourite books shows her penchant for stories of heroism, lives of great men, romance and idealism. She found a way of emulating them through amateur theatricals, for which she had a natural talent, and saw in acting her means of escape from the stifling role her daily and domestic life imposed upon her:

June 1858: I was to do Widow Pottle, as the dress was a good disguise and I knew the part well. It was all a secret, and I had hopes of trying a new life; the old one being so changed now, I felt as if I must find interest in something absorbing. But Mr B. broke his leg, so I had to give it up; and when it was known, the dear, respectful relations were horrified at the idea. I'll try again by-and-by, and see if I have the gift. Perhaps it's acting, not writing I'm meant for. Nature must have a vent somehow.

Alcott continued to compare writing and acting. '. . . worked off my stage fever in writing a story and felt better' runs an entry in July 1858. Both activities projected an aspect of self into a fictional form, and helped her to adopt a persona in which she could express elements of her character that were allowed no other release. She was aware too of the other side of the theatrical coin. In many ways, her whole life was a performance, shielding her true feelings from the world. 'Pride made me laugh in public; but I wailed in private, and no one knew it' she disclosed to her journal in 1854. Her 1866 novella, *Behind A Mask*, features a character who has discovered that the whole secret of a woman's survival lies in acting. Jean Muir, the beautiful and vivacious heroine, succeeds solely through her capacity to create the right public persona and to adapt herself to a variety of stereotypic female roles: modest virgin; elegant hostess; charming mother; dutiful daughter. One of the story's most brilliant episodes describes Jean, who up to that point has been shown only in company with others, alone in her room. As she slowly removes her wig, her rouge and her false teeth, 'her mobile features settled into their natural expression, weary, hard, bitter'[6] and the real woman underneath the mask of youthful, alluring femininity is exposed. No more cynical moment exists in all Louisa May Alcott's writing, nor any more revealing.

Frequently Alcott's journal entries emphasise her solitude, and sense of separateness from those around her. The tensions between different aspects of her self, the adventurous spirit, with its Romantic aspirations, and the sense of duty to the tedious domestic routine, are exhibited on virtually every page. Denied expression during the day, her energies erupted at night. 'Dreamed that I was an opera dancer, and waked up prancing', she reported on 7 January 1868. The following day she went to see the famous British actress, Fanny Kemble, perform *The Merchant of Venice*, and noted admiringly how Kemble's fairly nondescript appearance – 'a short, stout, red woman' – could transform itself as the occasion required. Louisa's own disguise, her public face, was perfect. Her dreams show how she visualised herself, but that extrovert, sparkling, lively exhibitionist remained hidden from view in company. Unless she was in costume, a performer on the amateur stage, Alcott presented herself as shy and retiring. She did not dare for instance to speak to the great Fanny Kemble when she was invited to a post-show supper party with her, but was content to gaze from a distance on this magical, 'queenly' and successful actress who epitomised so many of Louisa's own ambitions.

Other dreams that Alcott reports in her journal demonstrate the same sort of division. In 1863, she contracted typhoid pneumonia, after a brief spell nursing soldiers wounded in the American Civil War. In her illness she became delirious and experienced fantastic nightmares. The 'most vivid and enduring' was of a romantic marriage with an exotic Spaniard, dressed in black velvet, 'with very soft hands, & a voice that was continually saying "Lie still, my dear"'. At the same time, however, this undeniably glamorous and dynamic lover was a frightening figure, appearing unexpectedly, making unwanted demands and 'threatening me dreadfully all night long'. The sexually ambivalent nature of this dream reveals Alcott's own confusions regarding her gendered identity. Unfulfilled desire finds expression in this fantasy, while fear of the unknown and terror of violation form an equally powerful resistance. Another recurrent nightmare was that she was 'being hung for a witch, burned, stoned, & otherwise maltreated'. She also had what were to her inexplicable dreams of worshipping the Devil. Images of deviance issued from her subconscious as she was simultaneously attracted and repelled by the idea of sexual and social rebellion. Typically, Alcott did not dwell on her dreams, just as she never allowed herself the indulgence of extensive self-analysis, but the fragments she noted down do indicate her state of uncertainty about herself, an uncertainty that was to be only partially resolved through her writing.

Louisa May Alcott's first published work was a whimsical collection of children's stories, entitled *Flower Fables*. It appeared in print in December 1854, and with it, in her mother's Christmas stocking, Louisa included a defensive note, apologising for its deficiencies and admitting that 'I hope to pass in time from fairies and fables to men and realities'. Characteristically she felt ashamed of the extravagant dimensions of her creative imagination, and this determination to repress fantasy and turn towards 'men and realities' shapes her journal entries of the same period. The style of these entries is laconic and factual, with little time wasted on what she had termed earlier 'sentimental musing'. Her emphasis on practical issues and her insistence on order and restraint reflects perhaps her unwilling adoption of patriarchal values, in conflict with her natural inclination. Having been taught to formulate her private desires according to a model of public acceptability, her journal contains ample evidence of repression. Her only apparent release was in literally running off her surplus energy. At one with her body in an unspoken expression of feeling, her return to writing was in effect a reminder of her own dislocated sensibility. As Ann Rosalind Jones has observed, 'A woman may experience *jouissance* in a private relationship to her own body, but she writes for others. Who writes? Who reads?'[7] These questions, 'Who writes? Who reads?', are crucial in thinking about Alcott's journal. Despite its alleged status as a private document, it seems to shun privacy by deliberately avoiding all suggestion of intimate revelation. It assumes throughout an implied and rather strict reader. There is little mention of personal feeling. It overtly suppresses anger, pain and suffering, although by describing the attempts to suppress these dark and dangerous emotions Alcott creates her own channel of expression. Her image of her mind as a room that needs tidying endorses her approach to language as a means of control, and her diary demonstrates her attempts to disguise her own 'voice' and to imitate instead the dominant, masculine, approved mode of discourse.

So Alcott's journal changed as she grew older and more famous. Her irrepressible joy at first being paid for writing soon gave way to a careful record of amounts earned. 'November 1855. – ... $20 earned by stories sent to the 'Gazette'; December. – ... Got $5 for a tale and $12 for sewing; January 1856. – C. paid $6 for 'A Sister's Trial', gave me more books to notice and wants more tales' (p. 83). Such details are typical of the entries of these years. She kept meticulous accounts and at the end of each year reckoned up the total amount she had earned by her writing. She started to see herself explicitly as the breadwinner for the family, taking over the role that her father had signally failed to fulfil. In a letter that she wrote to him from Boston in November 1856 she asserted that 'things go smoothly, and I think I shall come out right, and prove that though an Alcott I *can* support myself. I like the independent feeling; and though not an easy life, it is a free one, and I enjoy it. I can't do much with my hands; so I will make a battering-ram of my head and make a way through this rough-and-tumble world'.[8] It was at about this time too that Alcott became actively involved in the problems of independent single women. Although she was never a militant activist, she was keenly interested in Women's Rights. She was later to campaign for women's suffrage and in July 1879 she was proud to be the first woman in Concord to register her name as a voter. Yet, striving for approval, Alcott was always conscious of how far she fell short of her parents' ideals. The need to prove herself found an outlet in authorship, and payment for her services validated her labours and went some way to giving her the recognition she longed for. In 1858, reviewing the past year, which among other things had seen the death of her beloved sister, Elizabeth, she noted how suffering and hard experience had fuelled her creativity. 'I feel as if I could write better now, – more truly of things I have felt and therefore *know*. I hope I shall yet do my great book for that seems to be my work, and I am growing up to it' (p. 103). She had recognised that the market wanted realism, and felt that her own vivid, ephemeral imaginings were too immature to be ranked as 'great'. An entry for the following March said it all. 'Life is my college. May I graduate well, and earn some honours!'

Motivated continually by a desire for independence, both economic and psychological, Alcott saw in the act of writing the answer to her problems. Her journal provides illuminating insights into her working methods, together with the therapeutic effects of creativity during this period. In 1860 she began work on her first full length novel, *Moods*, a story which leaned heavily on her own unreturned love for Thoreau, and which tried to depict a woman of her own moody, dissonant temperament. Her diary records how in August of that year, 'Genius burned so fiercely that for four weeks I wrote all day and planned nearly all night, being quite possessed by my work. I was perfectly happy, and seemed to have no wants'. Writing at this stage was totally effective in dispelling her cares. Secure in her attic, she was removed from the outside world and its domestic demands. Literary activity was a solace and a companion. Alone with her imagination, she needed no exterior stimulus. Similarly, when revising the manuscript in February of the following year, 'From the 2nd to the 25th I sat writing, with a run at dusk; could not sleep, and for three days was so full of it I could not stop to get up . . . Mother wandered in and out with cordial cups of tea, worried because I couldn't eat. Father thought it fine, and brought his reddest apples and hardest cider for my Pegasus to feed upon. All sorts of fun was going on; but I didn't care if the world returned to chaos if I and my inkstand only "lit" in the same place'. The act of writing could not however, be matched by the act of publication. 'Wrote much on "Moods"'', she told her journal in September 1863. 'Long to have it printed, but dare not offer it.' Indeed, when she did get around to 'offering' it, *Moods* was rejected by publisher after publisher, and was not to appear in print until the end of 1864, after the appearance of *Hospital Sketches*. It was too personal perhaps and too unstructured. When it was eventually published, it was not well received, and she determined that 'My next book shall have no *ideas*, in it, only facts, & the people shall be as ordinary as possible, then critics will say its all right.' She began on another semi-autobiographical novel, optimistically entitled *Success* – it was later to be re-named *Work*, a mark of Alcott's growing cynicism – but gradually the message was getting through to her that her true feelings had to be hidden if she wished her work to reach a wide audience. She commiserated with another woman writer in a similar predicament, 'who says she never had any troubles, though she writes about woes. I told her I had had lots of troubles; so I write jolly tales; and we wondered why we each did so.' Ruefully she recognised that emotional concealment was a necessary precondition of the success she longed for.

Ironically, the first step on that road to success was to come from work which had originated with her journal and its learned system of control and factual reportage. In April 1861, Alcott noted excitedly in her diary, 'War declared with the South'. Her excitement, however, was tinged with resentment at being confined to a passive position, 'I long to be a man; but as I can't fight, I will content myself with working for those who can'. War to her seemed dramatic and glamorous, a chance for a sensation-seeker like herself to taste fresh delights, and eventually she could not keep away. On her thirtieth birthday she 'decided to go to Washington as nurse if I could find a place. Help needed, and I love nursing, and *must* let out my pent-up energy in some new way.' (p. 140) She left home for Georgetown in December 1862 'feeling as if I was the son of the house going to war'. The need to see herself in a male role is a recurrent feature of Alcott's journal. Here, the image of the adventurer and the artistic concept of heroic solitude helped to sustain her as she said goodbye to familiar things, to her family and her home life. The war diary that Alcott kept during her two months at the front is a masterpiece of emotional detachment in its concentration on external objects, sharp observations and rational commentary. Her own fatigue, ill-health, despair and sense of desolation are kept in tight rein, as if to surrender to her misery would be a betrayal of her position. An extract from her entry of Monday 4 January 1863, given as a prototype of the run of her days, shows her refusal to give way to the horrors of her situation, although by then she was becoming seriously worn down by the conditions and was to succumb to typhoid pneumonia only a few days later.

Up at six, dress by gaslight, run through my ward & throw up the windows, though the men grumble and shiver; but the air is bad enough to breed a pestilence & as no notice is taken of our frequent appeals for better ventilation, I must do what I can. Poke up the fire, add blankets, joke, coax, & command; but continue to open doors and windows as if life depended upon it; mine does, & doubtless many another, for a more perfect pestilence-box than this house I never saw, – cold, damp, dirty, full of vile odours from wounds, kitchens, wash rooms, and stables. No competent head, male or female, to right matters, & a jumble of good, bad, & indifferent nurses, surgeons, & attendants, to complicate the chaos still more.

After this unwelcome progress through my stifling ward, I go to breakfast with what appetite I may; find the uninvitable fried beef, salt butter, husky bread, & washy coffee; listen to the clack of eight women & a dozen men; the first silly, stupid, or possessed of but one idea, the last absorbed with their breakfast & themselves to a degree that is both ludicrous and provoking, for all the dishes are ordered down the table *full* and returned *empty*; the conversation is entirely among themselves, & each announces his opinion with an air of importance that frequently causes me to choke in my cup or bolt my meals with undignified speed lest a laugh betray to these famous beings that a 'cheild's amang them takin' notes'.[9]

Active verbs dominate this passage. Louisa herself is the agent in the first paragraph, forceful, brisk and determined. The fear she admits to is not so much of death but of chaos, the loss of control.

She needs to construct order from the confusion confronting her, and the life-threatening elements in the situation are mentioned almost casually. Her concept of herself as a child among the soldiers, a sly figure taking notes unobserved, was her means of detaching herself from the experience, from the sense of personal frustration and from the horror of the overcrowded, foetid ward where men died daily and where the anguished cries of the wounded who were left waiting for admission, sometimes for days, on the earth outside the door could not be avoided. The journal also invested her with a power that was denied her menial position, for she had to take orders from the doctor and nurse in charge. Private writing in such circumstances conferred status.

On 21 January, she was sent back to Concord, gravely ill, and was not able to sit up or eat properly until March. She took up her pen without enthusiasm in April, to comply with a publisher's request and wrote three hospital sketches, based on her war experiences. To her surprise they 'made a great hit; and people bought the papers faster than they could be supplied' (p. 150). Without realising it, she had struck on a formula that was to provide the cornerstone of her future literary career. More articles on the same subject were asked for and she offered versions of the stories which had filled her diary entries and her letters home from Georgetown. *Hospital Sketches* was immediately popular and Alcott's name began to be known, but the subsequent attention she received disconcerted her and disturbed her own already confused sense of identity. In October 1863 she confided to her journal, 'If ever there was an astonished young woman, it is myself; for things have gone on so swimmingly of late, I don't know who I am' (p. 154). Fame was heady, but she was insistent that the author who produced *Hospital Sketches* was not to be confused with the private individual. Caught by surprise, she disliked the notice she received from strangers. She hated the uninvited callers and those who claimed a hold on her because they had read her work. Curtly she noted in her diary, 'Admire the books, but let the woman alone if you please dear public.'[10] The sense of division she had always felt was becoming more, not less, pronounced as her ambitions began to be realised. The reception of *Hospital Sketches*, however, was only a mild foretaste of the adulation that was to come her way when her bestseller, *Little Women*, appeared in 1868.

Paradoxically, *Little Women* was a task for which Alcott felt the utmost reluctance. She was pushed into writing it by Mr Niles, an enterprising partner in the publishing firm of Roberts Bros, and his solicitations were strongly echoed by her family. In January 1868 she had made a New Year's resolution in her diary, 'I want to realize my dream of supporting the family and being perfectly independent, heavenly hope! . . . Perhaps we are to win after all, and conquer poverty, neglect, pain and debt, and march on with flags flying into the new world with the new year.' Characteristically, she employed military imagery to articulate her ambitions for the year ahead. 'March', a word appearing frequently in the journal, was the name she was to choose for her fictional family – an appropriate calendar month, more definite and purposeful than May, her mother's family name.

That spring, she began work on the 'girls' story' that everyone urged her to produce. 'Marmee, Anna and May all approved my plan. So I plod away, though I don't enjoy this sort of thing. Never liked girls, or knew many, except my sisters; but our queer plays and experiences may prove interesting, though I doubt it.' We could ask why Alcott was so tentative. Was it that the writing of *Little Women* forced her to confront her own past and to recall uncongenial memories? Or was it that in turning her attention to actual events, she was stifling her romantic imagination and with it her only outlet for psychological release? Her dislike of the commission surely relates to the sense of maladjustment that is so strong a presence in her journal. Her temperament failed to conform to the conventional womanly model and in writing a story that endorsed those conventional values, she was in many ways betraying her own integrity. Certainly she felt a conflict between her inclination and her economic and family responsibilities, a conflict that had dogged her throughout her life. But she fell to work and in two months had written twelve chapters, which she sent off for approval. Her publisher initially 'thought it *dull*; so do I. But work away and mean to try the experiment; for lively, simple books are very much needed for girls, and perhaps I can supply the need'. Compared with the exhilaration that Alcott had felt while writing *Moods*, the composition of *Little Women* was laborious indeed, a duty imposed upon her rather than an extension of her creative powers. On 15 July she was able to note with relief, 'have finished "Little Women", and sent it off – 402 pages', but when the proofs arrived at the end of August she found herself rather grudgingly admiring the effect 'Not a bit sensational, but simple and true, for we really lived most of it; and if it succeeds that will be the reason of it'. Alcott's move from sensationalism to realism was indeed the source of the book's success, but it had devastating personal consequences. In basing the story of the four March sisters and their parents on her own upbringing, Louisa had falsified her actual experience to make it palatable to both a wide readership and to herself. We have only to compare her version of childhood scrapes in *Little Women* with her journal record of the Fruitlands farm disaster to see how firmly her bitterness was now under control. In order to prevent herself dragging up too many unpleasant memories, she removed her father from much of the novel's action and by so doing sharpened the book's focus on women's communal solidarity. In part, her vision was softened by a visit she had made to Europe the previous year, when several thousand miles distance between herself and her family made their place in her life seem particularly poignant. From France and Switzerland she was able to gain a fresh perspective on those who had always been so close to her, and her homecoming in the summer of 1866 re-established her as a child in their affection. But in sentimentalising characters and events from her own past, Louisa May Alcott had, without realising it, created in *Little Women* a pervasive American myth. The presentation of the March family created an image of distinctively feminine values and of female strength that did not set out to disturb the status quo. At a time when women's suffrage was becoming a hotly debated issue in North American life, *Little Women* gave the public a positive, but highly conservative view of women's roles which was reassuring. Meg, Jo, Beth, Amy and Marmee emerged as individual personalities who could yet be linked to particular stereotypes and whose creative potential could be satisfied by their duties as mothers and homemakers. Even Jo, the unruly second daughter who carries the emotional sympathy of the novel, must learn that her aspirations and her behaviour have to be modified if she is to gain her parents' and correspondingly society's approval. Marmee's advice to this tomboy daughter to 'try with heart and soul to master this quick temper, before it brings you greater sorrow and regret than you have known today'[11] is repeated in the form of the novel itself. For in *Little Women*, Alcott subdued her own anger and her sense of burning frustration to give an unreal version of her family life that captured the public imagination.

No one would guess from reading the text how little she approved its message. When Marmee tells her daughters that 'To be loved and chosen by a good man is the best and sweetest thing which can happen to a woman; and I sincerely hope my girls may know this beautiful experience',[12] her voice was at odds with its author's principles. While delighted with the financial rewards from *Little Women*'s sales, Louisa was infuriated by the nature of the public response to the book. On 1 November she complained bitterly to her journal 'Girls write to ask me who the little women marry, as if that were the only end aim of a woman's life. I *won't* marry Jo to Laurie to please anyone'. (p. 201) Having witnessed at first hand the tensions of her parents' relationship, Alcott's attitude towards marriage was one of wry disillusionment. When *Moods* was published, she was asked how she, a single woman, had managed to acquire such insight into married relationships. Indignantly she wrote in her journal that the novel 'was meant to show a life affected by *moods*, not a discussion of marriage which I knew little about, except observing that very few were happy ones'. Just before starting work on *Little Women* she had in fact embarked on 'an article about old maids. 'Happy Women' was the title and I put into my list all the busy, useful, independent spinsters I know, for liberty is a better husband than love to many of us'. The ethos of *Little Women* stood in sharp contrast to such sentiments.

Alcott's biographer, Martha Saxton, has argued convincingly that *Little Women* marked the stultification of Louisa's creativity.[13] Its immense appeal vindicated her father's traditional view of women, a view which Louisa had always fought against. It also validated a view of her literary scope that she disliked: that she should focus on the home as the proper female subject, rather than allowing her imagination to seek out the realms of fantasy in which she could lose herself. It indicates too the ways in which market forces (including her father and her astute male publisher) determined women's literary sphere. For children's books were clearly acceptable in ways that fantasy or works of emotional intensity were not.

As a result of its popularity, *Little Women* bound Alcott to a myth that she personally found unpalatable. From the time of its publication, although her fame as a novelist grew, she lost that dynamic interest in writing which had sustained her when she was working on *Moods* and *Success*. Her journal from 1868 onwards reveals her pleasure in her increasing bank balance, but more and more her writing was treated as an onerous task that had to be undertaken if the bills were to be paid. In 1873 when travelling through Europe with her sister May, she 'wrote another sketch for "the Independent", – "A French Wedding"; & the events of my travels paid for my winter's expenses. All is fish that comes to my literary net. Goethe put his sorrows & joys into poems; I turn my adventures into bread & butter.' It is clear from this that writing had become for her nothing more than a money-spinning activity, an automatic task that did not draw on her emotional resources. Her intimate life was carefully guarded from public gaze. Unlike Goethe her 'joys & sorrows did not form the acknowledged subject of her writings, as they did in her earlier fictions. The American feminist Frances Perkins, skilled in public life, was to advise her daughter, 'Don't let anyone too close, don't reveal yourself'. [14] After *Little Women*, it was rare for Louisa May Alcott knowingly to disclose anything of importance in print.

Yet her journal still invites critical questions. Much of its later sections are devoted to descriptions of her travels abroad. The same interest in her bank balance is maintained; sums of money are precisely itemised. Just as precisely she recounts her descriptions of people and places, sharp sketches, factual and often dismissive. But the style she adopts with its brief comments on her published writings is in itself enigmatic. When Anna's husband, John Pratt, died, the news reached Louisa far away in Rome. Her reaction was immediate and practical. 'Began to write a new book, "Little Men", that John's death may not leave A. and the dear little boys in want . . . In writing and thinking of the little lads, to whom I must be a father now, I found comfort for my sorrow.' (p. 257) It is apparent that if anything writing had become for Alcott a means of avoiding feeling rather than expressing it. Quite naturally by this stage in her career, she was confident about her own capacity as provider. Yet the language she employs shows that her identity crisis was as unresolved as in her childhood years when she was not ashamed of admitting to her anxieties. Oddly she speaks of herself as 'a father', just as earlier going off to war she had 'longed to be a man' and had visualised herself as the son of the house. Uncomfortable with her gender, she adopted masculine terminology in order to deal with what she saw as her deviant personality. The critic Carolyn Heilbrun has commented that 'woman's most persistent problem has been to discover for herself an identity not limited by custom or confined by attachment to some man'.[15] It is a problem which certainly surfaces in *Little Women* where Alcott's fictional projection, Jo March, adopts boyish behaviour, whistles, uses 'unladylike' slang expressions, seeks out male company and, as her ultimate gesture of defiance, crops her hair – an act that confuses her as much as it liberates her and brings about a telling scene where she weeps for the loss of her feminine beauty without fully understanding why. The scene has its parallel in Alcott's journal when she has her hair, one and a half yards in length, shorn during her illness.

With no strong female models available for her to draw on, Louisa May Alcott could only refer to masculine identities to explain her own position. Writing in the mid-nineteenth century, she found her culture's polarisation of male and female characteristics too stringent to be of help in her own self-analysis, and consequently tried her best to keep that analysis at bay. Her journal documents numerous instances of this discomfort. During a stay in Switzerland in 1870 she was fascinated by a boys' school near her lodgings, and spent hours watching the pupils at play. 'I stand at the gate, like the Peri, longing to go in and play with the lads' (p. 248), but she never dared do more than gaze from a distance, just as years earlier she had been too timid to approach the actress, Fanny Kemble. Her ultimate satisfaction came from reminding herself of the financial freedom she had won with her labours. 'The cream of the joke is that we made our own money ourselves and no one gave us a blessed penny', she wrote home in 1870. 'That does soothe my rumpled soul so much that the glory is not worth thinking of.'[16] And in June 1872 she was able to celebrate the fact that at last the dream of twenty years before had become reality: she had paid off all the family debts. As provider for her family, bringing them not only solvency but a degree of material luxury that at one time had seemed beyond their reach, Alcott had successfully adopted the masculine role that her father had earlier abandoned.

Only occasionally did she allow the mask to slip. In 1874 during her mother's last illness, she was sufficiently moved by misery to cast an ironic glance at her own situation. It was not a pleasant picture. 'When I had the youth I had no money;' she bemoaned. 'Now I have the money I have no time; and when I get the time, if ever I do, I shall have no health to enjoy life. I suppose it's the discipline I need; but it's rather hard to love the things I do and see them go by because duty chains me to the galley ... Life always was a puzzle to me, and gets more mysterious as I go on' (p. 267). This is one of the few moments when Alcott reverts to the dissatisfied voice of her adolescent years, but it is a dissatisfaction which forms a permanent subtext to the journals. Occasional lines, 'I have no ambition now but to keep the family comfortable and not ache any more' and 'Got no sleep without morphine', expose the strain under which she lived, but which she never elaborated upon. In fact she had never recovered from her war illness, and had been in constant pain since then, a victim of the mercury poisoning which was an inevitable result of the calomel treatment she had received. Her best therapy, the remedy for all situations, was to be found in writing. 'Work is my salvation' she noted while attending her mother's sickroom, and even at the moment of watching over the dying woman she scribbled furiously away, for 'brain very lively and pen flew. It always takes an exigency to spur me up and wring out a book. Never have time to go slowly and do my best'.

Devastated by the death of her youngest sister, May, five years later, Louisa turned once again to literary activity to help her through the crisis. 'Father and I cannot sleep', she told her journal sadly. 'But he and I make verses as we did when Marmee died. Our grief seems to flow into words.' Learning to discipline herself was the hardest lesson Louisa May Alcott ever had to accept. Throughout her life, writing was one means of acquiring this self-discipline. Language was a tool whereby she could fashion her experience and by so doing place it at a distance when it became too painful to endure. Her journal shows us the contradictions of her life and the processes of her writing, as she trained herself to subdue her real feelings and to write a prose that would not give her away too nakedly.

7

The Life Apart:
The Diaries
of Edith Wharton

*I appear to myself like a new creature opening dazzled eyes on a new world.
C'est l'aube.*

Edith Wharton. *Diary*, 7 May 1908

In 1862, six years before Louisa May Alcott's *Little Women* was to
exert its powerful hold on the minds and imaginations of American
women, Edith Newbold Jones, later Wharton, was born into a
wealthy New York household. Although in later life, Wharton was
to make her home in Lenox, Massachusetts, barely a hundred
miles from Alcott's Concord base, the difference between the two
women could hardly have been greater. Whereas Alcott engaged
herself fully with the cultural and ethical debates of her age,
promoting in her novels images of family life that endorsed the
dominant values of her society, Wharton deliberately distanced
herself from the world she used as fictional material, offering a
view of American culture that was bitterly critical of its progress
and its development.

Indeed in her autobiography, Wharton, the purist, speaks dispa-
ragingly of reading *Little Women*, even as a child feeling 'exasper-
ated by the laxities of the great Louisa', whose use of language was
casually American rather than correctly 'English' in its tendencies.[1]
For Wharton, brought up on a diet of classical literature, and
accustomed to travelling abroad from her youth, soon became a
devotee of Europe and its civilisation, and it was from an essentially European perspective that in her fiction she submitted American
values and behaviour to her intensive scrutiny.

Edith Wharton's major novels are tough-minded cynical satires
on the mores of American society in the late nineteenth century,
the time of Wharton's own adolescence and young womanhood.
In them she offers a clear-sighted view of the historical and social

processes that affected a crucial era in American culture and she is unshrinking in her assessment of the particular implications that such processes had for women, caught up in an environment that simultaneously elevated their status and denied their rights to freedom. One of her most enduring fictional themes in the hypocritical nature of this social world and devastating effects it produced on women, insisting as it did on a sharp division between the public face and the private experience. The idea of an imposed public persona, controlled and impassive, often at odds with private grief and suffering, is a subject that Wharton addressed with growing intensity as her career developed. Among her earliest published works were writings on travel and on architecture and design – *The Decoration of Houses* in 1897 and *Italian Villas and their Gardens* in 1903 – works which concentrate on the exterior world, landscape, buildings and the forms and appearance of objects as she observed them. Her first stories too exploit her accuracy of observation in their exposé of a grasping materialistic society and the idiosyncracies of its inhabitants. It was only with the publication of *The House of Mirth* in 1905 that she showed how she could use her talent for ironic social commentary to suggest its obverse, the tragedy of the isolated individual, passionate and unfulfilled, destroyed by the pressures of conformism to a false ideal.

In many ways the story of Edith Wharton's own life appears to reproduce this pattern. Brought up in luxurious surroundings, and deeply impressed from her earliest years with codes of propriety, she initially found little difficulty in creating for herself a social role that satisfied the requirements of her milieu. In her carefully guarded autobiography, *A Backward Glance*, published in 1934, she describes how as a young girl having just 'come out', she enjoyed to the full the precious feeling of being part of 'a little "set" with its private catch-words, observances and amusements, and its indifference to anything outside of its charmed circle'.[2] Married at twenty-three to a man who, thirteen years older than herself, might well have represented to her the height of sophistication, Edith Wharton fell easily into the lifestyle of a modern young married woman, focusing her energies on house and garden, on style in dress and surroundings, and on travels abroad each winter, with little apparent resistance to the glamour such entertainments offered. Concurrently, however, through her growing intimacy with certain cultivated individuals, she was also being introduced to an intellectual and literary world that widened her horizons and helped to foster her own leanings towards artistic composition.

As Wharton grew older and these two worlds merged into that of the celebrated author, so a third life took shape, that which she called 'the life apart', the inner life of emotional longing and pent-up desire requiring release. Occasional comments in the notebooks of her later years hint at a reclusive spirit, tired of keeping up the polished and brilliant surface she so often seemed to embody. 'Oh the joy of being alone – alone!' she breathed rapturously to her diary in 1926, an idea that would never have been voiced by the gregarious extrovert of twenty years before. The sense of the separate worlds any sensitive individual inhabits, and the doubleness of human experience, forms a pervasive subject in Wharton's fiction. That it also formed an essential ingredient in her own life is revealed by a study of her personal writings, her diaries and to some extent her autobiography, which by its very attempt to give away as little as possible discloses more than its author could have realised.

The extant diaries among Edith Wharton's surviving papers are few in number, and with one exception, sparse in content. They consist of her pocket engagement diaries for 1905 and 1906, the period when she was engaged in the completion and publication of *The House of Mirth*; a notebook and a journal for 1908 covering the time of a liaison with an American journalist, Moreton Fullerton, in Paris; a notebook for 1910 which also contains material relating to subsequent years, mostly unconnected comments on her position as a writer plus occasional literary phrases which she wanted to keep for future reference; pocket diaries from 1920, and an exercise book dated for the years 1924 to 1934, but containing only fourteen pages actually filled. Yet even such irregular evidence of diary writing indicates something of the tensions that Wharton experienced between her need to maintain a public persona and the expression of her personal feelings. They reflect the separate areas of her life, the socialite, the writer and the private woman, and suggest her own awareness of a sharp distinction between the time spent on show in the company of others and the time she spent alone. To some extent the fragmentary nature of the diary material can be compared with the journal writings of Katherine Mansfield before they were organised into a definitive shape by her husband and literary editor, John Middleton Murry. For although Wharton's jottings are disordered and haphazard, especially in the later years of her life, collectively they can be read as a story of division, and as with the personal documents of other writers in this study, taken together they acquire far more than simple biographical meaning.

The line-a-day diaries that Wharton kept during the years 1905 and 1906, the period when she was beginning to be noticed as a novelist, show us a woman whose life was ordered, secure and under tight rein. Her days were occupied with entertaining a constant stream of guests to her magnificent New England home, The Mount, for luncheons, dinners and weekend parties, or taken up with the art of being a guest in other people's houses. In these diaries she recorded meticulously the arrival times of her visitors, the visits she made herself to distinguished company – 'Dined with Mrs Astor to meet Prince Louis of Battenburg'[3] – and the traffic conditions on the journeys she encountered to and from her palatial residence at Lenox – 'Left Hyde Park 9 am. Reached Lenox 2.15 pm. Actual time 4 hours, 1 hours delay on the road' she noted on 26 June. She worked hard at the business of being a hostess, taking seriously the details of the arrangement of rooms at The Mount and the beauties of her garden. 'Primrose, phlox, delphinium in bloom' she reported in November 1905, delighting in the unseasonally mild weather, while the following summer she recorded, presumably with some pride, her achievements at the local midsummer flower show, where she 'took 1st for 12 perennials. 1st 24 annuals. 1st Antirrhinums & gladiolus – premium for seeding phlox'. These diaries, succinct and factual, also make a point of charting the daily weather conditions, 'mild', 'rainy', 'blizzard', etc., together with the exact atmospheric temperature as measured in degrees Fahrenheit.

On their own they are hardly propitious material for a literary critic. Wharton's attention to the days' appointments reveals little of personal interest. There is no attempt to record an inner life, nor even to write continuous prose. They could be the engagement diaries of any busy hostess at the turn of the century who wanted a record of the efficient running of her household and to note (perhaps for future reference) the progress of her newly acquired motor car or the dates on which she entertained. But Wharton was not merely a busy hostess with nothing other than social affairs to occupy her mind. In March 1905 she completed *The House of Mirth* and in October the book appeared, to wide public acclaim. While keeping her writing clearly separate from her other duties –

marking aside the mornings as her time for literary endeavour –
Wharton turned to her diary to record the triumphs that affected
her so keenly. 'Wed 22nd March. Finished "The House of Mirth"',
she noted proudly. 'Begun about Sept 1903 – left off in Dec. –
Begun again Aug 1904 – & continued till today.' Her achievement
was indeed remarkable, a product of concentrated discipline, her
time for writing packed into a hectic social schedule. On Saturday 4
October she jotted hurriedly, 'House of Mirth appears. 40,000
printed –' between her notes on matters of more pressing urgency
relating to her guest list – 'S. Norton left' and 'Bayard Cuttings
came'. Throughout the autumn she continued to chart the progress
of her novel as it maintained its position on the best-seller lists and
went to press again and again for reprinting. On a blank page at
the end of the diary she made a careful note of the royalties
amassed by the success of her novel, and having said, 'Goodbye to
the good year 1905', she began a fresh notebook with a complacent
first entry, 'House of Mirth still the best-selling book in N.Y.', a
refrain that was becoming almost habitual.

Her industry was prodigious. In November 1905, having dashed
off a short story, 'In Trust', she began work on a new novel, *Justine
Brent*, later to be re-titled *The Fruit of the Tree*. Her diary for the next
few months stands as a tribute to her energy and perseverance, as
interspersed with the daily weather reports and the occasional
news bulletin – 'Frightful earthquake at Valparaiso, 7000 killed',
she reported on 16 August – she noted her word count with the
grim satisfaction of any author hurrying to meet a self-imposed
deadline. Three weeks from the first putting of pen to paper she
had written 20,000 words, and after a lengthy break during which
she collaborated on a dramatised version of *The House of Mirth* and
saw it through its first performances in September, she was able to
say with some exhilaration on 8 November, almost exactly a year
after she had begun, 'Perfect. Finished Book III of Fruit of Tree –
About 1,10000 [110,000] words done now!' Twenty years later, in
the light of experience, her very last diary entry describes the
stages of literary composition rather more feelingly, as she reached
page 166 of her then current enterprise, *The Buccaneers*. 'What is
writing a novel like?', she asked herself, and answered,

1. The beginning. A ride through a spring wood.
2. The middle. The Gobi desert.
3. The end. A night with a lover.

Wharton's boundless energy was a characteristic that remained with her throughout her life, whether directed into her writing or into her vigorous social and domestic activities, entertaining, travelling, sightseeing and establishing homes in France, England and the United States. The one departure from this pattern, in 1908, coincides with the production of a personal journal which is in both form and content a spectacular exception to the confident and consistent tenor of her life as it is portrayed elsewhere.

For while the early diaries are cursory documents, containing merely a brusque record of daily engagements and brief reminders of events, the journal which Wharton kept during the autumn of 1907 and spring of 1908 is a very different matter indeed. In late October 1907 at her home in Lenox, Wharton had received a visit from an American journalist, Moreton Fullerton, whom she had previously met in Paris, and who came to stay at The Mount for a few days. A special rapport was quickly established between them and, recognising that the ease of conversation she had enjoyed with Fullerton had liberated an expressive chord that was too precious to lose, Wharton, three days after Fullerton's departure, made the first entry in a diary that was to draw her into a compelling narrative of a type she had never attempted before.

The Mount. Oct 29th 1907

If you had not enclosed that sprig of wych-hazel in your note I should not have opened this long-abandoned book; for the note in itself might have meant nothing – would have meant nothing to me – beyond the inference that you had a more 'personal' accent than week-end visitors usually put into their leave takings. But you sent the wych-hazel – & sent it without a word – thus telling me, as I choose to think, that you knew what was in my mind when I found it blooming on that wet bank in the woods where we sat together & smoked a cigarette while the chains were put on the wheels of the motor.

And so it happened that finding myself – after so long – with someone to talk to, I take up this empty volume in which, long ago, I made one or two spasmodic attempts to keep a diary. For I had no one but myself to talk to, & it is absurd to write down what one says to one's self. But now I shall have the illusion that I am talking to you, & that – as when I picked the wych-hazel – something of what I say will somehow reach you. . . .

Your coming here the other day was marked by curious

symbols, for the day before you arrived we had our first autumn
snow-storm (we have October snow in these hills) & on the bank
where you & I sat we found the first sprig of the 'old woman's
flower' – the flower that blooms in the autumn![4]

It is clear from this that from the very beginning Edith Wharton
conceived this journal as a deliberate and discrete work of art.
Ultimately it develops to tell a complete story with its carefully
wrought opening and a formal ending, and is even accorded a title,
The Life Apart (*L'Âme close*). Whether or not Wharton at this stage, in
the autumn of 1907, saw her relationship with Fullerton as promising any special significance is less clear. She felt perhaps only that
she had found a kindred spirit, whose charm and sympathetic
manner had made her realise the emptiness of her own expressive
life. She already had a circle of men friends in whose company she
felt easy and confident, but the intimacy she had arrived at with
Fullerton was obviously of a different calibre. His interest and her
response had directed her attention towards an area of experience
that she had previously ignored and from which she now felt
excluded. Her need to voice her feelings through a diary and to
create the illusion of contact was a mechanism she adopted to
alleviate this sense of isolation or so her opening entry suggests.
Like all professional writers, she was fully aware that one of the
central problems facing the diarist was that of audience, and until
she could visualise a reader she was unable to exploit the potential
of the journal form to its full. The use of the second person
narrative, however, creating an imaginary confidant in Fullerton,
allowed her access to a range of expression previously untried. For
the style of writing Wharton used for this journal, unashamedly
romantic and often lyrical, is markedly different from the fictional
language of her novels, where she maintained the ironic perspective as a means of shaping her material. In the 1908 journal,
however, kept secret until the day of final departure from Fullerton
(when she emblematically allowed him to possess it for one night),
she indulged herself in recalling the detail of the moment and
constructed a framework of symbolic reference, beginning with the
image of the wych-hazel, to indicate the interaction between
mundane activity and the feeling heart. For the journal is a record
of the transforming effect of love on daily ordinariness, where even
simple actions such as smoking a cigarette or reading a letter
become invested with an emotional substance through the sugges-

tions of intimacy they convey.

In his biography of Edith Wharton, R. W. B. Lewis makes out a case for this 'love journal' as supreme evidence of a turning point in Wharton's life, her relationship with Fullerton awakening in her a recognition of an erotic nature that had previously lain dormant.[5] Certainly the journal tells a convincing tale of passion and the thrills of amorous experience, but how far can it be taken as an innocent piece of writing offering a direct line into the heart of its author? For above all the journal makes a feature of its own artistry, and as a self-conscious composition creates both a plot and a heroine equal in stature to anything in Wharton's more celebrated fictions. In her study of feminist biography, Carolyn Heilbrun has suggested that female lives are often written in terms of available and appropriate narrative structures, the most common of these for women being the erotic or romance plot.[6] Edith Wharton before 1908 was unusual in her avoidance of this conventional narrative strand, both in her own life and in the written works that she produced. In fact the persona that she invented for herself was if anything deliberately unfeminine, strong, assured and delighting in the masculine qualities of independence, wit and camaraderie.

The liaison with Fullerton, however, offered Wharton the opportunity of living out an acceptable feminine plot for the first time in her life, and the journal she kept during the months of intimacy with him was her only chance of writing the script. For as Heilbrun has commented, 'We tell ourselves stories of the past, make fictions or stories of it, and these narrations *become* the past, the only part of our lives that is not submerged'.[7] So during her love affair Wharton kept her journal regularly, making entries sometimes only moments after she and Fullerton had parted. The first occasion in that October after he had left The Mount was not followed up until they met again in Paris the following February, but throughout the spring of 1908 she wrote at length in the notebook, describing in some detail the hours they had spent together, always as if addressing Fullerton, but never shown to him until the final day of parting was reached.

How far then should we read this diary as psychological revelation, and how far as literary experiment? Certainly the journal did not replace correspondence between Edith Wharton and Moreton Fullerton, for the couple continued to write letters and to receive them from one another, not only when they were separated by the Atlantic Ocean but also during the months they spent together in Paris in the first half of 1908. It seems evident therefore that the journal was not designed primarily as a means of communication with Fullerton, even though it utilised the mode of personal address. It was essentially a private document, to be written and enjoyed in solitude. Simultaneously, in creating the illusion of a sympathetic reader, Wharton imagined a new role for herself, that of a woman awakened to the passionate dimension of romantic love, revitalised at a time when she had thought herself impervious to new experience. Given that Wharton was a writer whose major fictions centrally confront the issue of role-playing for women in society, it is particularly significant that the journal develops a consistent persona, a dramatised version of a female inner life, tremulous, confused, coming to terms with a profusion of intense emotions. 'Malgré moi, I am a little humbled, a little ashamed, to find how poor a thing I am, how the personality I had moulded into such strong, firm lines, has crumbled to a pinch of ashes in this flame!' she wrote on 25 April. 'For the first time in my life *I can't read* . . . I hold the book in my hand, & see your name all over the page!' What a striking contrast between her past authoritativeness and her present lack of control, with a concomitant realisation that the personality she had previously 'moulded' into shape was as fictive as any of her imaginary characters. The self-possessed androgynous figure that Wharton had so successfully established was to be replaced in the journal by a woman shaken from her composure and routine habits of mind to a discovery of a new self and a new voice. For Wharton needed to adapt her writing style to reflect the changed character of romantic heroine which she was engaged in constructing – a process fraught with difficulties.

By the end of the following February Edith Wharton was in Paris, where Fullerton worked as foreign correspondent for the London *Times*, and the couple could see one another on an almost daily basis. As the friendship between them deepened, Wharton turned to the literary medium which she found most suited her temperamental and expressive needs. A long entry in her journal on 21 February, describing their growing intimacy, shows Wharton veering between the personal and the metaphoric as she tries to find a suitable language to dramatise the ambivalent responses of a woman profoundly disturbed by sensations that are both intoxicating and deeply troubling.

All these months I thought after all I had been mistaken; & my poor 'âme close' barred its shutters & bolted its doors again & the dust gathered & the cobwebs thickened in the empty rooms where for a moment I had heard an echo . . .

When you came to dine . . . you said things that distressed me. At first it was exquisite. I had my work & you sat near the lamp & read me a page of Chevrillon's article in the Revue de Paris – the article on Meredith that I had told you about. And as I followed you, seeing your mind leap ahead as it always does, noting how you instantly singled out the finer values I had missed – discriminated, classified with that flashing illuminating sense of differences & relations that so distinguishes your thought – ah, the illusion I had of a life in which such evenings might be a dear accepted habit! At that moment indeed, 'the hour became the husband . . .'

Why did you spoil it? Because men & women are different, because – in that respect in the way of mental companionship – what I can give you is so much less interesting, less arresting than what I receive from you? It was as if there stood between us at that moment the frailest of glass cups filled with a rare colourless wine – & with a gesture you broke the glass & spilled the drops.

You hurt me – you disillusioned me & when you left me I was more deeply yours . . . Ah, the confused processes within us!

In reliving the experience through her journal, Wharton tries to reproduce the processes of emotional fluctuation that so deeply affected her, from her gradual realisation of the possibilities of the relationship, through the joy in shared intellectual companionship, to the sudden intrusion of a presumably erotic element for which, naively, she was unprepared. She frames the description with the two poetic images of the neglected house and the shattered crystal. It is as if in working through the delicate moments in which her feelings were alternately exhilarated and shocked, she found in techniques borrowed from another medium the only means of preserving the uniqueness of such transient experience.

It is important to recognise that through her journal Edith Wharton explored not just her response to love, but also its expression in writing. For the entries are filled with references to the written word and its value. On 20 April for instance she began her entry by confessing that 'I haven't written for six weeks or

more. I have been afraid to write . . . Since then I have had my 'day'
– two 'days' . . . one at Montfort, one at Provins. I have known
'what happy women feel' . . . with the pang, all through, every
moment, of what heart-broken women feel! Ah, comme j'avais
raison de vous écrire: 'I didn't know what it would be like'.' Her
quotations are taken from two previous entries, one on 22 February
when she spoke of having a 'day' alone with Fullerton, and one on
3 March when she described her joyous sensations as Fullerton
entered her box at the theatre and she said to herself 'this must be
what happy women feel'. Clearly Wharton made a habit of reading
her past entries before embarking on the next. Hers was no casual
approach to journal writing, nor did she use her journal for
probing self-analysis, as for example did Elizabeth Barrett, also
involved in recording capricious emotions day by day. Rather
Wharton's journal is a sustained record of a buoyant current of
feeling *and* a contrived narrative from the pen of a practised writer.
However genuinely Edith Wharton might have fallen in love, she
could not help herself creating a literary *tour de force* out of the
experience.

Perhaps the most telling example of her emphasis on the written
word is her entry for 27 April when she describes the daily ritual of
receiving a letter from her lover.

A note comes almost every morning now. It is brought in on my
breakfast-tray with the other letters, & there is the delicious
moment of postponement when one leaves it unopened while
one pours the tea just in order to 'savourer' longer the joy that is
coming. – Ah, how I see in all this the instinctive longing to pack
every moment of my present with all the wasted driven-in
feeling of the past! . . . And then comes the opening of the letter,
the slipping of the little silver knife under the flap which one
would never tear! The first glance to see how many pages there
are – the second to see how it ends & then the return to the
beginning, the breathless first reading, the slow lingering over
each phrase & each word, the taking possession, the absorbing
of them one by one, & finally the choosing of the one that will be
carried in one's thoughts all day, making an exquisite accom-
paniment to the dull prose of life. Sometimes I think the moment
of reading the letter is the best of all – I think that till I see you
again, & then, when you are there, & my hands are in yours &
my soul is in my hands then what grey ghosts the letters all
become!

Although the account ends with an admission that literary experience is merely a second-hand substitute for physical contact, Wharton portrays the procedure of opening the letter so graphically that it comes to resemble an erotic encounter in itself. The terminology – 'instinctive longing', 'wasted, driven-in feeling' – is emotionally heightened; the imagery – 'breathless', 'slow lingering' – is suggestive, and Wharton's reference to the prosaic quality of daily life emphasises the poetic aspects of her blissful sensations. A week later on 5 May we find her writing again about the fetishistic status of the love letter and its implications, transfixed by

> the queer letter paper with criss-cross rulings on which you write me at night *chez le restaurateur du coin*, on your way home! There seems to be more feeling in what you say on that humble poor paper, on which the fashionable & the conventional are never expressed. You say in your note of last night: 'we are behind the scenes together – *on the hither side. . .*'

She was fascinated by the idea of having broken through the facade of propriety into a world in which every sign and every word carried a resonance of private meaning undetected by others. Correspondingly the forbidden nature of this love finds its complement in the secret status of the journal.

Somewhat quizzically she noted how the force of passion had caused her to reassess her literary *métier*. It was poetry that now attracted her, that seemed a more appropriate medium for her current exalted condition, and both the style of the journal entries themselves and the experiments with verse interspersed among them show her move away from the cool rational prose that had previously characterised her literary approach.

'It is curious', she commented on 25 April, 'how the scraps of verses I wrote from time to time in the past, when – a wave of Beauty rushed over me, & I felt I must *tell some one!* – it is curious how they express what I am feeling now, how they say more than I then understood, & how they go straight to you, like homing birds released long long ago by a hand that knew not whence they came!'

Oddly, poetry, distilled and reliant on the power of the image, seemed direct in a way that logical explication did not. Indeed during the Spring of 1908, totally immersed in living and writing her love affair, Edith Wharton could no longer settle to her former disciplined working habits. Instead of continuing with the novel

she had begun a few months before, she poured all her imaginative
energy into the journal. The verses she included among its pages
have to be seen as an integral part of the text, a single composition,
mingling verse and prose to produce a literary statement on a
woman's experience of love, and an attempt to authenticate that
experience. The poem she wrote after she and Fullerton had visited
the cathedral at Senlis is typical of the way she used verse to
illustrate her feeling of the transcendent quality of their intimacy.

                    Senlis. May 16th
              Hung high against the perfect blue –,
              Like flame the belfry trembled higher.
              Like leafage let the bird-flights through
              Like incense wreathed its melting spire.

              From the dim vantage, lilac hung,
              Picked in the Roman rampart's strength
              We watched the foaming clouds that swung
              Against the church's island-length;

              We watched & felt the tides of time
              Coil round our hidden leafy place.
              Sweep on through hanging race & clime
              And leave us at the heart of space

              In some divine transcendent hush
              Where light & darkness melt & cease
              Staying the awful cosmic rush
              To give two hearts an hour of peace. . . .

              So deep the peace, so ours the hour,
              When night-fall & the fiery train
              Had swept us from our high-built tower,
              And out across the dreaming plain,

              Stillness yet brooded in our souls,
              And even our rushing chariot staged
              Loitering through aisles of silvery boles
              To some remote & star-laced glade,

              Where through the pale & secret night
              Past plains of water, depths of shade
              Under a low moon's golden light
              We felt the quiet fields outspread –

And there, on the calm air afloat,
While silence held the throbbing train
Some thrush from immemorial throat
Poured all the sweetness, all the pain.

The poem encapsulates many of the central ideas that dominate the journal as a whole, the sense of the magic of private moments within a chaotic cosmos, images of stillness, enclosure, and of time and space reduced and possessed through mutual love. The imagery contains a subdued eroticism, in 'throbbing', 'rushed', 'poured', which build up to the final image of the combination of pleasure and pain, while the contrasting concepts of stillness and movement, silence and noise, the cosmic and the personal suggest the division that Wharton was only too keenly aware of between the worlds that she inhabited. Dominated by time, as well as by space, she conceived of the hours she spent alone with Fullerton as outside the norms of daily routine although ultimately forced to bow to outside pressures.

This need to capture and to give permanence to the transient moment is a determining feature of the journal, within its compass as a literary genre. As Edith Wharton describes her meetings with Fullerton, the walks in the park, the trips to the theatre, the private dinners together, the sightseeing visits away from Paris, she makes continual reference to the fact that she knows her happiness is only temporary. 'I am always glad to go with you to some new place, so that in the empty future years I may say, going there alone: "We were here together once"', she wrote in her journal on the 19th May. 'It will make the world less empty.' In her conscious awareness of the lonely time that lies ahead, Wharton emphasises the ephemerality of the present moment that only the journal could validate. 'What a pity one cannot live longer in the memory of such hours', she mused, fully aware that the love affair with Fullerton, however intense, could only for her be an episode, not a way of life, just as the journal was merely an interlude in her literary career. Living out a romantic fiction, she made herself temporarily into the heroine of the sort of love story that her later novels take as their sub-text, a forceful reminder of the power of latent sexuality which creates disruptive currents in the shining surface of polite life. All is framed by her sense of time, her consciousness of her blank past and of a vacant future awaiting her.

Commenting on the journal, R. W. B. Lewis has remarked that 'it
led to a mode of expression that was at times uncharacteristically
adolescent (not surprisingly perhaps since urges stifled since
adolescence were among those being brought into play), and it did
not always escape the clichés upon which strong emotion tends to
fall back. To speak in chillingly aesthetic terms, the journal cannot
be ranked among Edith Wharton's best efforts. But there is a
wealth of honesty at its core, and behind the exclamations and the
underlinings there lie that toughness and fortitude of spirit that
were of her essence'.[8]

Lewis's criticism is tightly bound by the limits of conventional
evaluative criteria. For while recognising that the journal is a
formed literary work, he can only downgrade its achievement
critically as not one of Wharton's 'best efforts', and try to reclaim
his subject in terms of her moral qualities, her 'honesty', 'toughness' and 'fortitude of spirit'. Yet if anything the journal is a
declaration of weakness rather than strength, an alignment with
traditional feminine experience of the emotional dislocation that
accompanies seduction. And far from being honest, Wharton
presents herself as a conventional romantic figure, her 'clichés'
perhaps demonstrating her frustration at the lack of a suitable
female language for the expression of personal feeling. It could be
argued that it is the absence of a history of women's love
confessions which results in Wharton's reliance on already in-
scribed sentimental writings about women. As Juliet Mitchell has
observed,

I do not believe there is such a thing as female writing, a
'woman's voice'. There is the hysteric's voice which is the
woman's masculine language . . . talking about feminine experience.
It is both simultaneously the woman novelist's refusal of the
woman's world – she is after all a novelist – and her construction
from within of a masculine world of that woman's world.[9]

And Wharton was after all a novelist. Her sense of an inevitable
dependence on the romantic language of others was encouraged
by contemporaneous reading of European authors, all male. The
quotations entered in the pocket diary she also kept during this
period and which acted in part as a personal coded memorandum
show her responsiveness to works which dealt with illicit and
inescapable passion, from John Donne's appeal on behalf of

eroticism in 'The Extasie' to the adultery of Lancelot and Guinevere in William Morris's 'Defence of Guinevere'. These quotations provided both a justification of and a complement to the journal, the classical writings of men about women set side by side with a subjective account of a woman's passion.

As the end of May approached and with it the day of Edith's departure for the United States, she began to draw the journal to a close. On 21 May she began her entry with typical theatrical verve: 'My two months, my incredible two months, are almost over!'. Looking back over the brief but dynamic period of the relationship, she recalled how she had always guessed what life could hold for her, 'And the day came . . . the day has *been* – & I have poured into it all my stored-up joy of living, all my sense of the beauty & mystery of the world, every impression of joy & loveliness in sight or sound or 'touch'. Her use of the past tense here takes on an extra poignancy in her recognition that the affair is about to end and after she had completed this entry, with its pathetic reminders of the pre-Fullerton days when she 'used to weave sensations into a veil of colour to hide the great blank behind. . . .', she gave the complete journal to her lover to read. Her next entry, entitled *The Last Day*, re-enacts the characteristic tenor of the diary overall, in its reliance on nostalgia and the symbolic associations of everyday articles. In the midst of her packing, surrounded by trunks and valises, Wharton gazed on the dresses she had worn during her Paris idyll, each garment bringing back a vivid memory: 'the tea-gown I wore the first night you dined with me alone . . . You liked it, you said. . . . the dress I wore the day we went to Herblay. when, in the church, for a moment, the Veiled happiness stole up to me . . . the grey dress, with Irish lace.' Perhaps she was unconsciously recreating the scene she had written for her heroine Lily Bart who, approaching her tragic end, spreads out her clothes on the bed while 'the scenes in which they had been worn rose vividly before her. An association lurked in every fold: each fall of lace and gleam of embroidery was like a letter in the record of her past.'[10] Re-writing her own life on the fictional model she had already devised, Edith Wharton demonstrates how, as a critic has commented, in the attempt 'to constitute herself discursively as female subject, the autobiographer brings to the recollection of her past and to the reflection on her identity interpretative figures (tropes, myths, metaphors, to suggest alternative phrasing).'[11] She was to employ the technique to full ironic effect again in her later novels, where material objects are loaded with heavy significance. Just as these clothes are reminders of a femininity that indicates both sexual power and its accompanying uncertainties – 'Will he like me in it?' she had asked of herself as she dressed for her lover's approval – so as she sailed across the Atlantic, the names of the places she and Fullerton had visited together were told over like rosary beads, jewelled mementoes of transcendent joy. 'Herblay... Montfort... L'Amaury... Provins... Beauvais... Montmorency... Senlis... Meudon...', she entered in her journal. 'What wealth for a heart that was empty this time last year.' For Wharton the experience of love provided an opportunity to reassess her entire personality. 'I, who dominated life, stood aside from it, how I am humbled, absorbed, without a shred of will or identity left!' she commented with wry insight. Her journal shows her admitting to a vulnerability and confusion that she had kept fiercely hidden from public view, and which after the experience with Fullerton was to surface only rarely.

Indeed it is worth comparing the self-portrait Wharton cultivates in the journal with the picture of her life as she draws it in *A Backward Glance*, her official autobiography. In the journal she presents herself primarily as an emotional being, subject to intense moods, alternating rapidly between ecstasy and desolation. Her entry for 20 April for instance describes both times when she felt 'calm and exalted' in the certainty of being loved, and other 'tormented days' when 'comes the terrible realization of the fugitiveness of it all, the weariness of the struggle, the à quoi bon?, the failing courage, the mortal weakness – the blind cry: "I want you! I want you!" that bears down everything else...' Her autobiography, however, projects an essentially dispassionate figure, incapable of being moved by strong emotions. Her unhappy marriage to Teddy Wharton and the subsequent misery of her divorce in 1913 are dismissed in a couple of sentences. It is only in the journal that she allows herself to speak of being stifled in Teddy's presence, of hearing 'the key turn in the prison lock' of her marriage and of the terrible 'mortal solitude' she can hardly bear. In the autobiography the name of Moreton Fullerton is never mentioned and there is no reference to those heady days in Paris 1908. Furthermore Wharton denies categorically that she ever kept 'even the briefest of diaries' before the age of fifty-five, claiming that she found her life 'too uneventful to be worth recording. Indeed I had never even thought of recording it for my own amusement'. It is as if in her memoir she wished to sustain the fiction she had preserved so successfully in public life – that of the famous writer, virtually ungendered and certainly asexual, denying her susceptibility to impulse.

In addition the journal makes a point of identifying with a common store of female experience – 'I want to be ... like other women', she had written, noting that the old mask of nonchalance had slipped now that she understood both 'what happy women feel' and 'what heart-broken women feel'. *A Backward Glance* on the contrary, after its opening description of Wharton as a child revelling in new clothes and in male attraction, presents her career as one largely determined by intellectual ambition. In observing how her literary talents were out of step with the proprieties that governed female demeanour, Wharton deliberately cultivates the notion of her own difference from her New York contemporaries, and her alignment with men rather than with women is a salient feature of the book. She devotes pages to descriptions of her male friends – Henry James, Percy Lubbock, Robert Norton, Howard Sturgis, Gaillard Lapsley – with whom she, the lone woman, took her place as an equal. With this 'inner group' as she termed it she could laugh, joke, gossip and talk about literature, revelling in a bonhomie that she found it difficult if not impossible to achieve with women. She notes with some relish for instance how at Paris dinner parties her company seemed to be an embarrassment to the other women when they gathered together in the drawing room, 'my burdensome presence preventing the natural interchange of remarks on children, servants and prices which would otherwise have gone on between the ladies'.[12] Feeling perhaps that her credibility as an author would be compromised by too ready an admission of her femininity, Wharton preferred to deny that element in her make-up in proposing a view of herself for public consumption. The secret female knowledge, the sharing 'what other women feel', the nervousness, the longing and the fears, all these were confessed and confided only to the pages of her journal, remaining as background hints in the novels that as John Bayley has observed are 'built on rules and concealments'.[13]

Telling evidence that for Wharton sex and work were incompatible comes from the speed with which she resumed writing immediately after her parting from Fullerton in May 1908. On the boat taking her back to America and the husband she despised, she wrote 'The Choice', a short story about a woman tied to a frivolous playboy husband. In the arms of her lover she wishes for nothing more earnestly than her husband's death, but it is the lover not the husband who is killed. Wharton then recommenced work on *The Custom of the Country*, probably her most savage satire on the ideal of American 'progress'. Its horrific heroine, Undine Spragg, a 'monstrously perfect result of the system' which has spawned her, conspicuously lacks any solid identity, moulding herself to the requirements of the different social milieux she encounters, and correspondingly she fails to find any true form of satisfaction. Wharton's attack on social pressures in her novels and her exposé of the human suffering that conformism generates can be seen to have their roots in her own realisation of the sterility of a life which she had once endured without question. 'The secret of happiness is to have forgotten what it is to be happy', she wrote in her diary in 1924, the memories of the time with Fullerton still wielding their influence. And almost ten years later in a diary entry headed 'Alone at Ste Claire' (her villa on the Côte d'Azur), she took rueful stock of her position. 'Another year & the tired heart still beats as vehemently as ever', she noted without bitterness. 'Ah well – in summing it all up, let me say: "Love & Beauty have poured such glowing cups for me that when the last drop of the last is drained I shall go away grateful – if not satisfied."' As an afterthought she added, 'Satisfied! What a beggarly state! Who would be satisfied with being satisfied?'[14]

These later diaries, although kept irregularly, show Wharton as a woman who is no longer afraid to be reflective or romantic. At the beginning of the copybook she bought in 1924 she hoped that 'Perhaps at last I shall be able to write down some disconnected thoughts, old & new – gather together the floating scraps of experience that have lurked for years in corners of my mind.' The diary was to be an attempt to impose order on inchoate fragments and to articulate for herself a coherent identity. Although she never kept up the entries as regularly as she had originally intended, she did attach a particular significance to the notebook itself. When she mislaid it in 1928 she could not 'settle' to another, and made no more entries until she had recovered the original volume three years later. Similarly it was a source of frustration when she forgot to take the diary with her on leaving France for her travels in May 1933, 'I hunted in vain for it all summer, & now on my return, have just found it', she wrote in November. 'Again & again I wanted to write something down in it; but all the "somethings" have taken flight & must trail till others flit up.'

In the diaries and notebooks of these years Wharton is not afraid to confess her weaknesses. In 1913 for instance she recounts at length a dream that haunted her, 'a real dream' not a fiction, a graphic illustration of secret terrors lurking in the dark realms of the psyche threatening to break up the composure of her control.

A pale Demon with black hair came in followed by four black gnome-like creatures carrying a great black trunk. They let it down & opened it, & the Demon crying out 'Here's your year – here are all the horrors that have happened to you, & that are still going to happen!' dragged out a succession of limp black squirming things & threw them on the floor before me. They were not rags or creatures, not living or dead – they were Black Horrors, shapeless, & that seemed to writhe about as they fell at my feet.

In the dream, trying to destroy these unnameable horrors, she finally empties the trunk, turns to the devils and admits her worst fear, '"Are you sure it hasn't a false bottom?"'. The nightmare that lies beneath the collected surface of the well-regulated brilliant society that peoples her novels finds explicit expression in Edith Wharton's diary. So she had turned to the journal in 1908 to give voice to despair, after hearing from Fullerton that he could not meet her that autumn as they had planned. 'A distance seems to have widened between us since I read that letter', she wrote on 12 June. 'All hope forsook me & I sent you back a desperate word: "Don't write to me again! Let me face at once the fact *that it is over*."' Despite the correspondence between them, she needed the journal to satisfy both an emotional urge and a creative impulse – she was after all being given a perfect closing chapter to her story.

For even in her most private moments Wharton was a perfectionist. In her 1910 notebook the sentence 'It has always been my fate to suffer like a brute & to understand like a demi-god' has been altered, the word 'demi-god' replacing the crossed-out 'fool'. Never forgetting that she was an author, she retained her artistic standards in her personal writing, ever sensitive to style and language. Many of her later jottings consist of phrases for possible future use – 'Mr Vimpry had adopted disparagement as a career' or 'She walked through life on a narrow plank of prejudice, convinced that a slip on either side wd. plunge her into an abyss of immorality or vulgarity' – together with comments on literary procedure. 'Most novelists have too much subject & don't do enough with it', she observed. *'Each page shd be conceived & born separately*. The whole creative act shd. begin again every morning'. Her journal like her novels was first and foremost a creative act. Its precipitous negotiation between personal feeling and literary expression was for Wharton an experiment that was never to be repeated, nor was it ever intended for publication. But it was preserved, not destroyed, and neither the experience it described nor the style of writing were regretted by its author. 'Life is either always a tight-rope or a feather-bed', she wrote in her diary on 23 March 1926. 'Give me the tight-rope'.

8

The Mask Beneath the Mask: The Journal of Katherine Mansfield

Don't lower your mask until you have another mask prepared beneath – as terrible as you like – but a mask.

—Katherine Mansfield to John Middleton Murry, 1917

'True to oneself! Which self?' asked Katherine Mansfield in her notebook of 1920. It was a question which plagued her throughout her life, and one which forms a recurrent and haunting motif in her journal. Katherine Mansfield's search for a unified identity is both a central theme of her personal writing and one which informs her fiction, as she experimented with different 'voices' and filtered episodes from her own life through a variety of literary perspectives in order to catch the 'truth' of experience. 'Is it not possible', she asked in that same 1920 entry, 'that the rage for confession, autobiography, especially for memories of earliest childhood, is explained by our persistent yet mysterious belief in a self which is continuous and permanent;'[1] Mansfield's own attempt to recapture her childhood, her questioning style, her apparent artlessness of expression and her urgent need to reconcile contradictory impulses, are features of both her journal and her published stories. These two forms of writing, the private and the public, the confidential aside and the imaginative fiction, are closely bound together both in their approach and in their exploration of self. Written during a period of furious artistic experiment in England and abroad, Katherine Mansfield's journals centrally confront the nature of that experiment and link it with the displacement of the stable personality which was its complement. The enquiry into the concept of self was a crucial feature of literary modernism and in Katherine Mansfield's work in particular we see it used to challenge traditional stereotypic notions of women, while at the same time struggling to define and to resolve the confusions of femininity as they affected her own turbulent psyche. Romance, marriage, motherhood and sexuality, all conventional fictional subjects for women, are re-assessed in Mansfield's stories and the diffuse reality behind the fictions is exposed. Ironically, Katherine Mansfield's journal, a work which came to be celebrated for its openness and honesty, is in many ways as much of an illusion and a fabrication as were her stories, and not purely in its reflection of what was in many ways an enigmatic personality.

In 1927, four years after Mansfield's premature death from tuberculosis, *The Journal of Katherine Mansfield* was published, to be followed in 1939 by *The Scrapbook of Katherine Mansfield*, and in 1954 by a much weightier volume, the 'definitive edition' of *The Journal of Katherine Mansfield*. All were edited by John Middleton Murry, Mansfield's lover and later her husband. Yet Katherine Mansfield never kept a journal systematically, nor a scrapbook as such. The volumes that Murry produced were compiled from the voluminous mass of his wife's extant manuscripts, which incorporated her rather scrappy diaries for the years 1914, 1915, 1920 and 1922 with about thirty exercise books containing 'journal' type entries, as well as some sheets of paper showing work in progress and miscellaneous private jottings. Many of the dates we find in the final published version of the *Journal* are in fact not Katherine's but Murry's, based on his careful detective work and his attempt to construct some sort of order out of the fragments and uncollated memoranda she had left behind, and which she had hoped no one else would see. It is important to remember therefore when we speak of Katherine Mansfield's *Journal* that really such a document never existed. Although she tried many times to start a diary, she found it impossible to sustain and her good intentions of keeping 'this book so I have a record of what I do each week' (p. 271) remained an elusive ideal. Indeed any consideration of Mansfield's work must recognise that the idea of a consistent journal kept on any regular basis is a fiction, and, unlike the other diaries and journals treated in this book, it is a fiction partly composed by someone other than its narrator.

For in his 1927 edition of her *Journal*, John Middleton Murry presented a sentimentalised portrait of his wife as pure, childlike and romantic. Her best work, he argued, had its roots in her early childhood, 'as a life which had existed apart from, and uncontaminated by, the mechanical civilisation'[2] of the twentieth century. By describing her as 'natural' and her writing as 'instinctive', he undermined both her professionalism and her involvement in the intellectual climate of her age. Rather he suggested that 'she turned away from modern literature', and both his introduction to the volume and his choice of extracts promoted a view of Mansfield as miniaturist, limited as an artist by her commitment to the undeveloped literary form of the short story.

Despite the sporadic nature of the material, the study of Katherine Mansfield's journal is eminently worthwhile, for, more than many writers, Mansfield relied heavily on her recourse to private writings as a necessary corollary to her art. She was an energetic correspondent, especially in her relationship with Murry, to whom she wrote daily when they were apart, and she recognised how valuable a methodical personal notebook would be to her. Several times she announced her intention of keeping a journal, although she found 'DISCIPLINE' (as it appears in her notebook) frequently eluding her. Her approach to writing, like her life, was subject to her moods, full of passionate moments mixed with periods of gloomy inactivity. 'What a vile little diary!', she remarked with distaste in the notebook she began on 1 January 1915, 'But I am determined to keep it this year.' A mere two months later her New Year's resolution had foundered, and the following year she set to again, spurred on this time by the thought of eventual publication. The diary was to be the ultimate artistic form, direct and uncomplicated in its rendering of experience. 'I want to keep a kind of *minute book*, to be published some day. That's all. No novels, no problem stories, nothing that is not simple, open' (22 January 1916). She could not keep it up. Later, she referred to the 'huge, complaining diaries' that she kept in her youth, but these have not survived. Instead we are left with a series of personal entries in her notebooks, autobiographical fragments, outbursts of frustration at her own failures, unabashed confessions of love, and scraps of probing self-analysis.

For Mansfield, however, these haphazard jottings, apparently insubstantial and incomplete, served the same function as those solid nineteenth-century diaries which had helped women such as Dorothy Wordsworth and Louisa May Alcott to give substance and validity to their daily lives. They served as a record of her past and as a measure of the change in her attitudes. In December 1920, for instance, she re-read an entry she had made the previous August and carefully noted the alteration in her emotional condition. 'I don't love him less', she observed about Murry, 'but I do love him differently'. Six months later she read the entry over again, and it now 'seemed to me very stupid and strange that we should have hidden from each other. By stupid I mean of course stupid in me to write such stuff'. Her final comment on the matter occurs the following July, 'Neither stupid nor strange. We *both* failed'. (pp. 208–9) Clearly one value of the journal was the sense of continuous personality it transmitted to Mansfield herself, palpable proof of a mutually informing past and present. 'Life and work', she said, 'are two things indivisible. It's only by being true to life that I can be true to art'. (p. 236) It is this acknowledgement that makes her journal such a vital adjunct to an understanding of her literary position.

The very name 'Katherine Mansfield' is a mark of the uncertainties that dogged her. She was born Kathleen Mansfield Beauchamp in 1888 in Wellington, New Zealand, but throughout her life she was known by different names to her different friends, 'Kathleen', 'Katherine', 'Katie', 'Tig', Kassienska, K.M., each one indicating her shift of identity in any particular relationship and her own enjoyment of role-playing. From her earliest years Mansfield wanted to find a way of asserting her individualism in defiance of the values of her conventional family, in whose company she felt unloved and out of place. In 1903 she came with her sisters to school in London, but after her return to New Zealand four years later, her sense of alienation from the bourgeois world of Wellington society became more insistent and she turned to art where she found both a sense of personal fulfilment and (importantly for Mansfield) congenial company. Characteristically, she was at first undecided whether to pursue literature or music – she fell in love with a talented violinist, Arnold Trowell, the son of her cello teacher; a romantic entanglement which helped to muddy her sense of vocation – and it was not until 1908, when she came back to England, supported by an allowance from her father, that she made up her mind to become a writer. She continued to explore the manifold elements of her identity. Her bohemian existence, a series of unstable sexual relationships and her early writings, both fictional and non-fictional, all testify to her tentative hold on her own personality. She became pregnant by Garnet Trowell (the brother of Arnold), married a virtual stranger, George Bowden, had a miscarriage, and at some stage during this period contracted gonorrhoea, the debilitating effects of which were to prove permanent.

In 1911, Mansfield's first book of stories, *In a German Pension*, was published, based on her experience in Bavaria, where she had gone in 1909 after her discovery of her pregnancy. In the same year, she met John Middleton Murry and began the liaison with him that was to last until her death. They married after her divorce from Bowden was finalised in 1918. From the moment she came back to Europe, Katherine Mansfield's life was precarious in all senses, financially, emotionally, artistically and psychologically. She made friends easily, and lost them just as easily. Capricious in her relationships with both men and women, she acquired many enemies through her unpredictable behaviour and her casually sharp tongue. She abandoned herself to brief, passionate love affairs, and suffered bitterly when they ended. Her involvement with Murry was erratic, and they spent much of the time apart. In 1917 she discovered that she had tuberculosis, and she spent the next six years battling against the disease, frantically trying to find a cure, while also searching for a peaceful, secure environment in which she could continue to write. While retaining a base in England through Murry, she lived much of the time in France, where she died in 1923. One single consistent activity gave shape to the rootless and troubled last ten years of Katherine Mansfield's life, her commitment to writing. She produced brilliant, tough-minded reviews, four inspired collections of short stories, a mass of correspondence, and her sporadic but nonetheless revealing journal.

Like the stories and the letters, the journal shows Mansfield trying out different voices to suit her different roles. The lyrical tone of much of her writing mingles with prosaic observation, as she re-created her emotional condition through monitoring the world around her. In France, for example, with her marked talent for pictorial imagery, she noted how, 'Every morning the sun came in and drew those squares of golden light on the wall, I looked round my bed on to a sky like silk'. (p. 183) 'The street so smooth and arched like the curves of thought, and up there walked sailors with their bundles, very like flies carrying their eggs in the hot sun'. (p. 196)

Yet when dissatisfied with her surroundings, she could write petulantly, 'My room is horrible. Very noisy; a constant clatter and a feeling as though it were *doorless*. French people don't care a hang

how much noise they make. I hate them for it.' (p. 197)
     She could be comic:

> My sticks of rhubarb were wrapped up in a copy of the *Star*
> containing Lloyd George's last, *more* than eloquent speech. As I
> snipped up the rhubarb my eye fell, was fixed and fastened on
> that sentence wherein he tells us that we have grasped our
> niblick and struck out for the open course. Pray Heaven there is
> some faithful soul ever present with a basket to catch these
> tender blossoms as they fall. Ah, God! it is a dreadful thought
> that these immortal words should go down into the dreamless
> dust uncherished. (p. 121)

She could also be ironic at her own expense: 'Even if I should, by
some awful chance, find a hair upon my bread and honey – at any
rate it is my own hair'. (p. 120) And dramatic: 'Tearing up and
sorting the old letters. The *feeling* that comes – the anguish – the
words that fly out into one's breast; My *darling*! My *wife*! Oh, what
anguish! Oh, will it ever be the same?' (p. 194)
     Her voices changed as often as her moods, childish, romantic,
complaining, cynical, analytical and suffering. The multiform personality projected itself through a theatrical succession of roles,
roles which were to reappear in her stories. 'The solitary person
always acts', she stated in 1921, propounding her neo-symbolist
philosophy that being and seeming, life and art, fact and fiction
gradually become indistinguishable from one another.
     Despite her comment in 1916 about possible publication, ulti-
mately Katherine Mansfield did not intend her private writings
ever to appear in print. Indeed her will of 14 August 1922 left
explicit instructions that Murry should destroy her surviving
documents. 'I should like him to publish as little as possible and
tear up and burn as much as possible', she begged. 'He will
understand that I desire to leave as few traces of my camping
ground as possible'.[3] The journal was a deeply personal chronicle.
'I don't mean that any eye but mine should read this. This is – *really
private*' she wrote in 1921, and eighteen months before her death
she confirmed that 'One thing I am determined upon. And that is
to leave no sign'. As late as July 1922 she realised how heavily her
journal, that 'damning little notebook', compromised her. Much
criticism has been levelled at Murry for ignoring his wife's wishes
and for capitalising on her death. But however much we might

condemn his motives, in his exposure of what she wished to keep
secret Murry provided vital insights into the nature of Mansfield's
creativity, the deep links this had with her sense of herself as a
woman, and the essential correlation between Katherine Mansfield's journal entries and her crafted and polished fiction.

'I was nine years old when my first attempt was published and
have been filling notebooks ever since', (p. 252) Mansfield explained in a half-hearted attempt at autobiography in 1921. The
first entries available to us, however, come from the journal she
kept when she was fifteen. Clichéd and childish, with a rather
forced sentimental strain, these early jottings show her as a
self-consciously introspective teenager, reaching for a voice of her
own among the mass of fictional conventions that swamped her.

> This evening I have sat in my chair with my reading lamp
> turned low, and given myself up to thoughts of the years that
> have passed. Like a strain of minor music they have surged
> across my heart and the memory of them, sweet and fragrant as
> the perfume of my flowers, has sent a strange thrill of comfort
> through my tired brain. (p. 2)

Yet even in adolescence her ambitions were taking shape, and
several of what were to become insistent central themes in the later
journal begin to emerge. The pages of the notebook she kept
during 1906 are filled with memorable quotations from writers she
admired. They reflect her confusions and her hopes, her medita-
tions on the irreconcilable conflict between art and personal
happiness, her belief in the need to maintain individual integrity at
all costs, and they make clear the single-minded intensity of her
aspiration to succeed. A telling quotation from Marie Bashkirtseff
says it all. 'Me marier et avoir des enfants! Mais quelle blanchis-
seuse – je veux la gloire!' (p. 3). Bashkirtseff, the Russian painter
whose death from consumption at the age of twenty-four pre-
figured Katherine's own illness, had produced a series of journals,
which in their insistent and painful self-analysis provided a model
for the young Mansfield. Determined to avoid mediocrity in her
work, Katherine Mansfield was deeply influenced by reading
Bashkirtseff, recognising from the Russian's example how the
journal could be used as a positive step on her road to artistic
perfection. Consequently in Mansfield's hands, the journal became
an anchor for her literary progress. 'I'm surprised to have made

such a crude note', she commented for instance on a fictional fragment from October 1920.

> That's the raw idea, as they say. What I ought to do, though, is to write it, *somehow*, immediately, even if it's not good enough to print. My chief fault, my overwhelming fault is *not writing* it out. Well, now that I know it (and the disease is of very long standing) why don't I begin at least to follow a definite treatment? It is my experience that when an 'evil' is recognised, *any* delay in attempting to eradicate it is fatally weakening. And I who love order, with my mania for the 'clean-sweep', for every single thing being ship-shape – I to know there's such an ugly spot in my mind! ... Not one day shall pass without I write something – original. (p. 221)

Katherine Mansfield, using the metaphor of illness which held particularly poignant significance for her, was her own sternest critic, perceptive about her faults and keenly alert to the stages involved in composition. Her journal helped her to realise the artistic perfection she aspired to; it allowed her to work out her emotional confusions, to examine her own working methods, to try out preliminary sketches for her stories and to capture and recreate intense moments of experience that she did not want to lose sight of. 'Most women turn to salt, looking back' (p. 11), she noted. She was determined not to become one of them.

Three obsessive themes dominate Katherine Mansfield's journal. First comes her insistence on her own isolation. 'I hate society', she wrote in March 1914, a typical entry of this period. 'I feel a real horror of people closing over me' (p. 58). This desire for solitude spills over into the second predominant theme, that of her fraught emotional relationships, particularly her turbulent and lengthy liaison with Murry, which began in 1912. Miserable when parted from him, she was even more oppressed by his presence, which she often found stifling. 'It is the hopelessly insipid doctrine that love is the only thing in the world, taught, hammered into women from generation to generation, that hampers us so cruelly', she had written at the age of seventeen. 'We must get rid of that bogey – and then, then comes the opportunity of happiness and freedom.' (p. 37) Yet despite herself, she continually succumbed to the charms of love. Her journal describes romantic moments when Murry was 'the being that in a solitary world held my hand, and I his – was real among shadows, and ready to laugh and to run,' (p. 82) and desolate moments when the thought of his abandoning her caused intolerable anguish. 'Am I any man's *wife*? Is it all over?' she asked despairingly in 1920, a bitter if self-conscious reversal of her youthful bid for emotional independence. Intensely aware of the power of her own sexuality, she found it added a fresh, if disturbing dimension to her concept of self.

The third, and perhaps most striking, subject of the journals is Mansfield's rigorous attention to her own literary development, as she struggled to find the most perfect form of expression for her ideas. 'I long and long to write and the words just won't come' (p. 60) provides a repetitive strain in her early journal. Like women writers before her, she was continually frustrated by the inadequacies of the language available to her and much of her journal is concerned with how to overcome this problem. 'I thought and thought this morning but to not much avail . . . in my brain, in my head, I can think and act and write wonders – wonders, but the moment I really try to put them down I fail miserably', she wrote despondently in December 1916, the gap between idea and articulation seeming insurmountable.

These three recurrent themes are inextricably connected. Katherine Mansfield's early commitment to art necessitated, she believed, a rigidly self-imposed isolation. Only when she was alone could she maintain her integrity of observation, her thoughts uncorrupted by any outsider's perception or opinion. 'I really only have "perfect fun" with myself', she wrote in January 1915. 'I am so made that as *soon* as I am with anyone, I begin to give considerations to their opinions and their desires . . . Life with other people becomes a blur' (p. 81).

'I feel I must live alone, alone, alone – with *artists* only to come to the door', (p. 204) she wrote in 1920, fully sensitive to the danger that life's distractions offered to the world of art. 'Oh to be a *writer*, a real writer given up to it and it alone!' (p. 203) But as a woman, she knew that she needed to prove herself emotionally and sexually, a need which sat uneasily with the solitude that fostered her artistic creativity. More than this she understood something about the fear that motivated desire. 'Why I choose *one* man for this rather than many is for safety. We bind ourselves within a ring and that ring is as it were a wall against the outside world. It is our refuge, our shelter.' (p. 259) Alive to her own need for love and scrupulous in her analysis of its fluctuations, she craved companionship, despite the clarity of her insights into its dangers. It is this which is at the source of the tension conveyed by Katherine Mansfield's journals, a continual war between the messiness of love and human life, and the purified artistic construct she sought to build. The diary of January 1915 provides clear evidence of this, as her love affair with Murry deepened. 'I must work at my story tomorrow', she wrote on 2 January. 'I ought to work at it all day – yes, all day and into the night if necessary . . .' Two days later, she noted ruefully, 'I make a vow to finish a book this month, I *swear*. Told Jack who *understood*. But did not start that night for we were lovers'. By 8 January a tone of impatience had begun to creep in to her confession. 'J. interrupted me all day with my work. I did practically nothing'. The idyllic quality of their romance was soon to subside in competition with the more pressing passion of the demands of art.

For Mansfield the compulsion to write took on a quality of urgent desperation, and it is in her journal that this feeling of urgency is most powerfully communicated. 'Do other artists feel as I do – the driving necessity – the crying need – the hounding desire that will never be satisfied – that knows no peace?' (p. 47) she wrote in 1911. It was a feeling that was never to leave her, so closely bound was it with her quest for identity. The act of writing was the fulfilment of her prime creative energies, and when thwarted, left her with a sense of almost tangible failure as a personality. Frequently we find in her journal evidence of her frustration at her inability to perform the task she felt was her motive for living. Inactivity was anguish. 'Oh God, my God, let me work! Wasted! Wasted!', she pleaded in her journal at the beginning of January 1915. A few days later, her mental block had not lifted. 'O God, let me work to-day. It's all I beg', she prayed fervently, but her release from the paralysing spell could only take place when 'ah bless! I am alone for a little. I can write'.

The concern with writing is linked with Mansfield's examination of the origins of her creativity. In 1916, a period which several critics have seen as marking the emergence of her true artistic voice, she asked searching questions of herself that linked her need for storytelling with her craving for personal reassurance.

Now really, what is it that I do want to write? I ask myself, Am I less of a writer than I used to be? Is the need to write less urgent? Does it still seem as natural to me to seek that form of expression? Has speech fulfilled it? Do I ask anything more than to relate, to remember, to assure myself?

Narrative, memory and self-assurance: these three elements are the key to Mansfield's journal and her art. Her search for an authentic personality involved scrupulous analysis of the function of her journal. 'I must start my Journal and keep it day by day. But *can* I be honest?', she asked herself. 'If I lie, it's no use.' (p. 240) In wanting to understand her self she tried to eradicate pretension, to demolish the face she adopted for others and to speak as directly as was possible for her. At the same time she recognised the disadvantages of such self-confrontation. A letter to Murry in 1917 warns him of the risks of disclosure. 'It's a terrible thing to be alone. Yes it is – it is. But don't lower your mask until you have another mask prepared beneath – as terrible as you like – but a mask'.[4] Mansfield's journal, like her letters, exposes the paradox that self-projection inevitably involves impersonation. 'We all begin by acting and the nearer we are to what we could be the more perfect our *disguise*', she observed, stimulated by a reading of *Hamlet*. Investigating her position as a writer, she reflected on the interaction between self-awareness and artistic expression. 'To act ... to see ourselves in the part – to make a larger gesture than would be ours in life – to declaim, to pronounce, to even exaggerate. To persuade ourselves? Or others? To put ourselves in heart?' (p. 275) The dramatised consciousness which forms the basis of her fictional technique is a natural development of the narrative 'voices' we find in the journal. The processes of articulation incorporate theatrical devices, and it is, for Mansfield, an artistic paradox that the stuff of life needed to be magnified through language if its impact were to have any effect.

Self-definition is indelibly bound with memory, and it was only in 1916 that Mansfield realised that the key to her fiction lay in her personal past. Recollection became her means of recovering the identity which seemed so often to be fragmented and unreal. Some months after the death of her beloved brother, Leslie Heron Beauchamp (known as Chummie) in October 1915, her thoughts turned to their shared childhood, and New Zealand became both the acknowledged source of her psychological uncertainty and her means of realising it. As if addressing her lost brother, she formulated the aim which was to provide the inspiration for some of her best stories. 'I want for one moment to make our undiscovered country leap into the eyes of the Old World. It must be mysterious, as though floating', she wrote early in 1916. It was only by visualising an imaginary correspondent that she was able to break down the impasse that had prevented her writing easily, as she found a voice and a role with which she felt comfortable. 'Dear brother, as I jot these notes, I am speaking to you,' she wrote joyfully, as if explaining to herself the secret of her new articulacy. 'To whom did I always write when I kept those huge, complaining diaries? Was it to myself? But now as I write these words . . . it is to you'. Her next entry began, 'I have broken the silence'. The roles of sister and comforter gave her sufficient confidence to define her narrative approach. 'I always felt: He never never must be unhappy. Now I will come quite close to you, take your hand, and we shall tell this story to each other'. (p. 97)

Paradoxically, but not surprisingly, self-discovery relied on self-abnegation. In her recreation of her New Zealand origins she had to 'Lose myself, lose myself to find you, dearest'. (p. 98) Her notebooks show her experiments with straightforward autobiography and its fictional transposition, as she mingled first person narrative with the projection of her own experiences on to Kezia, the child who became her fictive persona. One thing she was certain of and that was the distinctive nature of her personal vision. 'Nobody saw it, I felt, as I did,' she wrote recalling her adolescent view of life. 'My mind was just like a squirrel. I gathered and gathered and hid away, for that long "winter" when I should rediscover all this treasure.' (p. 106) In 1916 that winter of her creativity had begun to release its buried wealth.

Katherine Mansfield's retrospective vision marks her both as a modernist, in the vanguard of literary experiment in the early twentieth century, as she strove to make sense of the inchoate nature of the world around her; and as a woman, drawing on essentially feminine modes of thought to establish her unique perspective on experience. Her journal continually emphasises the unorthodox and the uncategorisable in her approach to life, elements which she associated with female patterns of perception. In 1916 she described her college days in terms of her own non-conformism, her failure to assimilate the 'correct' information.

What coherent account could I give of the history of English Literature? And what of English History? None. When I think in *dates* and *times* the wrong people come in – the right people are missing ... Why didn't I listen to the old Principal who lectured on Bible History twice a week instead of staring at his face that was very round, a dark red colour with a kind of bloom on it and covered all over with little red veins with endless tiny tributaries that ran even up his forehead and were lost in his bushy white hair. He had tiny hands too, puffed up, purplish, shining under the stained flesh. I used to think, looking at his hands – he will have a stroke and die of paralysis ... They told us he was a very learned man, but I could not help seeing him in a double-breasted frock-coat, a large pseudo-clerical pith helmet, a large white handkerchief falling over the back of his neck, standing and pointing out with an umbrella, a probable site of a probable encampment of some wandering tribe to his wife, an elderly lady with a threatening heart who had to go everywhere in a basket chair arranged on the back of a donkey, and his two daughters in thread gloves and sand shoes – smelling faintly of some anti-mosquito mixture. (pp. 194–5)

As this extract demonstrates, Katherine Mansfield was an alert pupil, absorbed in her subject, even though the information she culled was not on the prescribed curriculum. Rejecting the 'coherence' of 'dates' and 'times', she prefers human detail, sporadic and undisciplined, her sentences gaining fluidity as her confidence in her personal vision strengthened. At lectures, instead of facts, she noted imagined possibilities of experience. College life for her 'might never have contained a book or a lecture', for it was rather a recognition of a 'pattern that was – weaving'. (p. 103) This assertion of an alternative perception, cutting across the structures of narrative logic and formal discipline, is indelibly entwined for Mansfield with the intrinsic nature of female experience and its consequent forms of expression.

Katherine Mansfield's comments on Dorothy Wordsworth's *Journal* place her own stance as a writer firmly in relation to her predecessor and suggest a fundamental disparity between male and female modes of apprehension. Quoting Wilson Knight's introduction to Dorothy's *Journal*, she notes his inability to understand the significance of trivia in women's lives. '"There is no need"', remarked Knight, '"to record all the cases in which the sister wrote 'To-day I mended William's shirts', or 'William gathered sticks', or 'I went in search of eggs' etc. etc."' 'There is! Fool!' is Katherine's caustic comment. For Katherine Mansfield, as for Dorothy Wordsworth, it was trivia which defined the quality of the individual life as it is lived and remembered. Only by recording these trivia could the fabric of experience be captured, and the life recreated. Thus for Mansfield, the journal method with its record at once both subtle and mundane needed to find its complement in an artistic form that would adequately render that 'mystery' of personal experience.

Continually her journal offers an analogy between literary creativity and the act of giving birth. The word 'mystery', the quality she wanted to convey in her stories, occurs in her description of birth as 'the most solemn mystery in the world'. (p. 245) Her initial vision of *The Aloe*, the story that as 'Prelude' most vividly encapsulated this 'mystery' in her New Zealand past, stresses the importance of childbirth in the overall scheme of the narrative, with the birth of Chummie providing both a conclusion to her tale and signalling the start of fresh experience.

> And now I know what the last chapter is. It is your birth – your coming in the autumn. You in Grandmother's arms under the tree, your solemnity, your wonderful beauty. Your hands, your head – your helplessness, lying on the earth, and, above all, your tremendous solemnity. That chapter will end the book. The next book will be yours and mine. (p. 98)

The labour of writing that particular story was to conclude by producing the image of female creativity which most eloquently communicated the confusions of female selfhood. Katherine Mansfield always saw the act of giving birth as incorporating both loss and discovery of female identity, producing new life by negating one's own personality in the process of motherhood. Linda Burnell, the mother figure in the New Zealand stories, tries in 'Prelude' and 'At the Bay' to find ways of rediscovering this lost self from the numerous roles imposed upon her. She simultaneously resents and adores the baby son whose demands confine her to the maternal function, and exclude her other, truer selves.

'She was broken, made weak, her courage was gone through child-bearing. And what made it doubly hard to bear was, she did not love her children ... No it was as though a cold breath had chilled her through and through on each of those awful journeys; she had no warmth left to give them,' reflects Linda, as she lies under the manuka tree in 'At the Bay'. Yet only a few lines later, she is irresistibly drawn to her baby son in an emotional contract that is instinctive and inescapable. 'The tears danced in her eyes; she breathed in a small whisper to the boy, "Hallo, my funny!" '[5]

This preoccupation with birth and its inherent contradictions recurs throughout the journal. Mansfield's poem, 'The New-born Son', placed by Murry in 1916, suggests something of the ambivalence of childbirth and the combination of love and sadness it inspires:

> So that mysterious mother, faint with sleep,
> Had given into her arms her new-born son,
> And felt upon her bosom the cherished one
> Breathe and stiffen his tiny limbs and weep.
> Her arms became as wings, folding him over
> Into that lovely pleasance, and her heart
> Beat like a tiny bell: 'He is my lover,
> He is my son, and we shall never part.
> Never, never, never, never – but why?'
> And she suddenly bowed her head and began to cry. (p. 118)

The confusions expressed here between the roles of mother and mistress suggest something of the contradictions of female psychology. The idea is taken up again in Mansfield's notes on Dostoevsky's *The Possessed*, when she comments on his portrayal of the agonies of childbirth.

> How did Dostoevsky know about that extraordinary vindictive feeling, that relish for little laughter – that comes over women in pain? It's a very secret thing, but it's profound, profound . . . Does this resemble in any way the tormenting that one observes so often in his affairs of passion? Are his women ever happy when they torment their lovers? No, they too are in the agony of labour. They are giving birth to their new selves. And they never believe in their deliverance. (p. 111)

Birth, sexuality, discovery, happiness and torment, laughter and pain – these are the elements which combine to produce the disconcerting quality of female creativity. In coming to terms with these contradictions Mansfield needed to find a technique which sufficiently incorporated them, a technique which moved towards openness and enquiry rather than towards closure and resolution.

Her journal is full of questions rather than answers, just as her
stories rely on broken, tentative phrases rather than fully rounded
sentences. 'No! No! No!' she protested when faced with Coleridge's assertion of 'the security, the comparative equability and
ever-increasing sameness of human life' (p. 223). For Mansfield life was
unpredictable and subject to continual change. It was this variety,
momentary and transient, that she sought to communicate. The
apparent hesitancy of her fictional technique, suggestive and
provisional, was formulated in her journal, where the often incohe-
rent style reflects the restlessness that dominated her.

Abandoning 'masculine' order with its rigid sense of development and emphasis on objective fact, she strove to formulate an
alternative in order to convey that indefinable sense of 'a mystery,
a radiance, an afterglow' (p. 94) which she had made her aim. It
was not easy. Too often she found herself falling back on available
models, inappropriate for her purpose. As she looked at her
finished version of her story 'Mr and Mrs Dove' in July 1921, she
was dissatisfied with the result, aware that:

> It's a little bit made up. It's not inevitable. I mean to imply that
> those two may not be happy together – that that is the kind of
> reason for which a young girl marries. But have I done so? I
> don't think so . . . I have a sneaking notion that at the end I have
> used the Doves *unwarrantably*. *Tu sais ce que je veux dire*. I used
> them to round off something – didn't I? Is that quite my game?
> No, it's not. It's not quite the kind of truth I'm after. (p. 256)

'Rounding off' was never Mansfield's 'game', but rejecting the
fictional conventions which preceded her was one thing; finding a
satisfactory substitute quite another. Frequently her sense of
frustration at her inability to solve the problem she had set herself
spilled over onto the page. In the middle of one unfinished story,
'By Moonlight', her exasperation at her own incompetence dis-
rupted composition completely. 'I am struck beyond words, and
again it seems to me that what I am doing has *no form*', (p. 262) she
wrote irritably, quite unable to continue. The same sort of infuriated outburst appears half way through the manuscript of 'Her
First Ball', a story that she did in fact complete and publish as part
of *The Garden Party* collection. 'All this! All that I write – all that I am
– is on the border of the sea. It's a kind of playing. I want to put *all*
my force behind it, but somehow I *cannot*!' (p. 258). 'All that I write

– all that I am': the two are here presented as indivisible. Mansfield's view of her art as a natural extension of her self suggests a provocative correlation between journal and fiction. Certainly the journal proved an essential part of the creative process, allowing Mansfield to merge her critical and artistic practice, as she searched for appropriate forms and language which would embody her essential vision.

Ironically, perhaps, some of Mansfield's most forceful attacks on her own idleness occur at moments of her greatest productivity. In the summer and autumn of 1921 she was in Menton, working hard despite her increasing debility. But her journal covering these months gives the impression of long periods of frustrated inactivity. 'Here I lie, pretending, as Heaven knows how often I have before, to write', she commented grimly in September 1921. 'Supposing I were to give up the pretence and really did try? . . . As it is every day sees me further off my goal.' The same months found her fuming at her inability to discipline herself – 'It's nothing short of loathsome to be in my state' – as she impatiently attributed her failings to inadequate conditions, the noise and activity around her that interfered with her concentration. 'I bitterly long for a little private room where I can work undisturbed', she moaned, resentful that Murry had appropriated the only private spot in the villa for himself, 'And it's not half so important for him'. (p. 257) Yet these weeks saw the composition of several of her most accomplished stories, including 'At the Bay', 'An Ideal Family', 'The Garden Party' and 'The Voyage'. Her output was prodigious but Mansfield the perfectionist was only conscious of how far her achievement fell short of her ideals.

As Katherine Mansfield developed as an artist she began to use her journal positively as a dynamic ingredient in literary production:

I must begin writing for Clement Shorter to-day 12 'spasms' of 2,000 words each. I thought of the Burnells, but no, I don't think so. Much better, the Sheridans, the three girls and the brother and the Father and Mother and so on, ending with a long description of Meg's wedding to Keith Fenwick. Well, there's the first flown out of the nest. The sisters Bead, who come to stay. The white sheet on the floor when the wedding dress is tried on. Yes, I've got the details all right. But the point is – Where shall I begin? One certainly wants to dash.

Meg was playing. I don't think I ought to begin with that. It seems to me the mother's coming home ought to be the first chapter. The other can come later. And in that playing chapter what I want to stress chiefly is: Which is the real life – that or this? – late afternoon, these thoughts – the garden – the beauty – how all things pass – and how the end seems to come so soon.

And then again there is the darling bird – I've always loved birds – where is the little chap? . . .

What is it that stirs one so? What is this seeking – so joyful – ah, so gentle! And there seems to be a moment when all is to be discovered. Yes, that is the feeling . . .

The queer thing is I only remember how much I have forgotten when I hear the piano. The garden of the Casino, the blue pansies. But oh, *how* am I going to write this story? (pp. 313–4)

Mansfield's thoughts about writing combine with imagined scenes, isolated images to be developed later, and fragments that can be incorporated into the story. The journal operates as a form of dramatised mental action, a preliminary stage in the machinery of composition. Writing it acts too as a brake on her impulsive charge at her material. 'One certainly wants to dash', she recognised at the same time that she saw the necessity for pace and control. These sections of the journal offer us a picture of Katherine Mansfield as mature artist, working through her creative problems with distance and judgement. A few pages further on, as the Sheridan story takes shape, she interrupts herself again to introduce a dissenting, critical voice, 'But this is not expanded enough or rich enough', and to suggest technical strategies for improvement.

I think still a description of the hour and place should come first. And then the light should fall on the figure of Mrs S. on her way home. Really I can allow myself to write a great deal – to describe it all – the baths, the avenue, the people in the gardens, the Chinaman under the tree in May Street. But in that case she won't be conscious of these things. That's bad. They must be seen and felt by her as she wanders home . . . That sense of flowing in and out of houses – going and returning – like the tide. To go and not to return. How terrible! The father in his dressing-room – the familiar talk. His using her hair-brush – his passion for things that *wear well*. The children sitting round the table – the light outside, the silver. Her feeling as she sees them all gathered together – her longing for them always to be *there*. Yes, I'm getting nearer all this. I now remember S.W. and see that it must be written with love – real love. All the same, the difficulty is to get it all within *focus* – to introduce that young doctor and bring him continually nearer and nearer until finally he is part of the Sheridan family, until finally he has taken away Meg . . . that is by no means easy . . . (p. 325)

As Mansfield talks herself in journal form through the story, she eventually approaches her goal. 'Yes I'm getting nearer all this . . . All the same, the difficulty is to get it all within focus'. The episode, with significant variations, is re-written, and Mansfield's final comment is a conclusive statement on the value of such experiment, for 'It's very strange, but the mere act of *writing anything* is a help. It seems to speed one on one's way'. This then is the ultimate function of Katherine Mansfield's journal in her later years, not a delaying tactic as she had once suggested, but a vital component in the artistic process. The act of journal-writing provided a departure point for her invention. 'It is time I started a new journal', she wrote in November 1921. 'Come, my unseen, my unknown, let us talk together. Yes, for the last two weeks I have written scarcely anything. I have been idle; I have *failed*. Why?' The unknown world she wanted to explore materialised only in the writing. The journal form incorporated her attempt to abandon conscious ambition, to avoid thinking of the end product, but instead to immerse herself in the performance. 'I must try and write simply, fully, freely from my heart. *Quietly* caring nothing for success or failure but just going on.'

In the last years of her life, Katherine Mansfield became increasingly worn down by her illness. Her journal documents her suffering from the first shock of seeing the red blood of her cough to the continuous exhaustion of her final months. Her initial terror turned to a weary acceptance of pain and weakness, but as her sense of doom became more insistent, so she turned to writing as the one effective therapy. 'It is only by acknowledging that I, being what I am, had to suffer *this* in order to do the work I am here to perform . . . that I shall recover', she wrote late in 1921. 'I have progressed . . . a little. I have realised *what* it is to be done – the strange barrier to be crossed from thinking to writing it'. (p. 272)

The idea of death pressed on her consciousness, making her ever aware of the brief time remaining to her.

> As a pure matter of fact I consider this enforced confinement here as God-given. But on the other hand, I must make the most of it quickly. It is not unlimited any more than anything else is. Oh, why – oh, why isn't anything unlimited? Why am I haunted every single day of my life by the nearness of death and its inevitability? I am really diseased on that point. And I can't speak of it. If I tell J. it makes him unhappy. If I don't tell him, it leaves me to fight it. I am tired of the battle. No one knows how tired. (p. 272)

Interestingly for a so-called 'liberated' woman, the compulsion to write resulted in part from the restrictions on speech. Like other women before her, Katherine Mansfield turned to her journal when other means of expression were withheld. 'The Man Without A Temperament', the story which depicts a long-suffering husband caring for his invalid wife, is a remarkable ironic projection of her situation in these last months, verbal communication between the couple reduced to banalities, the mutual psychological torture running as an undercurrent through the silences of their conversation. 'I am pursued by time', wrote Mansfield just a year before her death, and this awareness produced some of her most profound artistic insights. 'Pursued by time', her life began to re-enact the working out of the literary form she had developed and her journal notebooks dramatise that process. She knew that some sort of ending was unavoidable – 'It's always a kind of race to get in as much as one can before it *disappears* – and in life, as in art, she had to sacrifice something in order to achieve her aim. The compactness and orderliness of art could not incorporate everything that she as writer might wish, but in her rigorous selectivity she strove to define the nature of her own achievement.

> Art is not an attempt of the artist to reconcile existence with his vision; it is an attempt to create his own world *in* this world. That which suggests the subject to the artist is the *unlikeness* to what we accept as reality. We single out – we bring into the light – we put up higher. (p. 273)

9

The Safety Curtain:
The Diary
of Virginia Woolf

One must drop a safety curtain over one's private scene

—Virginia Woolf. *Diary*. September 1940

In her memoirs, Lady Ottoline Morrell describes a conversation she held with Virginia Woolf about their private diaries. 'When we were talking about keeping a journal, I said mine was filled with thoughts and struggles of my inner life', she records. At which, Virginia 'opened her eyes wide in astonishment'.[1] Recalling the episode in her own diary, Woolf remarked that it 'made me reflect that I haven't an inner life'. It is a revealing statement. For Virginia Woolf was a woman who appeared to put all her energies into self-expression, yet who never told the truth about herself. Her most intimate thoughts and feelings seemed perhaps to her too fragile to survive the transfer direct onto the page, and were kept so deeply hidden that only those closest to her were aware of those dark recesses. She noted quite cursorily in her own journal an occasion when she 'sat with Nessa & laid bare my sorrows', (vol. 1, p. 197) almost as if she were reluctant to acknowledge the existence of underlying misery. Certainly, for her, the diary was not the place to expand on it.

She knew full well what she was doing in this. Amidst the current vogue for confessional and lengthy intimate reminiscence, Woolf remained fixed in her determination to guard her privacy, although she did allow herself odd moments of quizzical reflection on her stance. 'How it would interest me if this diary were ever to become a real diary, something in which I could see changes, trace moods developing', she mused in February 1923. 'But then I should have to speak of the soul, & did I not banish the soul when I began?'. (vol. 2, p. 234) Her comment concedes her own rigid self-division and the consequent role she accorded the diary. From the beginning she saw it as a purely professional enterprise, not an opportunity for psychological scrutiny. As a twentieth-century writer, however, she was also a twentieth-century woman, and her diary establishes its own complicated confrontation with these aspects of her personality, while creating its own parameters of literary appropriateness.

What then do we find in Woolf's diaries if not the personal revelation or introspective enquiry? For her journal, kept up so conscientiously over nearly three decades, undoubtedly played a fundamental role in her life. Like so many of the other women studied here, she had first started writing a diary as an adolescent, but it was only in 1915, at the age of twenty-two, that she began to use the form in a way that seriously explored its capacity as a genre for expansion and flexibility. Whereas Ottoline Morrell took the traditional and at that time particularly fashionable view of the diary as confidante, Woolf's originality and literary seriousness completely bypassed such a function. Throughout her career Virginia Woolf never ceased in her artistic experiment, adapting different conventional models to her own explosive imagination. The novel, the essay, the review, the biography and the diary were transformed by her unique approach into fresh modes of expression. Journal-writing was a single strand in her myriad writing career, but it was a strand that she made a vital part of her total experience as a woman and as a writer. From the earliest entries to the notes she made just before her death she made it clear that the diary was the literary mode with which she felt most comfortable. 'Oh how gladly I reach for this free page for a 10 minutes scamper after copying & re-copying, digging in these old extract books for quotes all the morning!' she breathed with relief in November 1939, exhausted from the tedium of research for her biography of Roger Fry. She turned to the journal as a reward for having worked hard; a sort of private indulgence liberating her from the strictures of formal composition.

Virginia Woolf's diary formed a cornerstone for her total artistic undertaking. It was her only continuous piece of work, never completed because it did not contain within itself the mechanism for conclusion. To some extent this was its attraction for Woolf. As Margo Culley has remarked, 'While the novel and autobiography may be thought of as artistic wholes, the diary is always in process, always in some sense a fragment.'[2] While Woolf's other works were finite, determined by traditional prescriptive codes, the diary maintained its capacity for unlimited diversification, moving continuously towards discovery, inviting expansion rather than conclusion. In this it suited Woolf's female literary aesthetic. By its very nature it was an extension of 'the woman's sentence', a perfect example of the alternative, private tradition of women's writing she posited in her essays and in *A Room of One's Own*. Commenting in that treatise on the popularity of the novel form with the woman writer, she went on to ask 'who shall say that even this most pliable of all forms is rightly shaped for her use? No doubt we shall find her knocking that into shape for herself when she has the free use of her limbs; and providing some new vehicle, not necessarily in verse, for the poetry in her.'[3] The creative freedom that Woolf experienced in her journal had no counterpart in her other works. In all senses the diary was her major literary project, a permanent and continually evolving text, and as such she wanted to execute it to perfection.

In both her fictional and non-fictional writings, Woolf worked to develop an impressionistic perspective on experience, structuring her material subtly so as to shed illumination on the life around her. The prioritisation of art as a means of shaping the chaos of experience to this end was a central element in Bloomsbury sensibility. In a conversation she reported in 1918, Woolf and the painter Mark Gertler discussed how the obsession with form was a crucial issue facing all artists whatever their chosen medium. 'I advised him', Woolf told her journal, 'for arts sake, to keep sane; to grasp & not exaggerate, & put sheets of glass between him & his matter'. (vol. 1, p. 176)

It was this approach that became a consistent guiding principle in her diary. For her journal observations, certainly in the years 1917–30, turn away from any confrontation with emotion to focus on sharp analytical commentary. Through her emphasis on metonymic detail, Virginia Woolf brilliantly metamorphoses her friends and acquaintances into characters in a comic novel, Ottoline 'closely buttoned up in black velvet, hat like a parasol, satin collar, pearls, tinted eyelids, & red gold hair (vol. 1, p. 61); Carrington 'apple red & firm in the cheeks, bright green & yellow in the body, & immensely firm & large all over'; (vol. 1, p. 128) Koteliansky 'rather in the style of the solid lodging house furniture, but with an air of romance'; (vol. 1, p. 159) Harriet Weaver whose 'neat mauve suit fitted both soul & body'. (vol. 1, p. 140) This need to place her friends intrigued Woolf in as much as it provided an opportunity for comment on her own detached position. 'What a queer fate it is – always to be the spectator of the public, never part of it', (vol. 1, p. 216) she noted wryly in November 1918. Caught up in the maelstrom of two world wars, she yet managed to distance herself from their horrors by dispassionate observation of the mundane effects of shattering events. Her description of the 1918 armistice, for instance, presents her as an acute member of an audience in a theatre of curiosities, rather than a concerned participant in the event. London, seen as she and her husband Leonard were struggling to cross it, is a city apart, made abstract and general in her cool gaze.

> Taxicabs were crowded with whole families, grandmothers & babies, showing off; & yet there was no centre, no form for all this wandering emotion to take. The crowds had nowhere to go, nothing to do; they were in the state of children with too long a holiday'. (vol. 1, p. 217)

There is no suggestion here that the Woolfs themselves constituted any part of these crowds. They remain aloof from the celebration and the hysteria, precious beings in a magic circle of amused indifference. Here, as elsewhere in the diary, Woolf's critical mind is intent on seeking out formal problems rather than human issues. It is the shapelessness of the mass of humanity which catches her attention and its lack of direction on which she comes to focus.

Virginia Woolf's diary has most consistently been seen as a sort of literary training ground, a useful practice area in which she rehearsed her technique before applying it to her art proper. In his preface to his edition of what he termed *A Writer's Diary*, Leonard Woolf noted how his wife's diary 'discusses the day-to-day problems of plot or form, of character or exposition, which she encounters in each of her books as she conceives them or writes or revises them', including 'a certain number of passages in which she is obviously using the diary as a method of practising or trying out the art of writing.'[4] In his editorial work, however, Leonard gives a mistaken impression of the work as a whole. For only rarely did Virginia Woolf in fact use the diary as direct source material for her fiction or reviews. When writing *The Years* in 1933, for instance, she found it useful to refer to her past diaries to freshen her memory of the war. Similarly her original comments on Christina Rossetti, who 'starved into emaciation, a very fine original gift', (vol. 1, p. 178) appear reworked in her essay on Rossetti, later to appear in *The Common Reader*. But these examples are few and far between. If anything it is more remarkable that Woolf, obsessive in her perfectionism, appeared to need the diary so little for this purpose.

Instead, most frequently she used it to inscribe portraits of personalities, to preserve moments and features that might help her perfect her method of characterisation. As she explained in 'Mr Bennet and Mrs Brown', she felt strongly that 'It is to express character – not to preach doctrines, sing songs, or celebrate the glories of the British Empire, that the form of the novel, so clumsy, verbose, and undramatic, so rich, elastic, and alive, has been evolved.'[5] To capture that elasticity and richness in her novels, she needed to draw from life. But the journal as a working notebook had conspicuous defects.

'When people come to tea I cant say to them, "Now wait a minute while I write an account of you". They go and its too late to begin', she complained. 'And thus, at the very time that I'm brewing thoughts & descriptions meant for this page I have the heartbreaking sensation that the page isn't there; they're spilt upon the floor. Indeed its difficult to mop them up again'. (vol. 1, p. 139)

Should we assume from this that she saw life only as material for her art as a novelist? It is true that by keeping herself deliberately apart from the social experience, she gave the impression of waiting to transform it into something else, to sift it and modify its character. Distance enabled her to some extent to grasp the essence of individuals and to give her comic gift full rein, even if in the event it was also reductive. Her portrait of Edith Sitwell in the summer of 1930 is a case in point.

Edith Sitwell has grown very fat, powders herself thickly, gilds her nails with silver paint, wears a turban & looks like an ivory elephant, like the Emperor Heliogabalus. I have never seen such a change. She is mature, majestical. She is monumental. Her fingers are crusted with white coral. She is altogether composed ... We all sat at her feet – cased in black slippers, the only remnants of her slipperiness & slenderness. Who was she like? Pope in a nightcap? (vol. 3, p. 308)

As a genre the diary, like the novel and the review, imposed its own constraints on its author. The diary forced Woolf to select and to prune severely when confronted by the raw material of existence. 'I don't know how to put 3 or 4 hours of Roger's conversation into this page', (vol. 1, p. 150) she moaned after a stimulating evening with Roger Fry. A few days later, she found herself again at a standstill, 'paralysed by the task of describing a weekend at Garsington'. (vol. 1, p. 173) She was aware too of the pitfalls of boredom. The recounting of events brought a new slant and meaning to primary experience, but once a story had been told orally or by letter, it had already become tired, too wilted to include in the journal, for 'the telling leaves a groove in my mind which gives a hardness to the memory, stereotypes it, makes it a little dull'. (vol. 1, p. 150) In addition there were simple problems of memory. On 27 August 1918, writing after a five days' absence, she paused in her description of Sidney and Beatrice Webb's visit, having lost the thread from the previous entry, and with it her stimulus. Because she realised that 'I have let the first freshness of the Webbs fade from my mirror', (vol. 1, p. 193) she found it difficult to write about them effectively. A solution appeared only when she could light upon 'another metaphor which they imposed upon me', that of 'a waste of almost waveless sea, polish grey, or dented with darker shadows for the small irregularities, the little ripples, which represented character & life love & genius & happiness.' The picture provided her with an alternative perspective so that she could 'recapture the curious discomfort of soul Mrs Webb produces each time I see her'. Thinking in metaphors, she thus successfully reduced people to images. It was always through literary concepts rather than human dimensions that she could best encapsulate and transmit her vision.

In his introduction to the five-volume edition of Virginia Woolf's diaries, her nephew Quentin Bell quotes Clive Bell's account of Leonard Woolf reading aloud to friends extracts from his wife's journal. Suddenly Leonard felt compelled to break off, realising to his horror that the pages had 'not a word of truth in them'.[6] Does this mean that we should read Virginia Woolf's diary as another of her fictions, bearing little direct relation to the life that she encountered? 'To speak, invent, comment', she once noted, 'are tricks which human beings have devised for keeping the water fresh'. (vol. 2, p. 228) We should notice the hierarchy of this sentence and particularly the insertion of the word 'invent'. For Woolf, language superimposed its fictive quality on experience, and the act of description consequently was inevitably also one of imagination. With this in mind, she could build a complete character from a sketchy outline, using glimpses of strangers to fill out a portrait, to make the unknown knowable if speculative. Going up in the lift at Holborn tube station one day, she stood next to a boy of fourteen. Only his head was visible in the crowd. 'I noticed that it was an extremely interesting, sensitive, clever, observant head; rather sharp, but independent looking. One couldn't tell from his cap whether he was well off or not. I came to the conclusion he was the son of an officer with whom he stood. When we got into the street I looked at once at his legs. His trousers had holes in them. From that one could judge what a wretched affair his life will be'. (vol. 1, p. 124)

Although the diary remained very different in kind from her novels, Woolf recognised that the correlation between the two genres was close. 'I wonder whether I too deal thus openly in autobiography & call it fiction?', she speculated in January 1920. One could just as easily ask the question in reverse. Does her diary deal in fiction, disguised as autobiography? Certainly both modes are engaged in the business of recapturing the past. Half way through writing *Mrs Dalloway*, she observed how it had taken her 'a year's groping to discover what I call my tunnelling process, by which I tell the past by instalments, as I have need of it'. (vol. 2, p. 272) This technique, her 'prime discovery' as she termed it, may have only begun to permeate her mature fiction in 1923, but we can observe its operation in the method of her journal much earlier. Whether the past was recent or long gone, whether the memory was of childhood or of the hour just chimed, she could distil its essence through recollection and thus accommodate it. The year she began work on *To The Lighthouse*, the fictional work she tentatively defined as an 'elegy', she wrote in her journal that, 'The past is beautiful because one never realises an emotion at the time'. (vol. 3, p. 5) Through the diary, deliberate evocation of the past became an activity engrained into the texture of her days, a conscious re-working of the material of life to fashion it into a product she was able to control. Although Virginia Woolf was on occasion to speak of the diary as an essential stage in the formulation of her art as a novelist, it was never limited solely to a supportive role. In transcending the function that Leonard was later to ascribe to it, the diary is a supremely poised and confident text, frequently commenting on its own range and achievement. In

April 1919, she wrote an extensive note on the diary as independent genre. It was not the only time she was to pause for this sort
of analysis, but it is the first significant example of the status she
ascribed to the work which regularly kept her occupied for half an
hour after tea each evening.

> 'There looms ahead of me the shadow of some kind of form
> which a diary might attain to. I might in the course of time learn
> what it is that one can make of this loose, drifting material of life;
> finding another use for it than the use I put it to, so much more
> consciously & scrupulously in fiction. What sort of diary should I
> like mine to be? Something loose knit, & yet not slovenly, so
> elastic that it will embrace anything, solemn, slight or beautiful
> that comes into my mind. I should like it to resemble some deep
> old desk, or capacious hold all, in which one flings a mass of
> odds & ends without looking them through. I should like to
> come back, after a year or two, & find that the collection had
> sorted itself & refined itself & coalesced, as such deposits
> mysteriously do, into a mould, transparent enough to reflect the
> light of our life, & yet steady, tranquil, composed with the
> aloofness of a work of art. The main requisite, I think on
> re-reading my old volumes, is not to play the part of censor, but
> to write as the mood comes or of anything whatever; since I was
> curious to find how I went for things put in haphazard, & found
> the significance to lie where I never saw it at the time. But
> looseness becomes slovenly. A little effort is needed to face a
> character or an incident which needs to be recorded. Nor can
> one let the pen write without guidance; for fear of becoming
> slick & untidy'. (vol. 1, p. 266)

There are two separate emphases here: one on Woolf as writer,
fascinated by the methods of her own production, and one on
Woolf as reader, finding additional value in the conjunction of
phrases she originally offered without prevision of their ultimate
design. The succeeding, fluid recreation of the work by the reader,
albeit herself, suggests the innate instability of the original text.
Re-reading made her vividly aware of the formal properties of the
diary and the way in which she became an increasingly adept
practitioner of the genre. In 1919, for instance, she noted critically
how the diary she had written in 1918 seemed to be a technical
improvement on the previous year's effort. Although diary-writing

might have been a more relaxed activity than producing novels or reviews, this is not to say that she treated it casually. Discipline was essential if she were to avoid 'slovenliness', and her twin fears of verging towards the extremes of slickness or untidiness haunted her pursuit of perfectionism. 'Disgraceful! Disgraceful! Disgraceful!' she was to admonish herself when she failed to keep up the entries with her usual attentiveness. (vol. 2, p. 176)

The self-reflexive quality of the diary as a whole is closely bound up with the literary stylisation of modernist writing during this period and in particular with the associated suspicion of language as a vehicle for conveying meaning directly. The general lack of confidence in realist values that critics have come to identify as one of the hallmarks of post-war literature surfaces most prominently in the innovations of technique in texts by writers as different as T. S. Eliot and Dorothy Richardson. It is in this context that we need to place Virginia Woolf's diary. Its value rests not in seeing it as providing the groundwork for her fiction, but as a text which by its very nature makes a vital contribution to modernist artistic practice, offering the same insights into literature's capacity (or incapacity) to deal with experience as do her novels. Woolf's obsession with the diary as genre and its status as a construct is one of its most consistent themes, and it is one to which she returns throughout the years. After all, 'Of what should I write here except my writing?' she asked rhetorically in 1924. (vol. 2, p. 317)

But while at the forefront of the literary avant-garde, Woolf's revisionist approach was also fundamentally determined by her sense of herself as a woman and the traditional restrictions on female expression. She was convinced that 'Somehow the connection between life and literature must be made by women', (vol. 2, p. 184) and aware that 'they so seldom do it right', set out to rectify this situation. Her diary, not based on any conventional literary models, marked a distinct liberation from establishment forms. Explicitly linking female understanding – 'the relationship so secret and private compared with the relations with men' (vol. 2, p. 320) – with the ease of diary-writing, she commented on how the journal had 'greatly helped my style; loosened the ligatures'. Her imagery is worth noting. As she had once complained that Mrs Enfield, a 'popular' woman writer of her acquaintance, was too bound by 'the chain' of imitating male writing, (vol. 2, p. 183) so she perceived the masculine approach to language use as restrictive and fixed. In contrast the diary was fluid, a female form, not tied by the weight of inherited structures of emphatic linear progression. It was this engagement with writing which helped Woolf to identify herself as a gendered being – 'Now I am a woman again as I always am when I write', (vol. 3, p. 231) she commented to the journal, luxuriating in the freedom of private composition after the tension of public display.

Her diary perfectly conforms to her own requirements for a female literature, being composed of the trivia of what recent critics have tended to call 'dailiness'. For reading Virginia Woolf's diaries can often seem like reading a story full of non-events, as if she were determined to assert the value of the inessential. 'Shall I say "nothing happened today" as we used to do in our diaries when they were beginning to die', she wrote on 29 January 1915, 'It wouldn't be true. The day is rather like a leafless tree: there are all sorts of colours in it, if you look closely. But the outline is bare enough.' This was the challenge provided by the diary, to construct texture from the merest hint of structure, and by so doing to demonstrate the equation between form and content that was one of the hallmarks of modernism. In *A Room of One's Own*, Woolf was sharply critical of the power of the male literary canon, and the way it had come to distinguish between the relative value of men's and women's writing. 'This is an important book, the critic assumes, because it deals with war. This is an insignificant book because it deals with the feelings of women in a drawing-room',[7] she wrote with some acerbity. Her diary, even more determinedly than her novels, places the fabric of a woman's life at its centre and insists on its validity as subject. Although subsequent readers have appreciated Woolf's diary for the picture it provides of an extraordinary life, with its intimate glimpses of celebrated literary and artistic figures, she herself saw her life as commonplace, concerned like other women's with the problems of managing servants and shopping. Her anxieties about her appearance and her clothes feature prominently in her journal, mingled indiscriminately with details of the weather, train times, country walks, bath water, furnishings of rooms and all the paraphernalia of domestic existence.

In this Woolf was aware of her own position as recipient of a literary heritage of private writing. She read the work of other diarists, and their impact makes itself felt in her daily entries. 'And so to bed', she ended on more than one occasion, recalling Pepys,

or even 'and so to lunch', in semi-mocking recognition of her
celebrated predecessor, whose own diary had most famously made
apparent the circularity of individual lives. She read Fanny Burney's diaries, Dorothy Wordsworth's and Boswell's, noting how
they made her feel 'as if some dead person were said to be living
after all'. (vol. 3, p. 237) Deeply impressed with the maturity of
André Gide's journals, she found that 'diaries now pullulate', (vol.
5, p. 227) so that it became impossible for her to settle to any other
kind of writing. The diary as an artistic construct absorbed her
imaginative effort. Others' diaries also affected her sense of self,
always a particularly troubling area for Woolf. In 1926 she read *My
Apprenticeship*, Beatrice Webb's memoirs which had been composed from her diary extracts. For a moment she was drawn into
comparing her own life with Webb's as a literary subject. In a more
personally interrogative entry than most on 27 February 1926, she
noted the great social and political causes that had inspired her
contemporary and concluded somewhat despairingly that her own
life had no similar motivating force.

'I have some restless searcher in me', she pronounced, lured into
metaphysical speculation. 'Why is there not a discovery in life?
Something one can lay hands on & say "This is it?" My depression
is a harassed feeling – I'm looking; but that's not it, – that's not it.
What is it? And shall I die before I find it?'. (vol. 3, p. 62) Her
melancholy induced in her 'a sense of my own strangeness' and a
despondency at her failure to define a fixed identity, a task which
Beatrice Webb had seemed to approach with such certainty.

Yet it is precisely this lack of definition which marks Virginia
Woolf's diary as a distinctively female modernist document, creating substance from the elusive and ephemeral 'envelope' of
experience. In 1939 she asked herself how she could possibly
'compete with the compression & lucidity & logic of Gide writing
his Journal? Well, the plain truth is I can't'. (vol. 5, p. 244) Rather
her solution was to discover an alternative mode entirely, based on
a technique of amorphousness and inclusiveness, to accord with
her divergent experience. The rapid pace which she had noted as a
feature of her diary was an essential ingredient in her approach, for
'the advantage of the method is that it sweeps up accidentally
several stray matters which I should exclude if I hesitated, but
which are the diamonds of the dustheap'. (vol. 1, pp. 233–4)
However impressive a tool, logic was ultimately restrictive for
Woolf. It was the very diffuseness of the diary form that appealed,

together with the reliance on contingency that revealed hitherto unthought-of significance and ascribed meaning to apparently random experience.

Despite all this, however, Woolf's diary, like those of many other women, became useful to her in more commonplace ways. 'I solace my restlessness as usual . . . upon this book', she noted irritably in August 1934. It operated as a pacifying activity, helping her to order the jumble of impressions in her mind, and on 8 August 1921, frustrated by illness and inactivity and with 'nothing to record', she used the diary specifically to write away 'an intolerable fit of the fidgets'. 'No one in the whole of Sussex is so miserable as I am; or so conscious of an infinite capacity of enjoyment horded in me, could I use it,' she scribbled melodramatically, only to find that, 'There! I've written out half my irritation'. (vol. 2, pp. 132–3) Similarly she turned to her diary to assuage her resentment and calm her heightened feelings. 'I am now writing to test my theory that there is consolation in expression', (vol. 3, p. 81) she reported after she and Leonard had quarrelled over politics during the General Strike of 1926. The diary also served as a timewaster – 'I snatch at the idea of writing here in order not to write Waves or Moths or whatever it is to be called' (vol. 3, p. 259) – and, more gently, as entertainment. 'I have spent the whole morning reading old diaries, & am now (10 to 1) much refreshed', she wrote in 1932. 'This is by way of justifying these many written books . . . The diary amuses me'. (vol. 4, p. 167) She could also be dismissive about the diary. 'What do these diaries amount to? O merely matter for a book I think: & to read when I have a headache'. (vol. 4, p. 24) Yet such comments were symptomatic of her own disenchantment with life in general as she grew older, quite different from her earlier insistence that the diary was 'serious literature'.

So there is a danger in trying to extract any single unifying idea from Woolf's diary. It is a shifting document, covering a lengthy time span, and embracing a range of functions. Although one central recurrent topic is that of her writing, it is by no means the only subject of the volumes which follow the life of a woman for twenty-six years. Like those of other writers, Woolf's diary incorporates diverse voices, but in her case these voices constitute the essence of the text. In *To the Lighthouse*, she was to write about her famous symbol, 'So that was the Lighthouse, was it? No, the other was also the Lighthouse. For nothing was simply one thing.'[8] Similarly Woolf's diary cannot be reduced to any primary feature.

In a continuous process of experiment, she sampled different methods of writing to test their effectiveness. In September 1926, for example, during a period of extreme depression, she put out tentative stylistic feelers to try to recreate the precise quality of this special type of experience. Her entry for 15 September of that year began, 'Sometimes I shall use the Note form: for instance this' to introduce her new approach. What follows is written in a completely different tenor from the rest of the diary: 'eg. 'Woke up perhaps at 3. Oh its beginning its coming – the horror – physically like a painful wave swelling about the heart – tossing me up. I'm unhappy unhappy! Down – God, I wish I were dead. Pause. But why am I feeling this? Let me watch the wave rise. I watch. Vanessa. Children. Failure. Yes; I detect that. Failure failure'. (vol. 3, p. 110). Tellingly, she used this 'note form', terse, fragmented and potentially reductive to try to convey internalised moments of intense horror, episodes which seemed to resist the method of coherent description she deployed so efficiently in recording external events.

She was quite clear-sighted about the mixture of literary forms the diary synthesised, and remained sensitive to the fluctuations of style as they were taking place. After one passage of philosophical speculation, she explained that 'I write thus partly in order to slip the burden of writing narrative, as for instance; we came here a fortnight ago. And we lunched at Charleston & Vita came & we were offered the field & we went to see the farm at Lime Kiln'. (vol. 3, p. 189) Yet even at such moments of self-parody she had not doubt that as a retrospective reader in years to come, 'facts' would be more interesting to her than abstraction. 'I shall want, as I do when I read, to be told details, details, so that I may look up from the page & arrange them too, into one of those makings up which seems so much truer done thus, from heaps of non-assorted facts than I can now make them, when it is almost immediately being done (by me) under my eyes.' Once again, she projected herself into the role of reader, a reader who would actively impose meaning and structure on the signs before her on the page.

With her compulsive interest in formal issues, she tampered obsessively with the diary's organisation. Looking back on her old journals she was most struck by the spontaneous pattern they created without apparent authorial intervention. In 1918, for instance, reading the diary for the previous year, she noted, 'how exactly one repeats one's doings', (vol. 1, p. 200) in the familiarity of life's natural rhythms. Still she could not resist the temptation to impose a narrative structure of her own. 'I keep thinking of different ways to manage my scenes', she wrote in November 1918, 'conceiving endless possibilities; seeing life, as I walk about the streets, an immense opaque block of material to be conveyed by me into its equivalent of language'. (vol. 1, p. 214) She began to organise her daily entries so as to draw attention to their narrative continuity, however artificial such continuity might have been. On Saturday 30 October 1926, sensible of the fact that she had not written up her diary for a month, Woolf began with the very phrase that she had used to conclude her entry of a month before. Grumbling then about the inroads made on her time by persistent visitors, she mimicked their pleas of 'When may I come & see you!' (vol. 3, pp. 113–4), continuing her next entry with the words 'Too true a prophecy!'. Not content to allow the spaces between the entries to speak for themselves, she felt compelled to provide a deliberate gloss to draw attention to the diary's narrative development. Similarly she wove a story from the routine details of daily shopping trips, travel arrangements and meetings with friends. On 14 November 1938, for instance, having just spent £5.10.0 on 'a very charming bookcase', she announced her intention of buying a dresser, only to begin the following entry for 15 November with the words 'I did not buy the dresser'. (vol. 5, p. 186) This method of isolating specific strands of her life to identify a narrative line suggests her need of a structural principle, however slight, to assure herself of her own control over the medium of her life.

In her emphasis on the artistry of the diary she introduced and closed individual entries in terms that explicitly banished any idea of their spontaneity. 'Let the scene open on the doorstep of number 50 Gordon Square', (vol. 2, p. 222) she wrote grandly to herald the simultaneous start of 1923 and the beginning of a new volume for that year. Towards the end of 1930 she hit on the idea of copying daily newspaper headlines into the diary. Brief slogans punctuate her account of the days' events. 'Spanish Revolution. Russian timber yard scandal. Burst water main in Cambridge Circus' on 12 December; 'Horror death of Douglas. Indian Conference. Fog, Intermittent. Weather to be colder' on the 22nd. (vol. 3, pp. 336–8) The effect is bizarre. Rather than adding continuity, as she claimed was their purpose, the headlines interrupt the flow of the narrative with the intrusive voice of another medium. The newspaper style of reportage, so general and objective in its approach to the external world, stands sharply at odds with the more discursive dominant tone of the main work.

The fascination with time, a recurrent subject throughout the years, is foregrounded in this contrived interaction between days. In the conscious recall of past events Woolf projects the radical modernist perspective on the relative nature of time itself. Repeatedly this is linked with her concentration on her own ageing process. 'Time Passes' she called the central, deeply-wrought episode in *To the Lighthouse*. It could well stand as a title for her diary overall. Her own birthdays were landmarks, approached with trepidation. 'The last day of being 35. One trembles to write the years that come after it: all tinged with the shadow of 40', she wrote on 24 January 1918. And three months later she mused disquietingly, 'Are we growing old? Are our habits setting in like the Trade Winds?' (vol. 1, p. 132)

The passage of time, the only apparent formal property that consistently determined the sequence of individual entries, was also a theme that was to haunt her all her life. Her preoccupation with the interweaving of temporal levels – the past, present and future lives – connects with her absorption with the self as subject. As the writer Joyce Carol Oates was later to remark in her own journal, 'We don't think of ourselves in the past tense: we are always present tense: to consciously record the past is therefore to invent a self to perform in it, consciously or unconsciously – that's where artifice comes in.'[9] This topic, explored with such seriousness in Woolf's novels, is crucial to the very concept of her diary. 'How queer to have so many selves. How bewildering!', (vol. 4, p. 329) she wrote in 1935. Her heightened awareness of the natural fragmentation of the personality through time and the affective changes this involved is embodied in the diary's format. She anticipated the future in the act of recollecting the past by imagining herself, in her early years as a diarist, as she might be at the age of fifty, using old volumes as an aid for her memoirs. Her natural dread at the approach of her thirty-seventh birthday was partly assuaged by such a thought. 'I admit I don't like thinking of the lady of 50', she wrote. 'Courage however. Roger is past that age, & still capable of feeling, & enjoying & playing a very considerable part in life'. (vol. 1, p. 234)

But the passage of time could also be deceptive. She continually commented on how old her friends were looking and whether or not their appearance belied their years. Encounters with others made significant inroads on her perception of self. 'We are not as old as Mrs Gray, who came to thank us for our apples', (vol. 3, p. 160) she remarked with relief (Mrs Gray was eighty-six), at the age of forty-five. In 1923 she took 'Middle Age' as a conscious topic for discussion, noting that she and Leonard had started to attach more importance to hours than they used to, a sign of encroaching elderliness. (vol. 2, p. 222) Yet ageing had its positive side. Her acute sense of the race against time found her 'quicker, keener at 44 than 24 – more desperate, I suppose, as the river shoots to Niagara'. (vol. 3, p. 117)

In investigating the relationship between the 'different selves' that Woolf herself identified, we need to recognise the anxieties the journal discloses about her public persona. Paradoxically, as Virginia Woolf discerned so unnervingly, the literary act was both an isolated and a shared event. Guarded in the privacy of her study, revised painstakingly in the light of her own stringent critical intelligence, Woolf's books when completed were then thrown to the public for consumption and comment against which she felt helpless.

'I'm a failure as a writer. I'm out of fashion; old; shan't do any better; have no head piece;' she wrote miserably after the premature publication of *Monday or Tuesday* in 1921. Sapping her self-confidence, the effect of the public reception on her productive output was also stultifying. 'They don't see I'm after something interesting. So that makes me suspect that I'm not. And thus I can't get on with Jacob', (vol. 2, p. 106) she noted, stopped in her tracks by the reviews. Her own sense of a coherent personality, whose private intentions were at one with her contemporary culture, was vital to Woolf's belief in her ability to communicate. Writing was the act which linked the personal and public aspects of self, and which consequently validated her authoritative identity.

Just as unfavourable criticism cast her down, so she was elated by praise. Her successive triumphs excited her temporarily, but did nothing ultimately to confirm her self-esteem, and each time the eve of publication arrived, she was overcome with terror at the thought of failure. As early as 1919, with the completion of *Night and Day*, she knew that her faith in her talent as a novelist could be easily shaken by the response of others. With youthful hope she felt that her confidence would grow with her skill. 'Is the time coming', she wondered, 'when I can endure to read my own work in print without blushing & shivering & wishing to take cover?'

(vol. 1, p. 259) On the contrary, as her literary reputation grew, her periods of desolation became darker and more prolonged. After writing *To the Lighthouse*, she was almost suicidal. Similarly the appearance of *The Waves* in 1931 was only one in a series of occasions in her long career as a writer which ground her down with severe misgivings about its reception and her own loss of face. Desperate for a response before the reviews appeared, she gave the manuscript to John Lehmann, then manager of Hogarth Press, to read. Yet waiting for his opinion was excruciating. 'Trembling under the sense of complete failure', she transcribed her neuroses into her diary, convinced that 'John L. is about to write to say he thinks it bad'. Leonard accused her 'of sensibility verging on insanity', but feverishly she analysed her 'tumult of feelings', furious at the thought that anyone 'shd be running about London saying the new V.W. is a disappointment – all about nothing – exquisitely written of course'. (vol. 4, p. 43) She experienced the same sort of panic when *The Years* was published in 1937. 'I'm going to be beaten, I'm going to be laughed at, I'm going to be held up to scorn & ridicule', she agonised, (vol. 5, p. 64) while at the same time aware that keeping notes on her own emotional fluctuations was in itself therapeutic, as 'thus objectified, the pain & shame become at once much less'. All these entries illustrate her reliance on the opinion of others and her recognition that the public self was a necessary ingredient in the formation of the private person. This is mirrored in the substance of her diary, which in the later sections increasingly merges the interior world of personal feeling with the earlier world of judgemental, opinionated social commentary.

As she grew older so Woolf's diaries register an increased 'tiredness & dejection'. (vol. 1, p. 248) Whereas the early volumes are characterised by a *joie de vivre*, the writer's mind so alive and crowded with impressions that they seem to tumble over one another to reach the page, the volumes from 1930 onwards are more subdued in tone, given over to meditation, often at the mercy of her extreme moodiness. She herself had noted the pace of the first section, 'the rapid haphazard gallop at which it swings along'. (vol. 1, p. 233) Yet from 1935 the diary became much more erratic. She failed to keep it with the same fidelity, and her entries grew more sombre, moving inwards rather than outwards for inspiration. She mentioned the recurrent blinding headaches, 'the galloping wild horses' which attacked her brain without warning. (vol. 4,

p. 124) She was plagued by self doubt, terrified that she would be revealed to the world as a 'plain dowdy old woman'. (vol. 4, p. 124) In this her diary follows a familiar pattern of female diary-writing, where, as one critic has noted, 'earlier and more decisively than for a man, the curve of a woman's life is seen by herself and society to be one of deterioration and degeneration. Men may mature, but women age.'[10] For Woolf this process was associated fundamentally with her artistic creativity. 'Why am I so old, so ugly, so – & cant write', (vol. 5, p. 208) she asked in a fit of despair in March 1939. Her faith in her own powers of expression was a direct product of a perception of self that automatically accommodated others' criticism and approval.

This sense of audience response, which had such a radical effect on her self-confidence, had always been a vital ingredient for Woolf in her approach to literary composition. Indeed the thought of writing purely for her own pleasure was actively inhibiting, for, as she acknowledged, by so doing 'the convention of writing is destroyed; therefore one does not write at all'. (vol. 3, p. 201) Virginia Woolf's diary relied for its fluency on the visualisation of a reader, even though that reader might only be herself at some future date, transformed by time into another person. In 1928, for instance, reading her most recent entry preparatory to beginning afresh, she questioned her own position as diarist. 'Shall I now continue this soliloquy', she asked rhetorically, 'or shall I imagine an audience which will make me describe?' (vol. 3, p. 190) This implied reader determined the variety of forms her diary was to take, and 'Whom do I tell when I tell a blank page?' (vol. 3, p. 239) was the question which troubled her as the diary verged on the brink of confessional, the mode she had sworn to avoid.

As Woolf veered between extremes of elation and depression, her diary took on a correspondingly frenetic quality. Nineteen-thirty-six began in a sort of frenzy. Fighting her headaches, her mind splitting with wild ideas that she could not control, she turned to journal writing to calm herself down, and to try to bring a sense of equilibrium into the mental world she inhabited, where reality receded at an alarming pace. The following year seemed to bring little relief. She felt 'like the man who had to keep dancing on hot bricks. Can't let myself stop'. (vol. 5, p. 55) Amidst 'mornings of torture', (vol. 5, p. 24) she felt herself unloved and unwanted, occupying a nothingness, 'As if I were exposed on a high ledge in full light. Very lonely . . . Very useless. No atmosphere around me.

No words. Very apprehensive. As if something cold & horrible – a roar of laughter at my expense were about to happen. And I am powerless to ward it off: I have no protection'. (vol. 5, p. 63) Accordingly the subject matter of her diary changed. Deeply affected by the deaths of friends and by an impending sense of her own isolation, Woolf appeared to find the present increasingly intolerable, and turned instead to nostalgic reflection. In the year before her death she thought more often of her parents, but what she called 'the platform of time' confusingly offered them to her from two angles 'As a child condemning; as a woman of 58 understanding'. (vol. 5, p. 281) The recognition of the dichotomy of self that this implied troubled her profoundly. 'If I read as a contemporary I shall lose my childs vision & so must stop', she realised, adding as a reminder of the dangers of such activity, 'Nothing turbulent; nothing involved: no introspection'. (vol. 5, p. 345)

The last year of Virginia Woolf's life, 1940, was a year dominated by the air-raids of the Second World War and the threat of German invasion. As the Woolfs moved backwards and forwards between London and Monks House, Rodmell, their country home in Sussex, so the diary communicates a pervading instability, its style broken and moving quickly from one subject to another. 'Another loud night Another bad raid', she reported in September 1940. 'Oxford Street now smashed. John Lewis, Selfridge, B & H, all my old haunts. Also British Museum forecourt'. (vol. 5, p. 323) It was as if her past was being destroyed before her eyes, and in the process her hold on life became increasingly fragile. Her diary remained one method of holding the inner chaos at bay. As she told both Ethel Smyth and the diary, 'one must drop a safety curtain over ones private scene'. (vol. 5, p. 323) Yet in spite of all her protestations, Virginia Woolf's diary does disclose an inner, private life however much she wished to avoid overt self-revelation. In its manifold composition, its amalgamation of voices and its stylistic experiments, it demonstrates her attempt to integrate the different aspects of her personality and her life's activities. These features also isolate its highly distinctive quality as an artistic product, its creation an incessant process most closely approximating that of her own experience. It is surely no accident that one of her latest plans for a new critical work involved using the diary form, the form which had allowed her the greatest artistic freedom. She called herself fortunate in having been able to mobilise her being in her writing. 'I have to some extent forced myself to break every mould & find a fresh form of being, that is of expression, for everything I feel & think. So that when it is working I get the sense of being fully energised – nothing stunted', she wrote in August 1934. It is in her diary that she most consummately realised this energising process.

10

Conclusion

There is hardly an example of a diary written out of a first-class creative mind.

—P. A. Spalding. *Self-Harvest: A Study of Diaries and the Diarist*, p. 12

In the eighteenth century when women as a group first began to make their mark on the literary scene, they adopted certain tactics and topics that helped to insulate them as a sex against overt criticism of their effrontery at daring to publish at all. They focused their attention on the subjects they were supposed to know best, on domestic life, with female characters and female conduct the object of their moral concern. Poems and novels by women could safely take love as their theme without being thought to poach on the male preserves of power politics or trenchant social criticism, and romance consequently figured as a major motif in these texts. Over the next two hundred years, as women established for themselves a distinctive place in literary history, these topics remained dominant in their work, appealing to a growing mass market of bourgeois literate women readers who found in women's writing reflections of the fabric and the fantasies of their own lives. Recent feminist literary critics have forcefully revealed the existence of dissident subtexts in literature of the eighteenth and nineteenth centuries and have analysed most perceptively the various tactics employed by women writers who wished to retain the approval of their reading public (and the favour of their male publishers) while yet registering their independent views. As the preceding chapters illustrate, the diaries of such writers offer a further insight into the extent of their alienation from popular images of female propriety and, by demonstrating their interest in areas not normally considered to be a female province, show how women's writing for publication was most carefully stage-managed so as to stay within accepted limits.

The journals of Fanny Burney and Louisa May Alcott, women from different cultures but yet both impressed with a distinctively female mythology of behaviour, reveal for instance a fascination with war and politics, subjects that they learned to treat with caution in their published fictions, Burney, partly through her involvement with the English court and partly through her marriage to a French refugee, felt personally implicated in the European Royalist cause. Her journal accounts of post-revolutionary France and in particular of the Napoleonic campaign of 1815 are a major literary undertaking. Similarly Alcott, born into a family with strong political ideals, campaigned forcefully for the anti-slavery cause, involved herself in the action of the American Civil War, and later in life allied herself with the movement for women's suffrage. The fight against injustice and her belief in individual freedom form a continuous and insistent refrain in her journal, despite the blandness that many twentieth-century readers now find in her most popular works.

Both these writers too assert an independence of spirit which was in opposition to the dominant ethos of their age. 'Singleness be mine – with peace of mind and liberty', wrote the young Fanny Burney after being relieved of an unwelcome proposal of marriage, while Alcott, confronted everywhere with evidence of male unreliability, consistently maintained that 'liberty is a better husband than love to many of us'. Yet both these women in their major novels promote traditional images of women's roles as essentially domestic and Alcott in particular creates the sense of home as being a centre of marital harmony, an ideal that bore little relation to her own experience. They are not alone in projecting personal images of female strength and resilience in their journals nor in their adoption of a personal life style which was often at odds with the femininity their cultures endorsed. As Anais Nin has remarked, 'It takes character to write a long, life long diary, a book, to create several homes, to travel, to protect others'.[1] So Burney, despite her alleged timidity, was prepared to ignore warnings and to travel alone through war-torn Europe in 1815, braving the perils of roads thronged with soldiers and with refugees in order to reach her wounded husband. Alcott, combining energy with idealism, determined to provide for her mother and sisters in a way that her father had signally failed to do. From her teens she lived away from home, struggling to earn her keep in a variety of jobs, as teacher, seamstress, nurse, and travelling companion to an invalid lady. Her career evocatively depicts the limited nature of employment opportunities for women of talent and imagination in the nineteenth century, and her diary records her vigorous resistance to the subordinate roles she was forced to adopt in her early life.

As well as in their careers as professional authors, women writers in their own lives, as told in their journals, often successfully defied conventional mores with a freedom that they did not always grant their more submissive fictional creations. Their lives were rarely bounded by conventional domestic limits. They travelled abroad, often unaccompanied. Several, including Fanny Burney, Mary Shelley and Elizabeth Barrett Browning, set up homes in foreign lands. Several others, including Louisa May Alcott, Edith Wharton and Katherine Mansfield, rejected the traditional idea of marriage as offering a definitive source of fulfilment for women and lived alone for much of their lives, independent career women who wrote in their fictions about wives and mothers, women as objects of male desire or as victims of a system which inexorably destroyed their individuality. Mary Shelley and Elizabeth Barrett scandalised their families by their elopements, both prepared to challenge convention in their personal lives. Even Dorothy Wordsworth, that most diffident of diarists, was seen as unconventional in her youth, playing hostess to an establishment of unchaperoned young men and women, a situation which shocked her neighbours, who circulated rumours of irregular conduct in the Wordsworth household.

Dedicated as they were to writing as a profession (even if, as in Dorothy Wordsworth's case, that profession was another's), it is not surprising that these women dealt centrally with this as a major topic in their journals. It did after all form the pivot of their lives, and their diaries record the long hours devoted to composition, the progress of their manuscripts, anxieties about completion and the difficulties of dealing with publishers. Often they were too busy to jot down more in their journals than 'Writing hard' – the sum of a day's entry for Elizabeth Barrett in January 1832. 'Write my story', reported Mary Shelley equally tersely in August 1816, and 'Wrote much; for brain was lively, and work paid for readily', noted Louisa May Alcott, summing up the month's achievement in September 1862. Few, however, with the exception of Elizabeth Barrett Browning in *Aurora Leigh* (written, incidentally, thirty years after her diary), were prepared to take a woman writer as a major literary subject in work offered for publication. Most significantly in Dorothy Wordsworth's case, she was to find herself, in much of her brother's published poetry, written out of experiences she had participated in and had celebrated in her journal. The committed female artist who could support herself and her family by her writing was clearly an inappropriate subject for serious literary treatment from the eighteenth to the early twentieth century. Despite the fact that women writers themselves were highly professional in their approach to their craft, the flavour of the amateur still clung to the popular picture of the authoress, that 'singular anomaly' as W. S. Gilbert was to term her in 1885. The already slight reputation of female artists was further tarnished by reviews and 'appreciations' of their work which concentrated on their family circumstances. James Austen Leigh's memoir of Jane Austen as his 'dear Aunt Jane', for instance, promoted a view of her as a talented naive, rather than a rigorous and skilled practitioner, a view which qualified critical opinion of Austen's achievement for over a hundred years.

Women authors correspondingly tended to marginalise female literary creation in their published fictions. Burney's Evelina confines her writing to private letters whose contents remain unsuspected by the society she moves in; Alcott's Jo March has to learn to subdue her literary leanings as incongruous with her women's role; Mary Shelley's representative of creativity, Frankenstein, is not a woman but a man, and one whose work nightmarishly returns to destroy him; George Eliot's women abandon artistic idealism for domestic compromise; Edith Wharton's heroines are perceived as art objects rather than creators, manipulating traditional versions of womanhood in order to obtain their illusory freedoms. Even the two modernist figures studied here, Katherine Mansfield and Virginia Woolf, both products of a Victorian heritage, both absorbed in their writing, shy away from a central focus on the writing woman, however radically their works deal with revisionist notions of gender.

Yet the journals of these and other women show how their days and their thoughts were dominated by the ideas and practice of literary activity. 'I live to write', declared Katherine Mansfield in her journal of May 1919. Conversely it must have sometimes seemed to Louisa May Alcott as if she wrote purely to live, so pressing were the requests from publishers for stories and articles that she could barely meet their demands. 'Feel quite used up', she recorded sadly at the age of thirty-six, 'but the family seem so panic-stricken and helpless when I break down, that I try to keep the mill going. Two short tales for L., $50; two for Ford, $20; and did my editorial work, though two months are unpaid for. Roberts wants a new book, but am afraid to get into a vortex lest I fall ill.'[2] Alcott's resigned acceptance of her situation shows how the early delight she had found in self-expression had become converted into drudgery. As her work became public property and market pressures became the driving force in her choice of subject matter, so she wrote to order, sacrificing her own health and mental happiness to satisfy her rapacious readers. She was still, however, able to find her private writing a refreshing change from the disciplined approach of every day. 'My pen will not keep in order & ink has a tendency to splash when used copiously & with rapidity', she wrote to her sister in November 1858, apologising for the messiness of her script while rejoicing in the liberation of casual composition. 'I have to be so morose & dignified nowadays that the jocosity of my nature will gush out when it gets a chance.'[3]

Women writers turned to their diaries to record projects finished and unfinished, their feelings of satisfaction and of failure as they embarked excitedly on a fresh enterprise or came up against writer's block. The diaries recount too the painstaking revisions, the intense self-discipline and the constant process of self re-appraisal that determined the pattern of their subjects' lives. They dramatise women's efforts to meet publishers' deadlines and their reactions, delighted or crushed, to reviews and the opinions of friends. 'Its the curse of a writers life to want praise so much, & be so cast down by blame or indifference', wrote Virginia Woolf in her diary. 'The only sensible course is to remember that writing is after all what one does best; that any other work would seem to me a waste of life; that on the whole I get infinite pleasure from it; that I make one hundred pounds a year; & that some people like what I write.'[4] Such good humour and clear-sightedness was not, unfortunately, always possible, either for Woolf or for her predecessors and surprisingly it is often those most polished writers who admit to the most profound misgivings about their own progress. George Eliot's journal during the composition of *Romola* reads like a catalogue of hopelessness that counteracts the confident impression given by the published text. 'Utterly despondent about my book', 'trying to write, trying to construct and unable', 'brooding, producing little', 'dreadfully depressed about myself and my work', Eliot admitted to her diary throughout October, November and December of 1861. 'Flashes of hope are succeeded by long intervals of dim mistrust'. Instead of seeing her ascendant career as one of continuous unerring accomplishment, as did her readership, she became increasingly stricken with doubt as to her own ability to produce. 'Horrid scepticism about all things – paralyzing my mind. Shall I ever be good for anything again? – ever do anything again?'[5] she asked herself, verging on a despair of which no trace can be found in the rational voice of the omnisicent narrator Eliot adopted in her mature novels.

In their obligation to their own development as creative artists, however, women writers found their personal journals not just a useful forum to expatiate on their own problems as writers but an active opportunity (conscious or not) to evolve a personal literary voice. Several of the journals discussed in the preceding chapters show women experimenting with style and mood, searching for a technique that would most closely approximate the persona they wished to create, in the process bringing to bear on their intimate writings the inescapable tones of external influences. 'Whatever book I read bubbles up in my mind as part of an article I want to write'[6] noted Virginia Woolf, ever responsive to the magnetism of other texts and appreciative of their value, for as she acknowledged, 'It is a mistake to think that literature can be produced from the raw'.[7] In the invaluable documentation of the authors' reading which diaries provide, and the interplay of tones within them, we find the palpable evidence of the debt that women owed to contemporary sources and the roots from which their distinctive and individual literary voices were to emerge.

For through their diaries, women tried to find their own position amidst the cultural maze, often via a process of amalgamation. Dorothy Wordsworth, awestruck by the ascendancy of Romanticism, was nonetheless able in her Grasmere journal to break through the weight of literary precedent in order to find an utterance that was her own, however much she might have underrated it. Similarly, at the age of twenty-five, dominated by a canonical idea of literary value, Elizabeth Barrett struggled in her diary to rid herself of an unwanted poetic and fictional inheritance, while simultaneously enthralled by it. Her abandonment of the journal form as ultimately too close to painful experience constitutes a decisive statement about the disjunctive effect of personal articulation. In a recent edition of *Antaeus*, the novelist Joyce Carol Oates has commented on the disturbing implications of the continuing practice of private writings. She speculates unnervingly on 'Why the journal distresses me, but also fascinates: I'm required to use my own voice. And to record only the truth (But not to record

All the truth ...)'.[8] Oates perceptively identifies the ambivalent
appeal of the journal for a professional writer, the demand for
'truth' that is one of its preconditions and the impossibility of
satisfying this demand to the full. As Katherine Mansfield had
earlier acknowledged, 'I must start my Journal and keep it day by
day. But *can* I be honest? If I lie it's no use'.[9] The search for an
authentic voice in the private journal is clearly fraught for professional writers by their habit of practised mimicry. For women, for
so long denied a voice of their own, and beset by public expectations of how that voice should sound, the dilemma of defining a
personal utterance gains added intensity.

The predicament is aggravated by writers' awareness of the
enigmatic nature of textual production. In a letter of 1920, Katherine Mansfield told John Middleton Murry: 'The Journal – I have
absolutely given up. I dare not keep a journal. I should always be
trying to tell the truth. As a matter of fact I dare not tell the truth. I
feel I *must* not.'[10] Torn between her desire for truth and her fear of
confronting it, Mansfield, like Elizabeth Barrett, recognised the
importance of artistic distance for her own writing. It was essential
for her to maintain the mediating filter of imagination in her stories
in order to retain artistic control, for as she commented in her
notebook, 'There is a very profound distinction between any kind
of *confession* and creative work'.

The compulsion to dispense with the supportive structures of
traditional literary conventions, which appears to make the diary
so attractive as a form, thus can be seen to contain inherent
dangers for a creative artist. As Anais Nin pointed out, 'The diary
proves a tremendous, all-engulfing craving for truth since to write
it I risk destroying the whole edifice of my illusions.'[11] Significantly, given the psychoanalytical context of her writing experience,
Nin's diary was ultimately to take over from fiction as her major
literary project. Launched initially as a letter to her father, it
evolved into a personal chronicle of emergent womanhood, as Nin
found in the diary form the most sympathetic mode for gendered
literary expression. However, the bridge between truth and illusion proved to be more nebulous than she had at first supposed,
and the genre by no means simple to manage. The tendency for
writers to insist on the sharp division between the two areas of
their literary experience is not always helpful. Gail Godwin, clearly
troubled by the compulsive call of the diary, has tried to explain the
distinction between the two forms:

I write fiction because I need to organize the clutter of too many details into some meaning, because I enjoy turning something promising into something marvellous; I keep a diary because it keeps my mind fresh and open. Once the details of being me are safely stored away every night, I can get on with what isn't just me.[12]

Godwin's comment on the function of the diary, while obviously useful in clarifying for her own benefit her separate approaches to writing, is not entirely satisfactory in explaining the complex nature of the genre as a whole. Her distinction between the diary and the novel as loose and structured forms respectively, fails to address the issue of the diarist's control over her medium. The diary, after all, is not just an aid to openness as Godwin suggests, a necessary stage in the training of a writer's mental alertness, but is in itself an alternative method of structuring experience through language, the degree of control shifted rather than abandoned. Debatable too is her affirmation of the diary's access to a genuine self, the 'me' the writer needs to grasp and exorcise before consigning it to a convenient place in her work.

For the more we read others' diaries, the more we become aware of the diary's fictive quality, and of the creation of a central character, established through an act of imagination as powerful as those responsible for stimulating writers' published works. In a study of 'private chronicles', Robert Fothergill has noted that the ego impulse so evident in diaries written by men is marked by its absence from women's diaries. Women, he claims, do not project the self as dramatic protagonist, but are much more self-effacing, their diaries operating as instruments of sensibility, dominated by a fear of self-display.[13] However, as Margo Culley has rightly observed, 'Even the most self-deprecating of women's diaries are grounded in some sense of the importance of making a record of the life'.[14] Indeed, although women might traditionally have been dogged by conventions of femininity which restricted the forms of their expression, they still have been able through their diaries to break with those conventions and to provide decisive, coherent images of self that operate as forceful complements to the public evasions they might transmit.

Marie Bashkirtseff's journal, for instance, presents her as a woman whose art accords her a specialised role in life. The central character in her journal's story is a highly romanticised figure, passionate, fanciful and ambitious, striving for a realisation of her artistic ideals. Art is what helps her to define her conception of personality. 'In the studio', Bashkirtseff suggests, 'all distinctions disappear. One has neither name nor family; one is no longer the daughter of one's mother, one is one's-self, – and individual, – and one has before one art, and nothing else. One feels so happy, so free, so proud!'[15] Through an apparent negation of genetic factors, Bashkirtseff fabricates another identity, that of the authentic free spirit. But we need to recognise that it is an identity as partial and as fictive as any of her other artistic creations. Bashkirtseff's diary shows her continually striking poses, trying out attitudes to find one that suits the present moment, while the persona that over-rides them all is that of the image maker, desperate to convince herself of her personal and artistic absolutism.

Although they might admit to uncertainties more readily than men in their diaries, women are still capable of constructing strong, independent identities for themselves. For professional writers, the diary charts their achievements, the goals they set themselves and the independent life style they create, often so different from those of other women of their day. Even when assuming the mask of diffidence, they describe activities which contradict the very demureness they are intent on promoting. Fanny Burney's diary balances her insistence on her modesty and weakness on the one hand with her description of events which portray her initiative and fortitude on the other. Her journal recreates her life as a series of perilous episodes, with Burney the heroine of an adventure story who survives the hazards of victimisation through her hold on the solid fact of her own identity. It is through the journal as a form of self-realisation that women are able to evoke and articulate the different and often contradictory elements that constitute their individual natures. Unlike the composition of a formal autobiography, designed with a preconceived idea of individual growth and written from a position of historical superiority, the personal diary charts the fluctuations of temperament on a daily basis without the benefits of hindsight. To some extent it is this very regularity which also functions as a stabiliser, endowing the diary with its identifiable voice, whether it be the intimate tone of confessional or the confident pitch of forthright opinion. When women set aside a special time of day for writing their diaries – 'the comfortable bright hour after tea' in Virginia Woolf's case, for instance – they isolate its unique purpose as a time for reflection and for conscious formulation of ideas that can contribute to a consistent self portrait. We see Woolf repeatedly trying in her diary to capture a view of herself as a writer, assimilating the diverse areas of her experience into an entity that she could more easily comprehend and pin down. 'What is to become of all these diaries?', she asked herself in 1926, speculating on whether or not they were substantial enough for Leonard to make into a book if she were to die. Yet, at the moment of asking the question, she knew that 'This is dictated by a slight melancholia, which comes upon me sometimes now and makes me think I am old; I am ugly. I am repeating things. Yet, as far as I know, as a writer I am only now writing out my mind.'[16]

One of the most outstanding examples of the genre's ability to create a vivid identity for a woman is found in the diary of Alice James, a work which serves as a fascinating footnote to the other diaries studied here. Overshadowed in public affairs by her more vocal brothers, Henry, the novelist, and William, the psychologist, Alice James retreated in her family and social life into the haven of feminine debility that provided a not uncommon escape route for frustrated Victorian women. Subject to bouts of illness from her late adolescence, she expanded invalidism into a career and began her journal in 1889, at the age of forty, only three years before her death. Fully conscious of her brothers' literary achievements she presented in her journal a view of her infirmity that made it seem analagous with their publications, a contrived work of art which she offered as a complement to their more celebrated accomplishments. 'Within the last year Henry has published *The Tragic Muse*, brought out *The American*, and written a play . . . and his admirable comedy; combined with William's *Psychology*', she pondered in 1891, 'not a bad show for one family! especially if I get myself dead, the hardest job of all.'[17] For Alice James, the diary was the book of the self in a grand way. It was a deliberate and highly controlled exercise in self-invention, and one that was kept hidden from everyone except her close friend and companion, Katherine Loring. Like Sylvia Plath's Lady Lazarus, dying for Alice James was an art that she did exceptionally well, as she concocted a role for herself as a doomed but gifted figure, together with a position from which she could comment on her own performance. The day after she had received the diagnosis of fatal cancer, she wrote in her diary how:

having it to look forward to for a while seems to double the value of the event, for one suddenly becomes picturesque to oneself, and one's wavering little individuality stands out with a cameo effect and one has the tenderest indulgence for all the little *stretchings out* which crowd in upon the memory.[18]

Continually she refers to herself in theatrical metaphors, remarking how the act of writing a journal creates a part 'easy to act as we walk across our little stage lighted up by our little self-conscious footlights', or lamenting the fact (nine months before she learned of the cancer) that her death 'will probably be in my sleep so that I shall not be one of the audience, dreadful fraud! a creature who has been denied all dramatic episodes might be allowed, I think, to assist at her extinction.' The ironic narrator of Alice James's journal explodes the myth of the diary's essential informality. Self-aware, assertive and monitoring her own behaviour from a perspective of amused detachment, she acknowledges explicitly the journal's part in structuring her experience. 'If I can get on to my sofa and occupy myself for four hours at intervals, thro' the day, scribbling my notes and able to read the books that belong to me, in that they clarify the density and shape the formless mass within, Life seems inconceivably rich', she observed in May 1890.[19] Her companion Katherine Loring, present at her deathbed, describes how even *in extremis*, the dying woman was intent on revising her diary, asking Katherine to make alterations to sentences when she herself could no longer hold the pen, for 'although she was very weak and it tired her much to dictate, she could not get her head quiet until she had written: then she was relieved.'[20] The diary was for Alice James her main literary endeavour, functioning not just as the record of daily events or of casual gossip, but as a careful artistic product.

Simultaneously deprecating the quality of her life and affirming its value, Alice James used the diary to imbue her life with meaning and to establish for herself a vital and original character that could counterbalance the persona of the fading invalid lady known to the world. Denied outlets for her talent by a family that had encouraged masculine potential but belittled signs of feminine intellect, she waited until middle age before she gave full expression to the witty raconteur that lay dormant within her. Yet, like women of a century earlier, she kept her journal secret, so that its discovery proved an astonishing revelation of her literary powers for her brothers after her death. In 1890 she described in her diary how her early bouts of hysteria had helped her to realise that life was to be 'a fight simply between my body and my will, a battle in which the former was to be triumphant to the end'.[21] The journal became her defence mechanism in this fight, allowing her to exercise her intellect, the only weapon at her command with which she was able to defy the weak female body that threatened to take over her identity. It became her only means of control over her environment, a powerful instrument for creating a view of herself as cynical observer, successfully able to reduce and manage events which surrounded her.

As she contrives it, Alice James's journal tells a complete story, with a heroine who battles valiantly against adverse circumstances and with a plot that moves inexorably, unusually for a diary, towards a single conclusion. Although she was not a published writer in her lifetime, Alice James was immersed in a literary milieu, notably through her brothers' achievements, and was certainly sensitive to the technical requirements of literary composition. She refers more than once to a possible readership for her journal and to the fact that she, unlike her brothers, has not 'ever written for the press'. Tartly she acknowledges that 'the domestic muse isn't considered very original'.[22] But the elegance of her phrasing, the conscious erudition of her remarks and her painstaking approach to revising her work all demonstrate that she regarded the diary as a serious literary enterprise. In a similar way, the journals of other women writers show how they bring their literary expertise to bear on their private writings. Through these apparently careless and fragmented memorabilia, they construct narratives of individual lives which, to the attentive reader, are as compelling in their fast-moving representations as the more orthodox works written for an impersonal public. After reading extracts from Anais Nin's diary, her analyst Otto Rank commented to her: 'Here in your diary we have the story written by the woman herself, and yet it is essentially the same story we find in tradition.'[23] The life path that Nin plotted for herself in her journal resembled to the Jungian psychiatrist, Rank, the archetypal scenarios of myth, in its reconstruction of fundamental patterns of female experience within family structures.

Rank's interpretation of Nin's diary raises an interesting critical question relating to the problematics of reading in general and these informal texts in particular. From his position as analyst, he saw the diary as a material indication of his patient's psyche and thus identified certain elements in it which helped to validate his therapeutic methods. As literary critics or as common readers we need to be aware of the perspectives we too bring to bear on our reading of these documents. Diaries and journals, so often relegated to the margins of the literary academy, are nonetheless exacting literary projects, of great significance to their subjects – frequently, as in the case of Fanny Burney or Virginia Woolf, underlying all their other writings. The sequential organisation of the diary provides the basis for its plot in the connection between daily entries. Writers often re-read previous entries before starting to write the next, aware of the structural relationships they create. Yet we can interpret the narratives which journals comprise in different ways. A diary, such as Elizabeth Barrett's or Edith Wharton's single attempt at the genre, can be a love story, following the progress of a romance from the first hints of attraction through to fulfilment or to disillusionment. It can be, as with Hester Thrale's children's book, a family history, documenting the chronology of family and social life, and isolating the high points of domestic activity. Many writers' diaries, like Louisa May Alcott's, are *Bildungsromans*, stories of individual career development from tentative scribblings to triumphant publication and the dubious rewards of success. Women write their lives as adventure stories, projecting themselves in heroic guise, like Fanny Burney or Alice James; as sentimental narratives, as in Mary Shelley's later journal; as travelogues, as in George Eliot's diaries of her journeys abroad; or as moral tales of endurance, a message we can elicit from Dorothy Wordsworth's patient record of life at Dove Cottage.

Most frequently diaries contain elements of several of these genres, weaving single discrete narratives with a distinct beginning and end into the fabric of the main plot, as their authors embark on different stages of their lives. 'In their form', Suzanne Juhasz has observed, 'women's lives tend to be like the stories that they tell: they show a pattern less of linear development towards some clear goal than one of repetitive, cumulative, cyclical structure.'[24] While not necessarily agreeing with this in its entirety (for with the diaries of professional women writers we can frequently identify clear goals), Juhasz does make a useful point about the relationship between female experience and women's writing. Pattern and repetition certainly feature in a number of journals. Fanny Burney writes the same story – of panic and survival – again and again as she goes through her life from one apparently terrifying encounter to the next. Dorothy Wordsworth makes a virtue out of the sameness of days – the Lakeland scenery, the domestic routine, the neighbours' gossip – celebrating both the sense of reassurance in this continuity and the uniqueness of each individual episode.

In examining the private diaries of published women writers then, four main critical perspectives emerge. First and most tantalising perhaps is the investigation of the relationship between this informal writing and other material written specifically for publication. The differences in subject matter and in tone between private and public writings are particularly noticeable in texts produced by nineteenth-century women, and suggest the existence of tensions between these versions of their experience. Similarly we can see the emergence of a private persona which is often at odds with the public image of feminine propriety. Alternatively of course, the similarities we find between diary material and work prepared for publication can be just as telling in illuminating the overlapping nature of the two literary forms. Katherine Mansfield's journal, for instance, shows the same searching after theatrical effect in the interplay of different voices as do her short stories, worked on so painstakingly as individual dramatic pieces. To some extent too the journal can be seen as a form of relaxation for these women, as they revert to a mode of writing not controlled by formal literary constraints. The personal diary, removed from certain demands of artistic standards and a critical public audience, liberates a freedom of expression which need not take others' strictures into account. When these factors are related to a literature produced by a sex which has traditionally been trained in suppression rather than expression, we can see a dynamic relation operating between the forms of private and public writing.

The second approach concerns methods of literary production. Can a study of writers' diaries inform our reading of their published work in terms of revealing their sources of inspiration, their working methods, the market forces which determined their subjects and other pressures on them to produce? How far do private journals act as working notebooks, providing a constant source of reference for writers who revise the substance of daily life to produce a more polished rendering? Certainly the diary can allow a writer to experiment with material or to develop a concept of individual style that can be refined and transferred to published work. The expression in diary form of anxieties that beset writers over the processes of production informs our understanding of the genesis of a text and the problems surrounding it. This interest in creative output, highlighted for instance by Leonard Woolf's editing of his wife's diaries, marketed as *A Writer's Diary*, is not of course confined to women alone, but in considering writers who are also women, sensitive to their position as gendered authors, often with other, domestic claims on their time, the subject acquires a significance which says much about the whole position of the woman writer and her exceptional circumstances.

Thirdly, the diary is a form of autobiographical writing, subject to many of the same theoretical approaches that apply to that genre. The differences between the diary and other types of autobiography relate both to formal features of organisation and their implications – the daily entry as opposed to the retrospective view from a distance of years for example – and to the ways in which the text explores and constructs versions of the self (however problematic a concept that might be). For the diary is not able, as are memoirs or autobiographies written for publication, to stand back from past events with a clear detached view, and the diarist herself is a constantly changing factor, shifting from day to day, in the active production of the work which is always in progress, never completed. The sort of fictional persona which ultimately emerges helps to elucidate the nature of the diary as literary genre and to relate it to the social context which produces it.

The last and perhaps the most provisional of these perspectives concerns the diary as literary text and how we read it. For the diary is not merely a daily record of events, but a continuous narrative, and as such a highly self-conscious piece of writing. No longer can we retain the idea of an innocent narrator, uncontrolled and existing in a vacuum. In dealing with women who were engaged in the craft of writing as a profession, aware of the formal difficulties of literary experiment, and in most cases in touch with a sophisticated theoretical scheme of literary practice, we should not assume any naivety in composition. The journals that these women kept, however diverse, create structured narratives, which follow the development of individual lives. Written with sometimes more than half an eye on a possible reader, journals become deliberately fashioned works, capable of great formal flexibility but nonetheless subject to unspoken disciplines and generic conventions such as governed the poetry and prose produced by the same writers for the public market.

It is unfortunate that even today, when their work is being

granted a critical attention it was often originally denied, the diaries of women writers are still seen merely as a footnote to their main oeuvre, offering useful biographical insights but ignored as important literary documents. This study has attempted to redress the balance. 'The core of us is an artist, a writer', wrote Anais Nin in her diary. 'And it is in our work, by our work, that we reassemble the fragments, re-create wholeness.'[25] The diary itself, that uniquely 'feminine activity',[26] crucially dramatises this process of reassemblage and as such it is a major work of art, re-creating the core of the artist who produced it.

Notes

Chapter 1: Women and their Diaries

1. Oscar Wilde, *Complete Works* (London: Collins, 1981) p. 357.
2. Marie Bashkirtseff, *The Journal of a Young Artist*, in Mary Jane Moffatt and Charlotte Painter (eds), *Revelations: Diaries of Women* (New York: Random House, 1974) p. 48.
3. Margo Culley (ed.), *A Day at a Time: the Diary Literature of American Women from 1764 to the Present* (New York: Feminist Press at the City University of New York, 1985) p. 11.
4. Gail Godwin, 'A Diarist on Diarists', *Antaeus*, no. 61, ed. Daniel Halpern, New York, Autumn 1988, p. 9.
5. *The Journal of Katherine Mansfield, 1904–22, Definitive Edition*, ed. J. M. Murry (London: Constable, 1962) p. 255.
6. Hester Thrale, *Thraliana: The Diary of Mrs Hester Lynch Thrale, 1776–1809*, ed. K. Balderston (Oxford: Clarendon Press, 1942) vol II.
7. *The Early Diary of Frances Burney 1776–1778*, ed. Annie Raine Ellis (London: Bell, 1907) p. 19.
8. Ibid, p. 18.
9. Ibid, p. 20.
10. *Memoirs of Mrs Laetitia Pilkington 1712–1750 By Herself* (London: Routledge, 1928) p. 31.
11. Ibid, p. 90.
12. *The Diary of Anais Nin*, vol. 1 (New York: Harcourt Brace, 1966) p. 58.
13. Felicity Nussbaum, 'The Female Autobiographical Subject', conference paper given at the Institute of Historical Studies, University of London, November, 1988.
14. Felicity Nussbaum, 'Eighteenth-Century Women's Autobiographical Commonplaces', in S. Benstock (ed.), *The Private Self* (London: Routledge, 1988) p. 154.
15. Elizabeth Berridge (ed.), *The Barretts at Hope End: the Early Diary of Elizabeth Barrett Browning* (London: John Murray, 1974) p. 235.
16. Hester Thrale, *The Family Book*, in Mary Hyde, *The Thrales of Streatham Park* (London: Harvard University Press, 1977) p. 21.
17. Ibid, p. 203.
18. *Salem Gazette*, 7 Dec. 1830, quoted in L. Hoffman and D. Rosenfelt (eds), *Teaching Women's Literature From a Regional Perspective* (New York, MLA, 1982) p. 84.
19. *Thraliana: The Diary of Mrs Hester Lynch Thrale, 1776–1809* (Oxford: Clarendon Press, 1941) vol. I, p. 459.
20. *The Unpublished Diary of Abigail Alcott*, Houghton Library, Harvard University.
21. *The Diary of Virginia Woolf*, ed. Anne Olivier Bell (London: Hogarth Press, 1982) vol. 4, p. 178.
22. 'Glimpses Into My Own Life and Literary Character', quoted in Berridge, op. cit.

23. *Queen Victoria in her Letters and Journals,* selected by Christopher Hibbert, (Harmondsworth: Penguin, 1985) pp. 13–14.
24. *The Diary of Tolstoy's Wife 1860–1891,* quoted in Mary Jane Moffatt and Charlotte Painter (eds), op. cit., p. 142.
25. Jane Austen, *Persuasion* (London: Dent, 1966) p. 201.
26. May Sarton, *Journal of a Solitude* (London: Women's Press, 1985) p. 83.
27. Quoted in Simon Brett (ed.), *The Faber Book of Diaries* (London: Faber, 1987) p. 380.
28. *The Diary of Virginia Woolf,* op. cit., vol. 3, p. 201.
29. Ibid, vol. 2, p. 24.
30. Edith Wharton, *Unpublished Diary,* Beinecke Library, Yale University.
31. Woolf, op. cit., vol. 5, p. 205.
32. *The Journals of Mary Shelley 1814–44,* eds Paula R. Feldman and Diana Scott Kilvert (Oxford: Clarendon Press, 1987) pp. 459–60.
33. Barbara Pym, *A Very Private Eye* (London: Macmillan, 1985) p. 163.
34. Sidonie Smith, *A Poetics of Women's Autobiography: Marginality and the Fictions of Self-Representation* (Bloomington: Indiana University Press, 1987) p. 5.
35. *The Diary of Virginia Woolf,* ed. Anne Olivier Bell (Harmondsworth: Penguin, 1979) vol, 1, p. 266.
36. 15 October 1884, quoted in Harriet Blodgett, *Centuries of Female Days: Englishwomen's Private Diaries* (New Brunswick: Rutgers University Press, 1988) p. 76.
37. Robert Fothergill, *Private Chronicles: A Study of English Diaries* (Oxford: Oxford University Press, 1974) p. 91.
38. James Olney, *Autobiography,* quoted by Linda Anderson, 'At the Threshold of the Self', in M. Monteith (ed.), *Women's Writing: A Challenge to Theory* (Brighton: Harvester, 1985) p. 59.
39. Moffatt and Painter, op. cit., p. 51.
40. Joyce Carol Oates, 'Selections from a Journal January 1985–January 1988', *Antaeus,* no. 61 ed. Daniel Halpern, New York, Autumn 1988, p. 332.
41. Culley, op cit., p. 8.
42. Hoffman and Rosenfelt, op. cit., p. 56.
43. Mansfield, op. cit., p. 203.
44. Quoted in Joanna Russ, *How to Suppress Women's Writing* (London: Women's Press, 1984) p. 102.
45. Suzanne Juhasz, 'Towards a Theory of Form in Feminist Autobiography', in Estelle Jelinek (ed.), *Women's Autobiography: Essays in Criticism* (London: Indiana University Press, 1980) p. 223.
46. Ibid, p. 223.
47. Lyndall Gordon, *Virginia Woolf: A Writer's Life* (Oxford: Oxford University Press, 1984) p. 178.
48. Quoted in Brett, op. cit., p. 380.

Chapter 2: The Journals of Fanny Burney

1. 27 March 1768. *The Early Diary of Frances Burney 1768–1778,* ed.

Annie Raine Ellis (London, 1907). All quotations from Burney's diaries of the period 1767–78 are from this edition.

2. Patricia Meyer Spacks, *Imagining a Self: Autobiography and the Novel in Eighteenth-Century England* (London: Harvard University Press, 1976) p. 174.
3. *The Journals and Letters of Fanny Burney (Madame D'Arblay) 1791–1840* in twelve volumes, ed. Joyce Hemlow and others (Oxford: Clarendon Press, 1976–86) vol. VI, p. 363. All quotations from Burney's diaries from the period 1791–1840 are taken from this twelve-volume edition.
4. *The Diary of Fanny Burney*, ed. Lewis Gibbs (London: Dent, 1971) p. 117. All quotations from Burney's diaries from the period 1778–91 are taken from this edition.
5. Thomas Babington Macaulay, *Edinburgh Review*, January 1843, p. 545.
6. Ibid, p. 549.
7. Ibid, pp. 550–1.
8. I am indebted to the information given by Joyce Hemlow in her introduction to *The Journals and Letters of Fanny Burney*, op. cit., pp. xxi–ii.
9. Frances Burney, *Camilla* (Oxford: Oxford University Press, 1972) p. 8.
10. Letter to Fanny Burney from Samuel Crisp, 1774, in the *Early Diary*, op. cit., vol. I.
11. Hemlow, op. cit., vol IV, pp. 167–8.
12. Macaulay, op. cit., p. 280.
13. Hemlow, op. cit., Sept. 1811.
14. Ibid, June 1823.
15. Barbara Johnson, 'My Monster/My Self', *Diacritics* 12 (2) 1982, pp. 2–10.

Chapter 3: The Journals of Dorothy Wordsworth

1. *Journals of Dorothy Wordsworth*, ed. Mary Moorman (Oxford: Oxford University Press, 1971) p. 129. All subsequent references are to this edition.
2. *The Letters of Dorothy Wordsworth*, ed. Alan G. Hill (Oxford: Oxford University Press, 1985) vol. II, no. 214.
3. Ibid, vol. III, no. 586.
4. Thomas Mallon, *A Book of One's Own: People and their Diaries* (New York: Ticknor & Fields, 1984) p. 125.
5. Robert Gittings and Jo Manton, *Dorothy Wordsworth* (Oxford: Clarendon Press, 1985) p. 31.
6. Ibid, p. 33.
7. Thomas De Quincey, *Recollections of the Lakes and the Lake Poets*, quoted in Elizabeth Hardwicke, *Seduction and Betrayal* (London: Wiedenfeld and Nicolson, 1974) pp. 155–6.
8. Gittings and Manton, op. cit., p. 150.

208   *Notes*

9.   Margaret Homans, *Women Writers and Poetic Identity* (Princeton, NJ: Princeton University Press, 1980) p. 73.
10.   Ibid, p. 41.
11.   Letter to Lady Beaumont, 20 April 1806, in Hill, op. cit.
12.   *Irregular Verses I*, quoted by Susan Levin and Robert Ready, 'Unpublished Poems from Dorothy Wordsworth's Commonplace Book', *The Wordsworth Circle*, vol. 9, 1978, pp. 33–44.
13.   *The Poetical Works of Wordsworth*, ed. Ernest de Selincourt (Oxford: Oxford University Press, 1964) p. 65.
14.   Ibid, p. 152.
15.   Thomas Frosch, 'Wordsworth's Beggars and a Brief Instance of Writer's Block', *Studies in Romanticism* 21, Winter 1982, p. 629.
16.   *Poetical Works*, op. cit., p. 152.
17.   Gittings and Manton, op. cit., p. 167.
18.   Ibid, p. 154.

Chapter 4: The Journal of Mary Shelley

1.   Mary Jacobus, 'Is there a Woman in this Text?' *New Literary History*, Fall 1982, pp. 117–41.
2.   3 Nov. 1823, Mary Shelley, *Letters*, vol. 1, ed. Betty T. Bennett, (Baltimore: Johns Hopkins, 1980).
3.   Ibid, 5 March 1817.
4.   Ibid.
5.   Entry for 2 Oct. 1822, *The Journals of Mary Shelley 1814–1844* in two volumes, eds Paula R. Feldman and Diana Scott Kilvert (Oxford: Clarendon Press, 1987). Subsequent references are to this edition.
6.   Edward Trelawney, *Records of Shelley, Byron and the Author*, 1878, quoted in *The Journals of Mary Shelley*, op. cit., pp. 68–9.
7.   Mario Praz, *The Romantic Agony*, quoted in Ellen Moers, *Literary Women* (London: The Women's Press, 1978) p. 144.
8.   *Journals*, op. cit., 19 Oct. 1822.
9.   *Letters*, op. cit., 7 Oct. 1817.
10.   Mary Poovey, *The Proper Lady and the Woman Writer* (Chicago: University of Chicago Press, 1984) p. 143.
11.   Christopher Small, *Ariel Like a Harpy: Shelley, Mary and Frankenstein* (London: Victor Gollancz, 1972) p. 30.
12.   Letter to Baxter, quoted in Poovey, op. cit.
13.   Mary Dunn, *Moon in Eclipse: A Life of Mary Shelley* (London: Wiedenfield and Nicolson, 1978) Preface.
14.   Virginia Woolf, 'Women in Fiction', *Collected Essays II*, (London: Hogarth Press, 1942).
15.   Poovey, op. cit., p. 138.
16.   Adrienne Rich, *On Lies, Secrets & Silence* (London: Virago Press, 1980) p. 162.
17.   As do for example Ellen Moers in *Literary Women*, op. cit., and Sandra Gilbert and Susan Gubar in *The Madwoman in the Attic: The Nineteenth-Century Woman Writer and the Literary Imagination* (New Haven, Conn.: Yale University Press, 1979).

18. Mary Shelley, *Frankenstein or, The Modern Prometheus* (New York: Dell, 1979) p. 171.
19. Ibid, p. 166.
20. *Letters*, op. cit. 28 Jan. 1826.
21. As for example in Gilbert and Gubar, op. cit., Barbara Johnson, 'My Monster/My Self', *Diacritics* 12, 1982.
22. *Letters*, op. cit.
23. Mary Jacobus, 'The Difference of View', *Women Writing and Writing About Women* (London: Croom Helm, 1978).
24. *Edinburgh Review*, March 1818, quoted Dunn, op. cit., p. 171.
25. *Journals*, op. cit., note, p. 390.
26. Patricia Meyer Spacks, *The Female Imagination* (London: Allen & Unwin, 1976) p. 143.
27. *On Lies, Secrets & Silence*, op. cit., p. 186.

Chapter 5: The Early Diary of Elizabeth Barrett Browning

1. Letter to Richard Hengist Horne, quoted in Elizabeth Berridge (ed.), *The Barretts at Hope End: The Early Diary of Elizabeth Barrett Browning* (London: John Murray, 1974) p. 26.
2. Elizabeth Berridge, *ibid*, p. 212. All subsequent references to Elizabeth Barrett's diary are to this edition.
3. Margaret Forster, *Elizabeth Barrett Browning: A Biography* (London: Chatto & Windus, 1988) p. 33.
4. Elizabeth Barrett Browning, *Aurora Leigh* (London: Women's Press, 1983).
5. Angela Leighton, *Elizabeth Barrett Browning* (Brighton: Harvester Press, 1986) p. 4.
6. Elizabeth Barrett Browning, *Selected Poems*, introduced by Margaret Forster (London: Chatto & Windus, 1988) p. 22.
7. For example Angela Leighton, op. cit., Alethea Hayter, *Mrs Browning: A Poet's Work and its Setting* (London: Faber, 1962).
8. Cora Kaplan, introduction to *Aurora Leigh*, op. cit., p. 16.
9. Elizabeth Barrett Browning, *Poems* (London: Eyre & Spottiswoode, n.d.) pp. 331–2.
10. *Selected Poems*, op. cit., p. 228.
11. *Aurora Leigh*, op. cit., p. 70.

Chapter 6: The Journal of Louisa May Alcott

1. *Louisa May Alcott: Her Life, Letters and Journals*, ed. Ednah D. Cheyney (London: Sampson Low, Marston; Searle & Rivington, 1889). All subsequent references are to this edition unless otherwise stated.
2. Abigail Alcott, unpublished *Diary* for 1842. Houghton Library, University of Harvard.
3. Ibid.
4. Louisa May Alcott, *Good Wives* (Glasgow: Blackie, n.d.) p. 24.
5. Ibid, p. 213.

6. Louisa May Alcott, *Behind A Mask* (London: Hogarth Press, 1985) p. 12.
7. Ann Rosalind Jones, 'Writing The Body: Toward an Understanding of *L'Écriture Feminine'*, in *The New Feminist Criticism*, ed. Elaine Showalter (London: Virago Press, 1986) p. 373.
8. Quoted in Cheyney, op. cit., p. 89.
9. Louisa May Alcott, unpublished *Journal* for 1863, Houghton Library, University of Harvard.
10. Ibid, June 1865.
11. Louisa May Alcott, *Little Women* (Harmondsworth: Puffin, 1978) p. 119.
12. Ibid, p. 140.
13. Martha Saxton, *Louisa May: A Biography of Louisa May Alcott* (London: André Deutsch, 1975) p. 16.
14. Carolyn G. Heilbrun, *Reinventing Womanhood* (London: Victor Gollancz, 1979) p. 72.
15. Ibid.
16. Louisa May Alcott, letter 30 May 1870, quoted in Cheyney, op. cit.

Chapter 7: The Diaries of Edith Wharton

1. *Edith Wharton, A Backward Glance* (London: Century Hutchinson, 1987) p. 51.
2. Ibid, p. 79.
3. Edith Wharton, unpublished *Diary* 1905, Beinecke Library, Yale University. All references to the diary material of 1905 and 1906 relate to the unpublished diaries from this collection.
4. Edith Wharton, unpublished *Journal* 1907–8, Lilly Library, University of Indiana. All subsequent references are to this unpublished journal.
5. R. W. B. Lewis, *Edith Wharton: A Biography* (London: Constable, 1975).
6. Carolyn G. Heilbrun, *Writing A Woman's Life* (London: Women's Press, 1988).
7. Ibid, p. 51.
8. Lewis, op. cit., p. 224.
9. Juliet Mitchell, 'Femininity, Narrative and Psychoanalysis', *Modern Criticism and Theory: A Reader*, ed. D. Lodge (London: Longman, 1988) p. 427.
10. Edith Wharton, *The House of Mirth* (New York: Scribner's, 1969) p. 317.
11. Sidonie Smith, *A Poetics of Women's Autobiography: Marginalities and the Fictions of Self-Representation* (Bloomington: Indiana University Press, 1987) p. 47.
12. *A Backward Glance*, op. cit., p. 290.
13. John Bayley, 'From the Battlefield of Society', *Times Literary Supplement*, 1–7 April 1988, p. 348.

Chapter 8: The Journal of Katherine Mansfield

1. *The Journal of Katherine Mansfield 1904–1922 Definitive Edition*, ed. J. Middleton Murry (London: Constable, 1962) p. 205. All subsequent references are to this edition.
2. *Journal of Katherine Mansfield*, ed. J. Middleton Murry (London: Constable, 1927) p. x.
3. Katherine Mansfield, *Letters and Journals*, ed. C. K. Stead, (Harmondsworth: Penguin, 1977) p. 10.
4. Ibid, p. 81.
5. Katherine Mansfield, 'At The Bay', *Collected Stories of Katherine Mansfield* (London: Constable, 1973) p. 223.

Chapter 9: The Diary of Virginia Woolf

1. *The Diary of Virginia Woolf*, ed. Anne Olivier Bell, in five volumes (Harmondsworth: Penguin, 1979) vol. 1, p. 79, note. All subsequent references to Virginia Woolf's diary 1915–24 (i.e. vols 1 & 2) are to this edition. References to Woolf's diary 1925–41 (vols 3, 4 & 5) are to the Hogarth Press edition, London, 1980–4.
2. Margo Culley (ed.), *A Day at a Time: The Diary Literature of American Women From 1764 to the Present* (New York: Feminist Press at the City University of New York, 1985) p. 19.
3. Virginia Woolf, *A Room of One's Own* (Harmondsworth: Penguin, 1975) pp. 77–8.
4. Virginia Woolf, *A Writer's Diary*, ed. Leonard Woolf (London: Hogarth Press, 1953) p. viii.
5. Virginia Woolf, *Collected Essays*, vol. 1, (London: Chatto & Windus, 1966) p. 234.
6. *The Diary of Virginia Woolf*, op. cit., vol. 1, p. xiii.
7. *A Room of One's Own*, op. cit., p. 74.
8. Virginia Woolf, *To The Lighthouse* (Harmondsworth: Penguin, 1975) p. 211.
9. Joyce Carol Oates, 'Selections from a Journal January 1985–January 1988', *Antaeus*, no. 61, ed. Daniel Halpern, New York, Autumn 1988, p. 347.
10. Cynthia S. Pomerau, 'The Emergence of Women's Autobiography in England', in *Women's Autobiography: Essays in Criticism*, ed. E. Jelinek (Bloomington & London: Indiana University Press, 1980) p. 37.

Chapter 10: Conclusion

1. *The Diary of Anais Nin*, vol. 1 1931–4 (New York: Harcourt Brace, 1966) p. 69.
2. April 1869, Ednah D. Cheyney (ed.), *Louisa May Alcott: Her Life, Letters and Journals* (London: Sampson Low, Marston; Searle & Rivington, 1889) p. 202.
3. Ibid, p. 107.
4. Woolf, op. cit. vol. 1, p. 214.
5. George Eliot, *Journal* in Gordon S. Haight, *George Eliot* (Harmondsworth: Penguin, 1985) pp. 351–78.

6.   Woolf, op. cit., 18 Aug. 1921, vol. 2, pp. 132–3.
7.   Ibid, p. 193.
8.   *Antaeus*, op. cit., p. 342.
9.   Mansfield, op. cit., p. 240.
10.   5 Oct. 1920, in C. K. Stead (ed.), *Katherine Mansfield, Letters and Journals* (Harmondsworth: Penguin, 1985) p. 183.
11.   Nin, op. cit., vol. 1, p. 242.
12.   *Antaeus*, op. cit., p. 12.
13.   Fothergill, op. cit., pp. 87–94.
14.   Culley, op. cit., p. 8.
15.   Op. cit., p. 52.
16.   Woolf, op. cit., vol. 3, p. 54.
17.   *The Diary of Alice James*, ed. Leon Edel (Harmondsworth: Penguin, 1964) p. 211.
18.   Ibid, p. 208.
19.   Ibid, pp. 125, 135, 113.
20.   Ibid, p. 232.
21.   Ibid, p. 149.
22.   Ibid, p. 227.
23.   Nin, op. cit., vol. 1, p. 277.
24.   Jelinek, op. cit., p. 223.
25.   *The Diary of Anais Nin*, quoted in Joanna Russ, *How to Suppress Women's Writing* (London: Women's Press, 1984) p. 102.
26.   Ibid

Select Bibliography

Main Primary Sources

Louisa May Alcott: Life, Letters and Journals, ed. Ednah D. Cheyney, 1889.

The Barretts at Hope End: The Early Diary of Elizabeth Barrett Browning, ed. Elizabeth Berridge, London, John Murray, 1974.

The Early Diary of Frances Burney 1768–1778, ed. Annie Raine Ellis, London, Bell, 1907.

The Diary of Fanny Burney, ed. Lewis Gibbs, London, Dent, 1960.

The Journals and Letters of Fanny Burney (Madame D'Arblay) 1791–1840, vols. I–VI ed. Joyce Hemlow with Patricia Boutilier and Althea Douglas; vol. VII ed. Edward A. and Lillian D. Bloom: vol. VIII ed. Peter Hughes; vols IX and X ed. Warren Derry; Vols XI and XII ed. Joyce Hemlow with Althea Douglas and Patricia Hawkins, Oxford, Oxford University Press, 1972–84.

The Diary of Alice James 1888–92, ed. Leon Edel, Harmondsworth, Penguin, 1964.

The Journal of Katherine Mansfield 1904–22, Definitive Edition, ed. J. M. Murry, London, Constable, 1962.

The Diary of Anais Nin, New York, Harcourt Brace, 1966.

The Memoirs of Laetitia Pilkington: Written by Herself, London, Routledge, 1928.

The Journals of Mary Shelley 1814–1844, ed. Paula Feldman and Diana Scott Kilvert, Oxford, Clarendon Press, 1987.

Mary Shelley's Journal, ed. Frederick Jones, University of Oklahoma Press, 1947.

Thraliana, The Diary of Mrs Hester Lynch Thrale, 1776–1809, 2 vols, Oxford, Clarendon Press, 1941–2.

Unpublished diaries and journals of Edith Wharton from holdings in the Beinecke Library, Yale University and the Lilly Library, University of Indiana.

The Diary of Virginia Woolf, ed. Anne Olivier Bell, London, Hogarth Press.

Journals of Dorothy Wordsworth, ed. Ernest de Selincourt, London, Macmillan, 1952.

Journals of Dorothy Wordsworth, ed. Mary Moorman, Oxford, Oxford University Press, 1971.

Critical Reading

Abel, Elizabeth, Marianne Hirsch and Elizabeth Langland (eds), *The Voyage In: Fictions of Female Development*, Hanover, University Press of New England, 1983.

Benstock, Shari (ed.), *The Private Self: Theory and Practice of Women's Autobiographical Writings*, London, Routledge, 1988.

Blodgett, Harriet, *Centuries of Female Days: Englishwomen's Private Diaries*, New Brunswick, Rutgers University Press, 1988.

Brett, Simon (ed.), *The Faber Book of Diaries*, London, Faber & Faber, 1987.

Culley, Margo, *A Day at a Time: The Diary Literature of American Women from 1764 to the Present*, New York, Feminist Press at the City University of New York, 1985.

Franklin, Penelope, 'The Diaries of Forgotten Women', *Book Forum* 4, 1979, pp. 467–558.

Gristwood, Sarah, *Recording Angels: The Secret World of Women's Diaries*, London, Harrap, 1988.

Halpern, Daniel (ed.), *Antaeus (Journals, Notebooks and Diaries)*, no. 61, New York, 1988.

Heilbrun, Carolyn G., *Reinventing Womanhood*, London, Gollancz, 1979.

Heilbrun, Carolyn G., *Writing A Woman's Life*, London, The Women's Press, 1989.

Homans, Margaret, *Women Writers and Poetic Identity*, Princeton, Princeton University Press, 1980.

Jelinek, Estelle C. (ed.), *Women's Autobiography: Essays in Criticism*, Bloomington, Indiana University Press, 1980.

Lensink, Judy Nolte, 'Expanding the Boundaries of Criticism: The Diary as Female Autobiography', *Women's Studies*, vol. 14, no. 1, 1987, pp. 39–53.

Mallon, Thomas. *A Book of One's Own: People and their Diaries*, New York, Tickner & Fields, 1984.

Moffatt, M. J. and C. Painter, *Revelations: Diaries of Women*, New York, Vintage Books, 1975.

Olney, James, *Metaphors of Self: The Meaning of Autobiography*, Princeton, Princeton University Press, 1972.

Olney, James (ed.), *Autobiography: Essays Theoretical and Critical*, Princeton, Princeton University Press, 1980.

Smith, Sidonie, *A Poetics of Women's Autobiography: Marginality and the Fictions of Self-Representation*, Bloomington, Indiana University Press, 1987.

Spacks, Patricia Meyer, *Imagining A Self: Autobiography and the Novel in Eighteenth-Century England*, Cambridge, Mass., Harvard University Press, 1976.

Spalding, Philip A., *Self-Harvest: A Study of Diaries and the Diarist*, London, Independent Press, 1949.

Stanton, Donna C. and Janine Parisier Plottel (eds), *The Female Autograph. New York Literary Forum 12–13*, New York, 1984.

Willey, Margaret, *Three Women Diarists*, London, Longmans, 1964.

Index